specialtypress

Vigilante!

Vigila

A PILOT'S STORY

1,200 Hours Flying the Ultimate US Navy Reconnaissance Aircraft

CDR Robert R. "Boom" Powell, USN (Ret.)

specialty press
PUBLISHERS AND WHOLESALERS

Specialty Press
838 Lake Street South
Forest Lake, MN 55025
Phone: 651-277-1400 or 800-895-4585
Fax: 651-277-1203
www.specialtypress.com

Publisher's Note: In reporting history, the images required to tell the tale will vary greatly in quality, especially by modern photographic standards. While some images in this volume are not up to those digital standards, we have included them, as we feel they are an important element in telling the story.

Edit by Mike Machat
Layout by Connie DeFlorin

ISBN 978-1-58007-261-8
Item No. SP261

Library of Congress Cataloging-in-Publication Data
Names: Powell, Robert R., 1942- author.
Title: Vigilante : a history of the US Navy's Mach 2 reconnaissance aircraft / Robert Powell.
Description: Forest Lake, MN : CarTech, Inc., [2019] | Includes bibliographical references and index.
Identifiers: LCCN 2019026400 | ISBN 9781580072618 (hardcover) | ISBN 9781580072610
Subjects: LCSH: Reconnaissance aircraft–United States–History. | Vigilante (Bomber)–History.
Classification: LCC UG1242.R4 P69 2019 | DDC 359.9/4834–dc23
LC record available at https://lccn.loc.gov/2019026400

Written, edited, and designed in the U.S.A.
Printed in China
10 9 8 7 6 5 4 3 2 1

Front Cover: *Classic view of North American RA-5C (BuNo 156608) from Reconnaissance Attack Squadron 7 (RVAH-7) "Peacemakers of the Fleet," assigned to USS Ranger (CV-61) in 1979. (US Navy photo)*

Front Flap: *VAH-7 flight crew with A-5A Vigilante on flight deck of the USS Enterprise (CVAN-65). High-visibility orange cotton flight suits were US Navy standard until the war in Vietnam.*

Front End Paper: *Raw power of the RA-5C is shown as this RVAH-6 Vigi takes off with a night flasher pod under the wing.*

Title Page: *Showing the Vigilante's massive size for a carrier-based jet, North American test pilots pose proudly with the prototype A3J-1 at Columbus, Ohio.*

Table of Contents Page: *Simultaneous launch of A3J Vigilante and F8U Crusader from the USS Enterprise (CVN-65) in 1962.*

Rear End Paper: *A Douglas TA-4J Skyhawk leads two RA-5Cs (BuNos 147852 and 150837) in this dramatic formation of sleek gull gray–over–white RVAH-3 jets.*

Rear Flap: *Author Robert "Boom" Powell flew the A-4 Skyhawk and RA-5C Vigilante and served as a Landing Signal Officer (LSO).*

Back Cover Photos
Top: *While other RVAHs used a single color, RVAH-12 always had red, white, and blue markings.*

Middle: *Prototype YA3J Vigilante (BuNo 145157) on the ramp at North American's facility in Port Columbus, Ohio, prior to its first flight in 1958. (NNAM)*

Bottom: *The exact moment an RA-5C Vigilante becomes airborne during a catapult launch is captured in this dramatic painting by Mike Machat, aptly entitled Unbridled Elegance.*

DISTRIBUTION BY:

UK and Europe
Crécy Publishing Ltd
1a Ringway Trading Estate
Shadowmoss Road
Manchester M22 5LH England
Phone: 44 161 499 0024
Fax : 44 161 499 0298
www.crecy.co.uk
enquiries@crecy.co.uk

Canada
Login Canada
300 Saulteaux Crescent
Winnipeg, MB, R3J-3T2 Canada
Phone: 800 665 1148
Fax: 800 665 0103
www.lb.ca

TABLE OF CONTENTS

DEDICATION

PREFACE

I was an experienced A-4 Skyhawk pilot with a full combat cruise and two years instructing in the A-4 RAG. I was due for orders back to sea duty. I wanted to get out of Lemoore; the flying was great, but family life, not so much. I had a long chat with my aviation detailer (one of those officers back in Washington, DC, who decided pilots' futures with the stroke of a pen). The conversation went something like this:

Me: "There's still four fleet squadrons of A-4s in Alameda [my first duty station]. Any one of them would be great."

Detailer: "Not likely. See you have A-6s as second choice."

Me: "Oh, yes. I love blowing things up."

Detailer: "Would you go to the East Coast for A-6s?"

Me: "Sure. You certain Alameda is out?" Other chatter for several minutes, until . . .

Detailer: "I see you have Vigilantes as a third choice. You serious?"

Me: "Well, it's a good-looking airplane and would keep me in a cockpit."

Detailer: "OK" and hangs up.

Thus, the next seven years of my life were determined. Little did I realize what a wonderful assignment orders to RVAH would be. I was on my way to a community of professionals flying an exciting, if challenging, aircraft, the RA-5C Vigilante, in the shadowy and somewhat mysterious world of aerial reconnaissance.

My introduction was quirky and somehow fitting. When my written orders arrived, they had me reporting on Thanksgiving Day. I called BuPers in DC and was assured that that was the date the Recce Wing had specified. My wife and I left our kids with their grandparents and drove to NAS Albany, Georgia. The next day, I put on my dress blue uniform and went to the squadron to check in. There was no one there except the sailor on duty, and he seemed confused why this lieutenant was reporting on a holiday. He took my orders and logged me aboard.

I called the Vigilante group a community and do so to this day. In researching this book, I found the complete list of pilots and RANs who had more than a 1,000 hours flying the A-5. (NAA kept track and recognized that mark with an appropriate plaque and citation.) Of the 115 men on that list, I personally knew 97 of them. At any given time, there were not more than 70 pilots who were current. It was indeed a community and I am proud to be a member.

Publisher's Note: In reporting history, the images required to tell the tale will vary greatly in quality, especially by modern photographic standards. While some images in this volume are not up to those digital standards, we have included them, as we feel they are an important element in telling the story.

ACKNOWLEDGMENTS

Because much of this book came from so many members of the Vigilante community, it would take several pages just to thank them all, but they, like myself, would rather hear about our airplane. So, a general thank you for digging into shoeboxes, the back of closets, and almost forgotten files for cherished photos and memories.

Little could I guess when I began training in the Vigilante that classmate Al Plunkett would far outlast me in the community. We reported to RVAH-3 in the fall of 1969. I wound up in RVAH-6, and Al made his first cruise with RVAH-12 before rolling back to RVAH-3 for instructor duty, then went to RVAH-13 for another Mediterranean deployment. Upon disestablishment of the RVAH-13 *Bats*, he had RVAH-6, "Engraved on my nametag."

Assignment to what would be the last CRAW-1 Staff resulted in what was to be the official history of Recon Attack Wing One. Alas, the history was never published due to a lack of funding, but Al was smart and saved it. As he said, "This project has been one of personal interest. Reviewing the pages of research material and files of information brought back many memorable occasions; some happy, some sad."

Although we only actually flew together less than a dozen times and were squadron mates only a few months (although that did include the great adventure of volcano hunting), George Cannelos's way with words added much to this volume.

Tom Myers was another who took pen in hand—or the modern equivalent—and recoded stories. Besides being the last CO of a RVAH squadron, he was deeply involved with the community for most of his career.

Jim Stark was not only quotable but also a good source of photos. Ken Carlton and Chuck Hoskin are two more Vigi vets who knew the value of taking pictures. Their names are in many photo credits.

Many parts of this book first appeared in my Catwalk column; articles in the Journal of Carrier Aviation, *The Hook*; or in articles I wrote for *Flight Journal* magazine. My thanks to those editors for allowing me to use them.

INTRODUCTION

In 1953, the US Navy had 51.22 accidents for every 10,000 hours flown. One of every 4½ aircraft crashed; that was 5 percent of the fleet. A sobering total of 423 aviators died.

A major change was needed, and a new emphasis on safety was placed at all levels of command. A navy-wide safety center was created and the Naval Aviation Training and Operating Procedures Standardization (NATOPS) system was put into effect. The Vigilante was born in this time of change; no longer just an airplane, but a weapons system. Manufacturer involvement with introduction and support intensified. Maintenance procedures were revamped from top to bottom. Aircrews received more comprehensive and better overall training.

NATOPS

With NATOPS, individual squadrons no longer did things "their way." Procedures were standardized and annual conferences for each type of aircraft updated procedures, exchanged ideas, and made improvements. The NATOPS manuals became the "bibles" of naval aviation.[1]

The Vigilante NATOPS evolved into a 592-page book with everything you needed to know to operate that sophisticated weapons system. The binding was awkward but made the annual replacing of changed pages possible, if not simple. Even not counting the performance charts, there were 407 pages covering the aircraft, navigation and recon systems—a complete how-to.

The RA-5C NATOPS was a major reference for this book.

Sources

My other major reference source was the people who worked with, navigated, and flew the Vigilante. Before the internet, collecting memories from such a dispersed group would have taken months. Now, exchanges of information take just days, if that long.

I have maintained an email collective of more than 80 names—a great collection of timely, firsthand stories. The ensign bombardier-navigators (BNs) in the A3J are in their late 80s. The last nugget pilots are in their 60s. The community was small with a web of friendships that continued past navy retirement. On the list of 115 aircrew who flew more than 1,000 hours, I was personally acquainted with more than three-fourths.

Names

Vigilante was not the easiest word to say, so it was usually shortened to "Vige" or "Vigi." *Vige* has one syllable and rhymes with ridge. *Vigi* is spoken with two syllables; like orange and purple, it has no known rhyme. Because of its size and difficult spelling, the word reconnaissance was also usually abbreviated to "recce" or "recon."

Pat O'Gara, who commanded the Vigi RAG (training squadron) RVAH-3 and then ReconWingOne, began a crusade to abolish the term "heavy" left over from A-3 Skywarrior days (e.g., VAH-10 was called "Heavy Ten"). At meetings, O'Gara went to the board, scrawled RVAH in large letters, and crossed off the A and H as obsolete. Vigilante veterans can be identified as to when they joined the community by whether they say "Heavy" or "Recce" Three.

The word "squadron" is often treated as a singular noun (e.g., "It went to sea."). However, accepted practice is to treat it as a plural noun (e.g., "They went to sea."). I use the plural in this book.

Numbers

Every navy airplane had three identifying numbers. Vigilantes each had a sequential number from the North American Aviation Company. Some of these added a C number for conversions. Each also had a US Navy–assigned Bureau Number (BuNo). Bureau numbers were not sequential for an aircraft type; there were gaps all the way through. Each block as contracted had its own series. The factory number and the BuNo did not change over the life of the airplane. They remained with it the entire time.

Once assigned to a squadron, every airplane was given an identifying side number. This consisted of two letters for the air wing and usually a three-digit number within the squadron. These changed with each new squadron, sometimes within a squadron or air wing. Matching the bureau numbers and the side numbers for any given time is difficult, as such records were temporary and usually not kept for long.

Images

A note on photographs: In reporting history, the images required to tell the tale will vary greatly in quality, especially by modern photographic standards. While some images in this book may not be up to current digital standards, they are included because they are an important element in telling the story.

Provider's names are supplied when possible. Most are US Navy via individuals. Two major sources are the National Naval Aviation Museum (NNAM) Emil Buehler Aviation Library in Pensacola, Florida, and the Tail Hook Association (THA) headquartered in San Diego, California. Any uncredited images are from my collection.

Insignia

An important factor in a squadron's morale and cohesiveness is its badge, emblem, crest, insignia (all mean the same thing). They may show up on the sides of airplanes, large or small and on official, and unofficial, documents. They may be decals or stencils or embroidery. For this book, I have sought pictures of them as they were displayed rather than neat graphics.

Related to a squadron's insignia is its name; it has two. One officially assigned for use in radio communication, the other a nickname (sometimes earned, sometimes contrived). Sometimes, they are the same. Sometimes, one becomes the other.

In Conclusion

I hope this book gives the Vigilante the coverage it deserves, but I admit there are still many more tales to be told. I used to say, tell them to me when we meet for happy hour in the O'Club, but the Puritans are winning and officer's clubs have turned into rental venues for rare special occasions. I do want to hear your stories, TINS or otherwise, and if I can't share a cocktail, you can at least send them to me electronically. I could post my current e-address, but so much changes so fast, it is smarter just to find me online.

PROLOGUE

Late-model RA-5Cs of RVAH-1. (Carlton)

The path that led to the Vigilante began with the dropping of the atomic bombs over Hiroshima and Nagasaki in 1945.

Strategic bombardment became the watch word, and after Hiroshima, strategic bombardment meant nuclear weapons. If the US Navy wanted a share of defense dollars, it had to establish its capability to deliver nukes. The problem was that the size of the bombs in the inventory didn't fit in anything but large bombers. The Mark III was an updated version of the Nagasaki bomb "Fat Man," which weighed 10,300 pounds, was over 12 feet long from nose to box fins, and had a girth 5 feet in diameter. Even the B-29 Super Fortress needed its bomb bay modified to carry the bomb.

There was no thought whatsoever when the Vigilante was conceived that it would ever be used for anything but bombardment. That the navy was wise enough to not waste a highly developed aircraft because the navy's role had changed is the story that follows.

The air war in Vietnam coincided almost exactly with the RA-5C. The reconnaissance Vigilante was the perfect airplane for the time.

RA-5C of RVAH-3, the "Recce RAG" after catapult launch from USS Coral Sea (CV-42) during carrier qualifications.

Reconnaissance Run

The coast of Vietnam appears in the tropical haze. The RAN has had the coast-in point—a distinctive cape—on the radar almost since launch. You push the throttles past the detent and feel a shove against your back as the afterburners light. As the Vigilante accelerates in the dive, you trim out pressure with tiny movements of a ridged wheel set in the control stick. At 550 knots, the narrow part of North Vietnam is crossed in minutes.

A look over your shoulder shows the Phantom in good position on your right. The first turn will be north to follow a section of the Ho Chi Minh Trail along the border with Laos. You level off between three and five thousand feet.

From the back cockpit, "Follow steering. Cameras coming on." In front, there is nothing but jungle-covered hills. The distance rolls to zero. "Right to 020. Follow steering." The Vigi feels smooth and solid at this speed. A precise course is sacrificed for constantly changing altitude and heading to throw off gunners on the ground.

The oblique cameras have a small green light on the pilot's glare shield that flashes when the cameras fire. Imagery is clearer if the airplane is steady and wings level when the cameras fire. A good Vigilante pilot times his jinking maneuvers to come between exposures. The green light winks, roll fast and pull, level the wings, wink, roll, pull, wink, reverse, pull, wink.

"I see the trail. It's bearing off right," says the RAN with his view straight down. You adjust your course between winks. Farther along you see a stretch of dirt road between the trees. You head for it.

Over a ridge there is a bombed-out bridge across a stream. The earth is red and pustuled with craters. In the fast glimpse you have, the bridge seems to be down. The cameras will tell the truth. It may be that the Vietnamese have rebuilt the bridge just below the surface of the water.

Your escort calls flak from the left. You watch yellow streaks come from the jungle and float behind and low. The RAN notes the coordinates. Fifteen minutes have passed. The terrain is higher and the safety of the water of the Tonkin Gulf is farther away. A cluster of red and yellow balls appears on your nose. They seem to float unmoving. No time to do or say anything. None hit. Someone says an expletive on the radio. The radar warning array beeps and shows a dotted line.

You start thinking which way to evade if a SAM is launched. Five miles to the end of the assigned route. Wink, bank, pull, wink. The beeping is persistent, loud. The distance counter reaches zero then spins up with the heading and distance to the carrier, to "Homeplate."

"We're outta here. 100 heading." The warning stops as you turn away from the hills.

Stay at low altitude, climbing would slow you down. You also fight the urge to jam the burners up to max and get the mission over with. Across the white, sandy beach—one mile, five, then ten. Begin a climb, deselect afterburner, slow down.

Peel off your oxygen mask and let it dangle to the side. The air in the cockpit is cool.

Chapter 1

THE BOMB GOES TO SEA

P2V-3C Neptune JATO assisted takeoff from the USS Franklin D. Roosevelt *(CVB-42) in February 1950. The dense smoke delayed work on deck and the launch of the next Neptune; one of the many reasons the concept was flawed. (USN)*

Something was needed to carry heavy atomic bombs off navy ships and fly to targets hundreds of miles away. The obvious solution was to adapt an airplane already in the inventory. The precedent was the selection of North American B-25s for the raid on Japan from the sea.

Lockheed was building the P2V Neptune patrol bomber for the navy. One of them, *The Truculent Turtle*, had set a long-distance record in September 1946 by flying 11,200 miles; farther than a B-29 could fly. The Neptune bomb bay, usually filled with torpedoes or depth charges, was cavernous enough to carry a Mark III weapon.

A moment in time at NAS Sanford: A-3 Skywarrior and brand-new RA-5C (wavy demarcation line and Navy and BuNo in pale blue) both with Hooter green-stripe tails and Air Wing 3 tail code, AC. The squadron was changing from VAH-9 to RVAH-9 and still had both types. This undated photo was probably taken in the spring of 1964. (M. Johnson)

The Preposterous P2V-3C

The concept was to load nuke-capable Neptunes on the new Midway class aircraft carriers (CVB). The carriers would steam to a launch point and the planes would take off using rocket power assist (JATO bottles), fly to their targets, drop a bomb, escape, and land at an airfield in a friendly nation. Squadrons were formed and crews trained. Navy Composite Squadron Five (VC-5) was the first. The use of the vague term "composite" for the nuclear mission may have been to conceal the mission.[1] Feasibility and practice launches were

Early Nuclear Bombs

Bombs were designated with Mark (Mk) numbers until 1968, and with "B" numbers after that.
- Mk1: 10,000 pounds
- Mk3 and Mk4: 10,000 pounds and bigger. Same type as the "Fat Man" bomb dropped on Nagasaki. In use until 1954.
- Mk7: 1,600 pounds, 15 feet long, 2.5-foot diameter. Implosion type, multipurpose tactical bomb. 8–61 kilotons. In use 1952–1967.
- Mk8: 3,300 pounds, gun-type Highly Enriched Uranium (HEU) weapon designed for penetrating hardened targets. 25–30 kilotons. In use 1951–1957.

Mark III "Fat Man" implosion-type nuclear weapon with a solid plutonium core at 5 tons, 10.5 feet long, 5-foot diameter. Replica on display at the National Naval Aviation Museum (NNAM) in Pensacola, Florida.

made. The VC squadrons deployed to Morocco to be close to the carriers in the Mediterranean ready to strike European targets.

Pilots for the P2V-3Cs were a mix; some from backgrounds in carrier tactical aircraft and many from patrol squadrons who had not flown from a ship since flight training. The attitude back then was that a naval aviator could fly anything.

A better solution was on its way. North American Aviation (NAA), builders of the B-25, had developed an atomic bomb–carrying airplane that could fly off and land on a carrier.

"A" for Attack, "J" for North American

The navy-designated AJ Savage was a hybrid with two conventional, and proven, Pratt & Whitney R-2800 engines on the wings and an Allison J33 jet engine in the tail to assist takeoffs and give it a dash speed over the target. The flush jet intake was on top of the fuselage and the exhaust below the tail fin. The Savage could take off at a gross weight of more than 50,000 pounds, which included a bomb and enough fuel for a long range. Another asset of the AJ was

that it could operate off all navy carriers, not only the three large CVBs. The eccentric VC squadrons transitioned to the Savage and more were formed as VAH (Navy, Attack, Heavy) squadrons. VAH-5, -6, -7, -8, and -9 went on to fly the A-3D Skywarrior and the Vigilante. (When VAH-8 transferred from the West Coast to the East Coast it became VAH-11 to match the navy's odd number east/even number west designation system.)

AJ-1 Savage of VC-6 on board the USS Midway *(CVB-41).* Daijobu *is Japanese for "Okay." (THA)*

The size of the AJ-1 Savage is apparent in this picture taken on board the USS Oriskany *(CVA-34) in August 1952. The number of red shirts (ordnancemen) and open bomb bay doors indicate this was probably a familiarization mission with the navy's new nuclear weapon delivery aircraft. (THA)*

Savage Sons

In the mid-1950s, VC-5 began flying the North American AJ Savage and was based at Sanford, Florida, so the new name, *The Savage Sons of Sanford* made sense. The word *savage* inspired a new squadron patch of a cartoon cannibal with wide eyes and a bone through his hair. A nickname of "Mushmouth" followed soon after. By 1962, the Mushmouth patch became officially unacceptable and was replaced with an Indian head and red arrow design. Unofficially, the Mushmouth lingered in the form of a Kilroy-like face peering over the tail stripe on the vertical fin of the squadron's RA-5C Vigilantes. An early bombing derby versus A3Ds from Whidbey was billed as, "The Wicked Warriors of Whidbey versus the Savage Sons of Sanford."

TINS: During a Mediterranean deployment, a group of African dignitaries were on board the carrier for a firepower demonstration. A removal of the Mushmouths was ordered and the cartoons dutifully painted over . . . on the Vigis on board. However, Murphy's Law was not to be denied. The RA-5C, which was trapped with the VIPs watching, came from the beach and still had the big-eyed caricature in full view.

A 156-series (post-1969) RA-5C with all three squadron insignia: *VC-5* Grim Reapers, *VAH-5* Savage Sons of Sanford, *and RVAH-5* Savage Sons. *(Stark)*

Squadron coffee mug. RVAH-5's nickname was the Savage Sons of Sanford *until the move to NAS Albany, when "Sanford" was dropped. Callsign* Old Kentucky. *(Craeger)*

High-altitude bombing required a bombardier.[2] The P2V had more than sufficient room, its usual crew was 5 to 10 men, but the Savage was much smaller to fit on carrier decks. What size should the crew be?

The basic layout of most multiengine aircraft was two men facing forward and the copilot replaced by a bombardier who also was the navigator. Roll control in case of an engine failure was easier with a yoke than a stick. The throttles were in the center. (The prototype and first model, AJ-1, had a stick with throttles on the left.) A third crewmember was added to assist with managing the fuel and engines.

"A" for Attack, "D" for Douglas

The A3D Skywarrior was an exceptional aircraft that served the US Navy (it was never exported) for many years after its original mission was over. Powered by a pair of Pratt & Whitney J57 turbojets in pods, the A3D could launch from a catapult at 76,000 pounds and had the speed and range to carry out nuclear strikes. Unheard of for most aircraft, the A3D (The AD was the famous Skyraider of Korea and Vietnam. The A2D was the Skyshark; a turboprop version that did not work out. Next in line was the A4D Skyhawk.) came in well under the contract specified weight and light enough that it could

A3D Skywarriors over Florida. Both have shore-based tail codes. The lead aircraft is from VAH-7 and has radar-aimed tail guns. The other A-3 is from VAH-3, which became the replacement training squadron for the A-3 and A-5 and kept the GJ code for its entire existence.

operate from flight decks smaller than CVBs as well as the new "super" carriers.

The Skywarrior firmly established the navy's ability to drop atomic weapons from high altitude; frequently equaling or besting in competition the US Air Force's very large bombers. Later, when small nuclear weapons were developed, the Skywarrior was able to do the low-altitude, under-the-radar toss bombing tactic as well as smaller aircraft such as the FJ Fury, F2H Banshee, and A4D Skyhawk. (In the early days, an engine pod occasionally ripped off during the pull-up into a loft maneuver. The result was a short hit with an unexpected and rapid roll.) Unfortunately, its size made the Skywarrior less than desirable on carrier decks.

By the time of the A3D, patrol plane pilots were still receiving orders to fly the twin-engine jet. Not always with good results. Bombardier-navigators were hard to come by. Using enlisted men was one answer (see sidebar "Navy Enlisted Bombardier-Navigators (NEBN)"), and drafting nuggets was another. A newly winged aviator (called a nugget) ordered to a VAH squadron spent a year or more in the right seat before flying the aircraft. As demoralizing as this must have been, many of these men became Skywarrior plane commanders and made the transition to the Vigilante without any problems.

The cockpit and control configuration remained the same as on the AJ, making the Skywarrior the only carrier-capable jet flown with a yoke. When the A-3 was first conceived, it had a rearward-facing 20mm cannon and a radar-directed mount in the tail. The third crew member sat backward, as in the Savage, which may also have given him, as the gunner, a better idea of what he was looking at on the radar scope.

There were no ejection seats. Emergency bailout was via a slide out the bottom (the slide had hand/foot holes for climbing to enter the cockpit). The difficulty of bailing out at low altitude gave rise to the unhappy expression that A3D stood for "All Three Dead."

If it had not been for the decision that an aircraft had to be supersonic to drop atomic weapons, the A-3 may have had a much longer life as a bomber. As it was, the Skywarrior turned into a long-lived aircraft with many other roles, including tanking and electronic warfare.

Speed and Speculation

In November 1953, North American Aviation's Columbus Division took the risky step of forming a team to design what the company hoped would become what the US Navy wanted for a new nuclear bomber. The program was North American General Purpose Air Weapon (NAGPAW). A fast aircraft, which hugged the ground to avoid detection going in, would execute the newly developed LABS bomb delivery maneuver, and use supersonic speed to evade the blast's shockwave. An unsolicited proposal was submitted and the Navy Bureau of Weapons (BuWeps) was interested. However, navy requirements for carrier work, especially zero-wind catapult launches, created a problem: The optimum wing for the rough ride at low altitude was incompatible with the lifting abilities needed for ship-based operations. A year later, a revised proposal included the change to a Mach-2 high-altitude weapons delivery. "Supersonic penetration of enemy defense was increasingly considered to be necessary for survivability in Congress, if not in combat."[3]

Navy Enlisted Bombardier-Navigators (NEBN)

How did enlisted men come to fly in the navy's most advanced jets? Be responsible for navigating the bomber to the target and arming and enabling the drop of atomic bombs?

Early carrier aircraft with more than a pilot included a gunner. When radios became common, the sailor became a radioman/gunner. Their electronics skills made the radiomen into radar operators when it came into use. Radar men also could navigate in bad weather. So when the US Navy took on a carrier-based nuclear weapon delivery mission, it made sense that such crewmen became bombardiers/navigators (BN).

Ray Williams

Ray Williams was one of the first enlisted sailors to become a qualified nuclear bombardier/navigator. During World War II, Williams was a radioman on the big Coronado flying boat in a specialized squadron based on Saipan transporting medical evacuees. By 1947, he was in VC-6, the navy's first operational nuclear delivery squadron. The squadron deployed with their P2V-7-3C Neptunes to the airfield at Port Lyautey in Morocco, ready to be loaded on a carrier should the need arise. He remained with the squadron during the transition to the AJ Savage and went to sea on the USS *Midway* (CVB-41) as petty officer first class. Williams remained enlisted for his entire career and may be the only one to have flown in all four types of aircraft requiring a bombardier/navigator.

Colin Pemberton

Colin "Pem" Pemberton was from Winthrop, Massachusetts, and was 17 when he enlisted in the US Navy. After boot camp, he was trained as an Aviation Metalsmith (AMH) and went to a development squadron at NAS Chincoteague, Virginia, where he worked on two dozen types of aircraft and was promoted to second class petty officer. In 1955, Pem received orders to Composite Squadron 7 (VC-7), one of the first AJ Savage squadrons, where after two years as a mechanic he was selected as a bombardier-navigator.

On his first carrier landing, the engine mounts broke and chunks of propeller sliced into the Savage's cockpit, inches behind his head. Pem made deployments on the USS *Essex* and the USS *Ticonderoga,* flying during both the Formosa and Lebanon crises.

NEBN Ray Williams with unknown pilot in front of A3J BuNo 147857, which was used in a variety of tests. The meaning of the dark bar on the fuselage is not known, and the orange arrow shape on the belly is partially obscured. The crew is ready for flight with torso harness and flotation gear over the MkIV pressure suits. The nosegear door is open and the "bath tub" is hanging down. (Williams)

NAA Savage with an engine mount that broke on landing, a common failing with the Savage. One propeller blade slashed into the fuselage side and cockpit. Enlisted BN Colin Pemberton was in the right seat for his first carrier trap. (USN)

A3J low over the desert floor. Tail marking is for Nuclear Weapons Experimental Facility (NWEF) Albuquerque. (Williams)

Ralph Feeback

Originally from Flagler, Colorado, Ralph Feeback earned the intriguing sobriquet of "Rotten" after enlisting in the navy. (He does not explain, but did keep it for his 30 years on active duty and into retirement.) Trained as an Avionics Technician (AT) he was sent to an advanced radar course at the Philco Company, working with the new APS-4 and APS-13 radars, which led to assignment at the navy's test center at Patuxent River, Maryland, where he was instrumental in establishing the US Navy's first Radar Bomb Scoring (RBS) facility. His expertise was recognized, and he was chosen by the Heavy Attack Training Unit (HATTU) to go to NAS Sanford, Florida, for training as a BN. Three years with VAH-11 flying in Savages from the USS *Essex* (CV-9), which had a straight deck, followed.

Feeback was the bombardier-navigator representing HATTU-1 in a bombing competition with the air force, an unusual event. Speculation was that it was to determine who would drop a hydrogen bomb in special tests at Bikini Atoll. Although the navy had better hits, politics dictated the USAF would do the drop. The last run of the competition was at the RBS site at Seattle. Ralph remembers the offset was 4,850 feet, so when he learned the SAC bombardier had almost spoiled the test by dropping a hydrogen bomb nearly 5,000 feet off target, he knew what had happened: The rather high-ranking air force bombardier had not taken the Seattle offset out of his calculations.

Crewing with and, especially, being graded by enlisted sailors was a recurring, if not frequent, problem. While in the RAG (Replacement Air Group), Feeback flew with a pilot who had problems landing the A3D Skywarrior in a crosswind. Feeback gave the pilot a "down" for his unsafe performance. The pilot was upset because Feeback was not only a non-pilot (he later earned his civil license) but was an enlisted man. For his recheck, the VAH-3 Operations Officer rode in the bombardier-navigator's seat so that an officer, a senior one at that, was the one to recommend the grounding.

Don Pierce

Don Pierce was a crewman in patrol aircraft for 10 years before joining the VAH-5 *Savage Sons of Sanford* and working his way from third crewman on the A3D Skywarrior to bombardier-navigator. With 1,800 hours of flight time and three cruises to the Mediterranean, he was a well-experienced first class petty officer when he joined VAH-3 as an instructor in the ASB-12 navigation system in the Vigilante. After one class, a pilot who had flown single-seat A4D Skyhawks wrote in his critique to get rid of Pierce: "No enlisted man is going to tell me how to fly my airplane." A meeting with the squadron training officer came the next day. After a few minutes, Pierce was dismissed while the pilot stayed behind. Next thing Pierce knew, the pilot was apologizing for not recognizing the importance of flight crew, no matter what their rank.

Denny Noto

Denny Noto was the last of the enlisted bombardier-navigators and became one by an unusual route—he was a TraDevMan (TD), a simulator specialist. Once at NAS Sanford, he volunteered to be a bombardier-navigator in the Skywarrior in 1961. His last flight was in an RA-5C in August 1969.

The Program

By the mid-1960s, the Naval Aviation Observer (NAO) program had become the Naval Flight Officer (NFO) program with a clear career path and the Training Command was producing as many bombardier-navigators and other specialties as needed. Individual enlisted bombardier-navigators were offered officer commissions. Many accepted and continued flying. Some opted to retain their enlisted status and go on to other duties. The majority of the 130 NEBNs stayed on active duty for 20 years or more. Arthur Critser claims 1,888 shipboard traps before retiring as a LCDR, which means he had more than any other NFO.

After his tour in VAH-1 (see chapter 3), Colin Pemberton was commissioned an officer, claiming that at 34½ he was the oldest ensign in the US Navy. His next assignment had him flying as a navigator in the electronic version of the Skywarrior, the EA-3, over Vietnam. On one of those missions, the aircraft went out of control in a typhoon at 28,000 feet and the crewmembers in the back bailed out while Pem and the pilot were trapped in the cockpit. The EA-3 finally leveled off at 3,000. The men who bailed out were never heard from again. After a brief time instructing, Pem was back at sea in the RA-5C, completing two full deployments to Vietnam and accumulating 17 Air Medals over 210 combat missions.

After commissioning, Ralph Feeback remained in RA-5C squadrons and flew in Vietnam. On a catapult shot from the USS *John F. Kennedy* (CVA-67), an engine failed and he and the pilot ejected. Before retiring, he was the commanding officer of a Joint Service Command in Philadelphia.

Although the NEBN program began as something of a stop-gap to fill the need for qualified bombardier-navigators at the height of the Cold War, not only was it successful but also an opportunity for talented and capable men to rise to the challenge.[4]

Wings worn by air crewmen other than pilots: (bottom to top) 1. Combat Air Crew, 2. Enlisted Air Crew, 3. Naval Air Observer, 4. Naval Flight Officer. (J. Powell)

Initial training cadre at NAA plant. Besides navy officers in khaki, three sailors appear in the back row. Factory Number-19 became BuNo 147857 and was used in testing before conversion to RA-5C. Before painting, the anti-corrosion coating gave the aircraft a greenish hue. (Williams)

Known problems with high-speed bomb drops from the company's B-45 Tornado's conventional bomb bay led to the internal, linear bomb bay. This arrangement became the Vigilante's distinguishing feature. Although the system was not accepted for operational use, its uniqueness caught the public's imagination. The first Monogram plastic model kit had a spring mechanism with which the builder could, "Trip the trigger . . . Eject the bomb . . . rearward!"

In later years, after the Vigilante became a reconnaissance airplane, people still said, "Oh, the Vigi, isn't that the one that 'spit' the bomb out the tail?"

Making the Airplane

Designed as a high-flying, high-speed, strategic nuclear bomber, the Vigilante may have introduced more new features than any other aircraft in history. Much of its development was in parallel with the F4H Phantom II. Both were the first with variable ramp engine inlets and boundary layer control (BLC), had two crew in tandem cockpits, and used the same GE J79 variable stator engines (and both used a new type of wingtip light). Indeed, the aircraft made their initial deployments jointly on the USS *Enterprise*.

The Vigilante had no conventional flight controls. The A-5 did not have ailerons, elevators, or a rudder.

Vertical Tail

The vertical tail was one-piece, slab-type construction, rather than having a hinged rudder. Like all jets, the Vigilante had a yaw augmentation system.

When you taxied behind another Vigilante, you could see the vertical slab move in response to the rudder pedals, which were used for nosewheel steering. The Yaw Aug responded to spurious inputs by shaking and shimmying the tail like a dog trying to get dry.

Nosewheel is turned as is the vertical slab as the Vigilante is positioning for takeoff.

YA3J Vigilante BuNo 145157 on the ramp at Port Columbus, Ohio, prior to its first flight in 1958. The nose is black and does not have a sensor probe. This aircraft was the only one to have the name in script on the fuselage. (NNAM)

Horizontal Tail

The horizontal tail surfaces were also one-piece slabs. Together, they controlled pitch and were adjusted separately for roll trim. The trailing edges were sharp enough that a rubber guard was fitted over them while on the ground or on deck.

While waving the Vigilante on board the carrier, Landing Signal Officers (LSOs) could see every tiny movement of the horizontal slabs because they were so big. (In area and shape, they were the same size as an A-4 Skyhawk's wings.) A well-flown Vigilante pass had the nose steady on speed while the slabs fluttered and twitched from the pilot's small, constant stick inputs.

Spoilers

Spoilers provided roll control and acted as speed brakes. The primary reason for spoilers on carrier-based airplanes is that they permit more of the trailing edge to be devoted to flaps.

In 1956, NAA modified a FJ-3 Fury with the spoiler-slot-deflector lateral control system that later was used on the Vigilante. The NACA

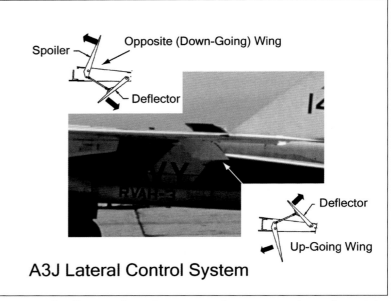

A3J Lateral Control System

Diagram of roll-control spoiler system that appeared on all models of the Vigilante. (T. Thomason)

tested it extensively in the wind tunnel at Langley. Interestingly, the test report was classified until 1964.

Using the spoilers to roll felt unusual for pilots used to conventional ailerons. Rather than the center of the roll axis being through the pilot's belly, as it is on most airplanes, it felt as if it were out on the high wing. Jam the control stick to the side and one seemed to drop as the roll started.

Wing

A manufacturing process was developed to make a wing that was strong for its weight. The entire wing was milled from a single piece of aluminum lithium alloy that facilitated designing a wing to meet the disparate requirements of high-speed and carrier operations. The leading edge had droops, which aided slow-speed flight and came down when the flaps were lowered.

Control System

Lateral and longitudinal fight control systems were electrically controlled and hydraulically operated with a mechanical standby system. This was the first use in a production aircraft of what later became known as fly-by-wire.

The description of Longitudinal Electric Control (the Lateral System was similar) from the NATOPS Manual follows:

"Normal control of the longitudinal system is electric. With the electric flight control system engaged, the longitudinal free play link is energized to induce some free play into the me-

Vigilante with wings folded and spoilers fully extended in speed brake mode. Vertical and horizontal tail surfaces are single pieces without elevators or rudders. (NNAM)

chanical linkage. With this free play induced, electrical system functions to control the master actuator. Potentiometers connected to the control stick linkage produce signals (as the stick is moved) which are amplified and fed to the longitudinal master actuator servo valve. As the servo valve responds (to electrical commands), the master actuator moves, mechanically positioning the control valve of the horizontal stabilizer actuators, causing movement of the control surface. A follow-up potentiometer, moved by the master actuator linkage, sends a position signal back to the amplifier, nulling the command signal when the proper control surface position is reached."

Flaps

Without ailerons, the flaps went all the way from the fuselage to the wing fold. The original extension was to 40 degrees down; it was increased to 50 degrees in the A3J-2/A-5B. Ducted engine bleed-air was blown over the flaps for improved lift and control at low airspeeds. An interconnect system changed the pitch trim when the flaps were lowered.

Folds

To better fit on aircraft carrier decks, the Vigilante not only had foldable wings but also could fold its vertical tail to the side (to clear the overhead on the hangar deck) and fold the nose, with its long sensor probe, up. This reduced the overall length by approximately 7 feet. Folding the nose also gave access to the radar antenna and Versatile Digital Analyzer (VERDAN) "ball." Wings and tail were folded hydraulically; the nose, electrically. A wing-shaped handle on the left console controlled folding with a switch to isolate the tail fold.

When parked on deck, the tail was rarely folded. Without hydraulic pressure, the wind from the side nudged the tip of the tail off its locks. If the wings did not lock while spread, the first remedy to try was to fold the wings, select tail fold, then spread them both. The mechanic's signal for tail fold was a somewhat silly hand wave on top of the head.

Engines

The General Electric J79 turbojet had variable inlet guide vanes and variable compressor stators. To accommodate these airflow demands, the Vigilante had variable

Variable intake ramps in the full down (supersonic) position.

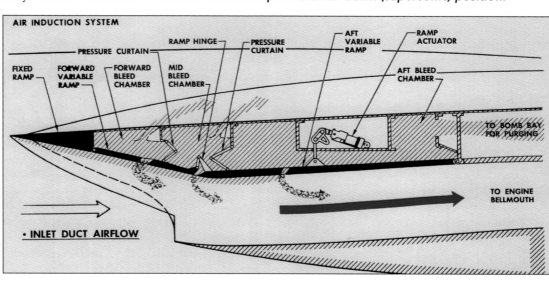

Diagram of engine air induction system from the NATOPS manual.

engine-throat inlets using horizontal ramp geometry for flight at high Mach numbers. (The open ducts on top of the intakes were susceptible to Foreign Object Damage (FOD) and were covered if work was done on top of the airplane.) The variable-thrust afterburners had primary and secondary exhaust nozzles. The engine bays had gold-plating to better reflect heat (the subject of many jokes about cost).

The Vigilante soon earned the sobriquet of *Elephant*. The length of the nose and the way it stuck far out in front of the nosewheel was part of the image, but more than that was the sound the J79 engines buried deep in the long, square intakes made when taxiing and on landing approach. Some wit described the pulsing, loud moan as the mating call of a female elephant. The name stuck and two or more Vigis moving on the flight deck preparing to catapult was called the "Dance of the elephants."

Mechanic looking up into the nose compartment exposed by lowering the bath tub hanging behind him. (Sharp)

Canopies

NAA developed a single-piece windshield providing undistorted vision and shatter protection for pilots of supersonic planes while saving weight. The new windshield was made from stretched acrylic, which, before being shaped, was pulled in both directions to rearrange its molecular structure to provide shatter resistance. The pilot's windshield was bird-proof and Mach 2 capable. The pilot's canopy had a plastic shield, called the radiation curtain, which could be pulled forward and down to prevent blindness from nuclear bomb bursts. The same worry gave the BN a solid canopy with only two small windows that had sliding panels to cut off the light. A side benefit was the bombardier-navigators did not have to bury their faces in a rubber boot to read the radar scope. When the new batch of Vigis was built in 1969, NAA offered to make the back canopy clear, but the reconnaissance attack navigators (RANs) said no for that reason.

Doors

Unlike most airplanes in which it is only a two-step process to raise or lower the landing gear, on the Vigilante it was a three-step process: To lower the landing gear, the main doors came open, the landing gear (struts and wheels) extended, and then the main doors closed, leaving the smaller doors open. To raise the landing gear after takeoff, the main doors came open, the landing gear retracted, and then the main gear doors closed. This closing of the large portion of the doors with the landing gear down was the third step.

North American aircraft have been doing this since the P-51 Mustang. (The F-86 Sabre and the F-100 Super Sabre did the same. The widely produced trainers, T-28 Trojan, and even the jet T-2 Buckeye did not have this feature.)

Therefore, to gain access to the wheel wells when the aircraft was on the ground, there were handles on the inside of the wheel wells that released the doors from their up locks. This is frequently seen in pictures of the Vigilante on the ground, especially the nose door,

which gave access to the electronics compartment and where flight crew stored their luggage on a trip. In addition, the interior nose area was protected by a hinged, fiberglass cover; officially a splash shield but always referred to as the "bath tub." This was unpinned and came down to allow access to the avionics bay area.

In-flight Refueling Probe

Techniques and equipment for in-flight refueling using the probe-and-drogue method were fully developed by the time the A-5 was being designed. All earlier aircraft used probes added to the basic

Extended air refueling probe. The doors remained open while the probe was out and made a lot of noise. If there was a problem with a door, it was not unusual to remove and fly without it. The F4H Phantom and the Vigilante were the first aircraft designed with extendable probes. This close-up shows applied markings on the canopy: The red item is an emergency lever to release the canopy from outside. The small black stripes when aligned indicate that the canopy is locked. The black square is where the hook on the boarding ladder should be placed. (Woodul)

model. Because of its speed, the Vigilante probe retracted and was covered by a set of doors (the F4H Phantom did the same). The best location to place a probe is in the pilot's forward field of vision, which NAA did on the left side.

Tanker Travesty

The idea of a supersonic tanker was silly but shows how desperate NAA was to establish the versatility of its multimillion-dollar airplane. Since the bomb-out-the-tunnel idea was not working, a hose and reel was installed in that space and plumbing added so that internal fuel could be transferred to another aircraft. The system worked fine. Both VAH-1 and VAH-7 used it during their deployments, but its major use was in the RAG, VAH-3, for training.

Escape System

The Rocket Assisted Personnel Ejection Catapult (RAPEC-II)/HS-1 ejection seat utilized a rocket (versus explosive cartridge) developed by the navy and refined by NAA for the Vigilante and the T2J Buckeye. Both had drogue chutes for stability, inflatable separation bladders, and an ejection interconnect system. When the pilot in the front cockpit initiated ejection, the interconnect system fired the rear seat 0.75 second before the front seat. Because of its training role with an instructor and a student riding in either cockpit, the Buckeye had a selectable lever so the rear cockpit could eject both seats. The Vigilante rear seat could eject only itself. The major difference between the two systems was the provisions made for extreme high speeds for the A3J:

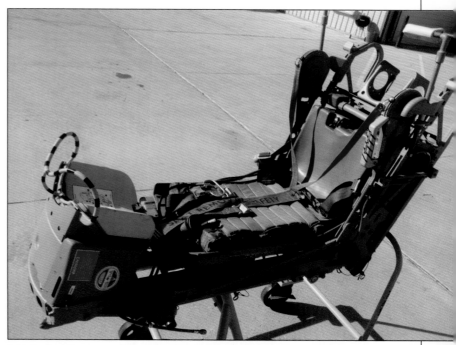

HS-1 ejection seat from the Frontiers of Flight Museum is transported on its back using a cart. The grips for the face curtain are rigid steel with wide openings to allow for the bulky gloves of a pressure suit. The yellow handle is for manual release from the seat. The leg restraints are extended forward. The twist-and-pull ejection handles on the seat sides are missing. (C. Woodul)

VAH-1 A-5A refueling from a tanker-configured Vigilante. The only tanker versions after VAH-1 and -7 became RVAH, were in the RAG for training. (NNAM)

- The face curtain handle was rigid metal and large enough to grasp while wearing the gloves of the MkIV pressure suit.
- Two alternate ejection handles were on the seat sides. When either one was twisted and pulled, the ejection sequence was initiated and the seat sides raised to restrain side motion and provide aerodynamic stability to the seat.
- On ejection, the seat pan bottomed out, a bar came up under the knees, and foot retractors swung down pulling the legs into a recess in the seat.

- Pilot and bombardier-navigators were supposed to wear a sleeve assembly which, through a complicated system of pull-tapes, pulleys, and cross connections, pulled the arms up against the chest and held them until seat separation. With the likelihood of high-speed ejections being remote and the restrictions to mobility, the sleeves were soon ignored. Veterans of the first deployed squadron "never saw a pair."

Unused Ideas

A couple of early design features that never got off the drawing board were twin vertical tails; a clear, rear canopy; and a rocket motor installed in the aft end of the bomb bay.

The first of these proposals—two short tails to fit in hangar decks—although installed on the first mockup, was rejected in favor of a single vertical tail, which, even with the mechanism to fold the tail, was simpler and lighter.

A clear canopy so the bombardier-navigator could see outside was assumed. However, when bomb flash protection was considered, it was simpler to make a solid canopy with closable windows than an extendable cover as on the pilot's canopy. A bonus was bombardier-navigators did not need a light-obscuring hood to read the radar scope.

The rocket motor was to be on the aft fuel can to provide high altitude and speed at the target. The fuels were to be JP-4 from the aircraft's normal tanks and hydrogen-peroxide (H_2O_2) in the linear fuel cans. Tests were flown with a rocket motor installed above the J65 exhaust in a NAA Fury fighter. Testing was successful with the Fury reaching Mach 1.4 at 70,000 feet. However, the idea was rejected because of the hazardous operating conditions with the special fuel, the consequent limited operating range, and the J79 engines proving adequate for the mission.

Since range was not a factor, NAA proposed the rocket in the tunnel to the USAF Air Defense Command as an interceptor with four air-to-air missiles on the wings. The air force did not buy the idea.

A letter of intent was signed in June 1956, and $86 million was awarded for two YA3J-1 prototypes and a static test airframe. The name

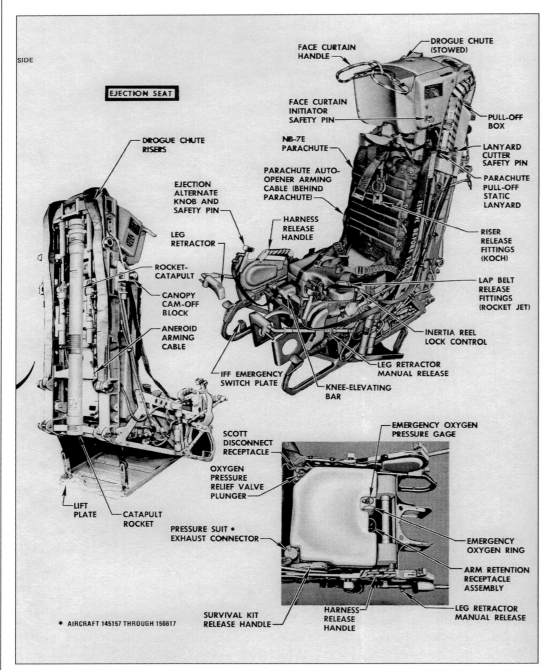

Diagram of HS-1 ejection seat from the NATOPS manual.

Loss of BUNO 149314, the RAN's Tale

The plane began its usual last-minute maneuverings (during Field Carrier Landing Practice [FCLP]). This particular plane, Bureau Number 149314, was on its second full day of flight operations after having been returned from a Progressive Aircraft Rework (PAR) program that updated all the systems and repainted the aircraft inside and out. It gave the feeling of flying in a brand-new airplane. We also carried a million-dollar camera in the reconnaissance pod. Usually, the camera was not used on the rough FCLP, but this plane was up, flyable, and needed. The navy policy of aircraft usage was when a plane was ready to fly, a crew was found to fly it. The constant pounding of the landings was hard on camera mounts and internal parts.

"I've got the ball, 4.8," my pilot said calmly.

"201, ball 4.8," I reported to the LSO.

"Roger ball," the LSO answered.

We staggered along as usual and made a nice pass with no comments from the LSO. The plane thumped its usual thump and accelerated as the pilot applied full takeoff power. We started to climb. I started to write down the landing and the fuel state on my pad in the well-lit small cockpit when I heard a sudden soft rushing sound to my right.

Just then my pilot said, in a slightly exasperated voice, "Oh, shit, starboard engine."

I immediately asked, as I started to put my pencil into its holder still listening to the whooshing on my right, "What's the matter?"

My pilot quickly answered me. "Standby, eject," he said in a terse, level tone of voice.

I immediately reached up with both hands and pulled the face curtain all the way down over my face and upper body.

Nothing happened.

The rushing sound continued as I looked down to see what was wrong and started to think that we were low and wouldn't have much time to do any of the manual procedures such as blowing off my canopy, unhooking myself from the seat, and jumping out. As it turned out, the delay was caused by the normal functioning of the seat firing sequence, which allowed three-quarters of a second for the seat to be set in the full down position. Since I was tall, I always had it in the full down position. I was still looking down when the rocket ejection seat fired. The cockpit was immediately filled with bright flame and I was ejected upward.

The original ejection seats were fired with explosive charges, but too many pilots suffered back injuries, so the seat was improved by having it propelled by a small rocket charge that reduced the initial shock on the back. The ride up was smooth.

After the bright flash of the rocket firing, I had just enough time to think that I hoped everything worked normally. I knew the complicated sequence that had to be followed precisely for me to live through this.

Just then, I felt a great tug and felt warm black sky all around so the knee restraints had retracted normally, the seat had bottomed out, my canopy had blown off, the seat had fired, the knee restraints had been popped off, the bladder behind me had inflated and separated me from the 600-pound ejection seat, my drogue parachute had deployed immediately since we were below 12,000 feet, my main parachute had opened, my face curtain was gone with the seat and I was coming down to earth under a parachute while breathing oxygen from my 10-minute bailout bottle.

My new silver flight suit had held and was comfortable. I did not know what had happened to my pilot. His ejection sequence is delayed one-and-three-quarter seconds to permit my ejection sequence to complete itself before his sequence commences. Without the delay, there was a chance of his canopy blowing into me as I was ejected upward.

As soon as I realized that the chute had opened, I saw a brilliant yellow flash down and to my left as my airplane hit the ground. I thought, "Just like in the movies." It hit and smeared a yellow flash in the night.

After a maximum of 3 seconds in the calm air after the chute opened, I abruptly hit the ground in a standing position and crumpled into a heap. During training, I was taught to roll upon landing, using the fleshy parts of my body to cushion the landing. They never mentioned what to do on a pitch dark night when the ground was invisible. As soon as I hit, I felt a sharp pain in my back but quickly got up and looked around. The burning plane was about 40 yards away, upside down, and making explosive noises. I was on a hard, flat, grassy field. I kept the oxygen mask on because the gas was cool and I knew it was clean. I put my blinking flashlight on my harness, as instructed in my training classes, and started to walk away to look for my pilot. I then took off the oxygen mask and breathed in the warm Florida night air. I laughed and thought, *I did it, and this is really something to talk about. I can't wait to tell the guys.* I shouted, "Mr. Butler, Mr. Butler." There was no answer, just the crackling of the burning airplane.

The next day, I woke up and my back was really hurting from a compression fracture of thoracic vertebrate six from the abrupt parachute landing. I went to work, was sent to the Dispensary where I was given some muscle relaxants for my back, and took two days off. I resumed flying and completed my training. The accident report revealed that a clamp, probably undone or not correctly tightened during the Progressive Rework, had become loose and was ingested into the starboard engine causing Foreign Object Damage (FOD) and a fire.[5]

Mockup of the proposed NAGPAW: clear canopy for the BN, scooped intake ducts, and two tails. (Carlton)

YA3J-1 Vigilante prototype posed for publicity photographs with a dressed crewman on the boarding ladder talking to pilot. There is no ejection seat in the rear cockpit because test instrumentation was later installed there. (EBAL)

Vigilante was approved. The rollout of BuNo 145157, the first Vigilante, was 16 May 1958. North American test pilot Dick Wenzel made the first flight from Columbus on 31 August that year.

NAA Columbus

North American Aviation (NAA) began building airplanes in 1934. The main facility was in Los Angeles, California. A pre–Korean War surge in air force and navy contracts caused an overload in production, and an additional production capacity was needed.

The Columbus, Ohio, airport (Port Columbus) had opened in 1929 as the eastern air terminus of the Transcontinental Air Transport air-rail New York–to–Los Angeles transcontinental route. During World War II, the airport became Naval Air Station Columbus. In 1950, NAA leased the extensive naval industrial reserve facility then occupied by the then rapidly sinking Curtiss-Wright Company. Eventually, it became an integrated, self-sufficient engineering and manufacturing facility.[6] With a 10,000-foot runway, the airfield was more than adequate for jet airplanes.

Besides Vigilantes, the Columbus Division built the swept-wing FJ Fury series, F-100 Super Sabre, T-2 Buckeye, T-28 Trojan, and OV-10 Bronco.

YA3J prototype in front of the NAA plant at Port Columbus, Ohio. The names of the plant's two previous products are displayed on top of the building.

Chapter 2

CONCEPT AND CONSTRUCTION

The Vigilante marked the end of the era when companies merely produced airplanes. The new concept was building a complete "weapons system." From its beginning, the entire aircraft was integrated with the latest systems and equipment. Success with a defined mission became the goal, not just going faster and higher. Technological advances dramatically increased mission capabilities and, at the same time, expanded pilot workload. The two-man crew became the rule; the McDonnell F-4 Phantom and Grumman A-6 Intruder are other examples. Each, in its way, was as sophisticated as the Vigilante.

Making a Weapons System

The navy designated the Vigilante's Weapon's-Navigation System the AN/ASB-12. The major components were a radar and television, REINS, and VERDAN. The technology was advanced and complex. It was a rare crew member who truly understood how the ASB-12 worked. Operating the system was the major task of bombardier-navigators, and they received specialized and extensive training in its operation. The Vigilante RAG had Douglas

A3J BuNo 147857, with its distinctive orange arrow fuselage paint, with boarding ladders to both cockpits. The first versions of the ladders had extendable hand grips at the top (the curved handles) and were built for lightness. Damage from rough handling aboard carriers eventually caused the ladders to be made with heavier metal tubing. The BN is Petty Officer Ray Williams (see chapter 1 sidebar "Navy Enlisted Bombardier-Navigators (NEBN)"). (R. Williams)

to measure acceleration/deceleration in all dimensions (up, down, left, right, forward, back) and integrate acceleration with time to get velocity, which is speed and direction. With a known and continuously updated velocity, navigation between any two points on Earth is possible.

Versatile Digital Analyzer (VERDAN)

For computing all the factors that went into navigation and weapons delivery, North American Autonetics developed the first airborne digital computer. It was one of the first solid-state

A pair of A-5As from VAH-1. Vigilante lead is "clean wing" (i.e., no pylons are installed). The Vigilante nearer the camera has a drop tank on the right wing and a practice bomb pod on the other. The tailhooks are retracted and doors closed. The A-frame portion is painted black and white to help LSOs check if the hook is down. (NNAM)

A3D-2T (TA-3B) Skywarriors, which had additional operating stations in the fuselage to train new BNs in operating the radar and navigation system before going on to the Vigilante.

Pilots knew the principles and capabilities but were happy to have someone else operate the system on missions. The simplified indicators for heading and distance in the front cockpit were sufficient. The most common instruction from the back seat was, "Follow steering."

Radar-Equipped Inertial Navigation System (REINS)

North American Aviation had experience with inertial navigation systems in its Navajo long-range cruise missile and made it the key element in the ASB-12. (The ram-jet-powered Navaho SM-64 project was canceled when the Atlas ICBM became effective. Its inertial navigation system was used in Polaris missile submarines as well as the Vigilante.) The basic principle of inertial navigation is

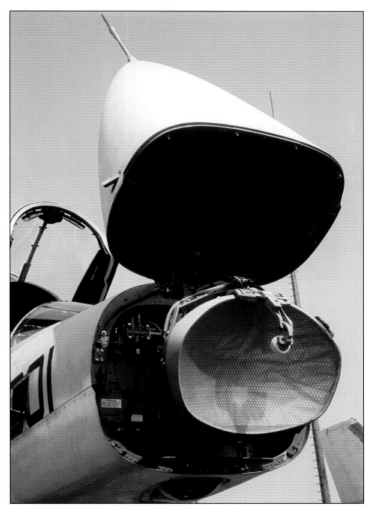

The radar antenna is a dual-surface paraboloidal reflector with a flexible Mylar diaphragm (without air pressure, the reflector wrinkles), which uses a vacuum pump to change shape. The antenna sweeps 45 degrees side to side and can tilt 30 degrees down. The rail in the middle of the pilot's canopy is for the retractable blast shield. On the forward upper edge are two rearview mirrors and a standby magnetic compass. (J. Woodul)

The nose cone is raised and the avionics platform lowered on support struts for access to the radar antenna, the VERDAN (computer) box, and the insulation-covered REINS (inertial platform) ball. (USN)

computer systems fitted to an aircraft. Corrections and changes could be inserted by the bombardier-navigator, especially updates to current position. Launching from a ship at sea, the starting position was not usually very accurate and an update on first "seeing" a known geographical location was vital to accurate navigation. There were three ways for an update:

- The radar was the first monopulse radar with terrain avoidance features (multimode Ku band using a flexible antenna).
- A television scanner head on the underside of the nose replaced the periscope of the AJ and A3D, which stuck out in the slip stream. The cathode ray tube (CRT) scope in the rear cockpit could be switched between radar and TV. Both displayed an azimuth line and range arc for target and checkpoint identification. The radar returns were orange colored; the TV presentation, nominally black and white, had a decidedly blue shade.

- The pilot could be linked to the system and use the multi-functional trigger on his control stick to "mark on top."

There were problems, especially in the early days. During the testing phase, the VERDAN computer had a mean time between failure (MTBF) of only 15 minutes. However, within a few years the computer's MTBF improved to a reasonable 240 hours.[1] The VERDAN required preheating and aligning the auto navigator platform, part of REINS, which took up to 30 minutes. (Some prankster redefined VERDAN as "Very Effective Replacement for a Dumb-Ass Navigator.")

"One of my early memories of the A-5 was the amount of support equipment required, especially that needed for alignment of the inertial navigation systems. About 30 minutes of external power and air conditioning was required for a proper alignment before power could be transferred to the aircraft itself. This could present a major problem at times, because the early support equipment was not always too reliable and many of the shore units were surplus army field units.

"Of course, the navy finally received its own RCPP 105 pods, containing electric power, air conditioning, and air start capability. These could be mounted on carts for mobility and could also be suspended from external bomb racks for emergency situations. These were relatively reliable compact units, but still took up a lot of space, especially onboard ship.

"As time went on, the carriers themselves were configured to provide power, air conditioning, and air start capability for the Vigilantes as well as inertial navigation information; this solved at least one of the early maintenance nightmares, as well as a shipboard handling problem."[2]

The Bomb Tunnel

The bomb bay tunnel determined the design of the airplane. The J79 engines, ducts, and afterburners on both sides along with the tunnel were enclosed in a box that became the fuselage. Wing and tail structures were attached and the crew accommodated in the streamlined nose section. It is ironic that the radical concept of the tunnel was not successful. As much as the tunnel influenced the design, and became a memorable feature of the Vigilante, it was never used as intended.

The tunnel also severely affected access for maintenance. The space was used for extra fuel and, in the RA-5C, the "can" for the Passive Electronic Counter Measures (PECM) system. Even once the Vigilante established it could accurately drop conventional and nuclear weapons from its wing pylons, no A-5 ever dropped a weapon in anger. (There were tales of annoyed crews dropping small practice bombs near fishermen who did not move away from the target range on Lake George.)

The concept was that the Vigilante would fly over the target at high altitude and very high speed. At the correct moment determined by the bombing computer, the tail cone would be blown off (one version had a decoy radar emitter inside of it) and the bomb train

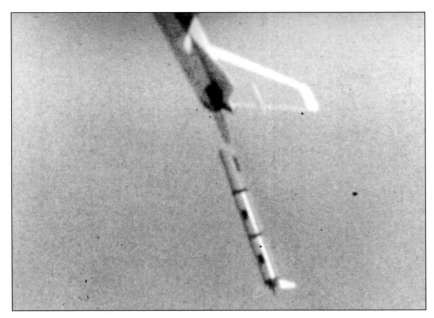

Frame from a movie taken during weapon release testing. The bomb train has cleared the tunnel and will continue upward to the top of a long arc before losing speed and nosing over. The maneuver gives the Vigilante time to use its high speed to get away from the blast. The bomb is on the front of the train, with two 295-gallon fuel tanks ("cans") fastened to it. Stabilizing fins at the rear have sprung open. (THA)

consisting of the bomb with its two attached, big, and now empty, fuel cans would follow. The cans would help stabilize the trajectory of the bomb. Being so high up, the Vigilante would remain above enemy air defenses. After bombs away, the altitude and speed of the Vigilante would keep it clear of the bomb blast.

When improvements in air defenses made the high-altitude high-speed attack method risky, the delivery tactic was changed to a loft maneuver. This had the aircraft coming in at high speed on the deck and pulling up at an initial point before the bomb released to go on a loft trajectory to the target. Both methods had complications. Computing exactly how much backward velocity was put on the ejected bomb was difficult, especially with the loft flight profile. In addition, test drops determined the aerodynamic forces tended to keep the bomb following along inside of the low-pressure area behind the aircraft. Accuracy was poor.

The sides and top of the tunnel held fuel lines, control cables, electrical wiring, wave guide, and radio antennas. The bottom had rails for the fuel cans; a creeper with wheels that fit it was made to ease mechanics' access.

Ed Gillespie flew many of the A3J supersonic bomb test drops . . . er, ejections. He was whipping along at Mach 1.6 over the Salton Sea when, on ground control's countdown, he punched the pickle. There were tremendous bangs, a whole lot of shaking, every light on the warning panels illuminated, and over his headset he heard a Los Angeles radio station with Louis Armstrong singing "When the Saints Go Marching In."[3]

Pilots and BNs of VAH-7 wearing MkIV full pressure suits on the flight deck of the USS Enterprise circa 1962. The unlikely formation, no cooling boxes, and no flotation devices on the suits indicate the photo was probably taken for publicity purposes. The pilot on the left (possibly Ken Enney, later CRAW-1) has removed one glove by unlocking the fastener ring.

High-Speed Drops

Another solution to the high-speed bomb dropping problem was a rotating bomb bay, which the British used on the Canberra (later the USAF B-57) and the Blackburn Buccaneer. The other aircraft designed for supersonic drops was the Convair B-58 Hustler, which used a large, streamlined pod carried externally on its belly. This meant the Hustler's landing gear were especially tall.

B-57, license-built Canberra by Martin Company. The internal bomb bay could carry a 10,000-pound bomb. (Wikipedia)

The Convair B-58 Hustler carried the bomb and additional fuel in the large pod that was dropped on target much like the bomb and fuel-can train ejected from the Vigilante. The B-58 had four J-79 engines with afterburners; the same engines as the A-5. (Wikipedia)

A3J over Patuxent River Test Center, 4 October 1960. The stylized W on the tail shows it is being flown by the Weapons Systems Test (WST) division. The two wing pylons have red-painted practice bomb dispensers. The Patuxent River is to the top and Chesapeake Bay to the right. The breakwater at the lower edge surrounds the seaplane ramp.

Space Suit

The human body requires extreme protection at the altitudes at which the Vigilante flew. Besides the lack of oxygen, above 50,000 feet atmospheric pressure is so low that human organs expand and fluids boil. To protect against these effects, BFGoodrich developed a high-altitude full-pressure suit.

In 1958, the standard high-altitude issue for US Navy squadrons was the USN MkIV, Mod 1, Type 1, which included helmet, full neck ring, detachable gloves, and integrated cloth shoes. The Mark IV, Model 3, Type 1 suit featured various enhancements in fit and ease of donning, as well as substantially improved pressurization control. It went on to be selected as the basic foundation of NASA's early Earth-orbital suit (the original Mercury prototype suits were specially reworked Mark IV suits). The suits were hot, uncomfortable, and awkward. Crews had to carry coolant boxes from the time of donning the suit until the aircraft's air-conditioning system was running.

Dave Sharp, whose first squadron was VAH-7 remembers, "We went to NAS Jax, got fitted, went to 70,000 feet in pressure chamber, experienced a decompression and watched a beaker of water boil. The instructor said in the headset that the water would be your blood if the suit wasn't on. He had you try to grab an imaginary throttle and stick and fly the aircraft. Always remember the considerable effort that took compared to astronauts in later years effortlessly bouncing around on the moon. We also walked around the bottom of a swimming pool wearing the suit. Fun time.

"Took them on the '64 cruise [the *Enterprise*] but never broke them out of storage. One mistake I've always regretted was that I never had a picture taken with it on."

For a while, the syllabus in the RAG used both the A-5A and RA-5C. Harry Klein wrote, "When I first flew the A-5A and they let me get to 60,000 and Mach 2, they didn't insist I wear a pressure suit with the retention system, and luckily, I didn't have to punch out."

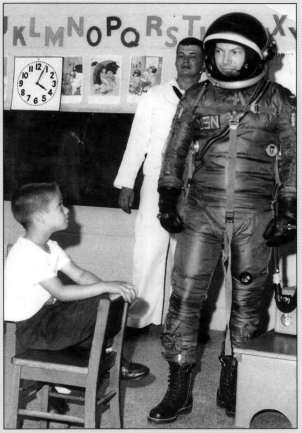

Enlisted BN "Rotten" Ralph Feeback was volunteered for a Sanford, Florida, elementary school's "Show and Tell" wearing the Goodrich MkIV suit. He explained, "It was on a Friday. Look at the clock. No way an officer was going to do it."

The sailor is a Parachute Rigger (PR) who provided the necessary assistance for donning and getting out of the suit. The box on the stool has a battery-powered blower to force air into the suit for cooling. Flight crews carried a box when going from the ready room to the aircraft. The MkIV had integral fabric socks and separate, normal flight boots. A suit pressure gauge is on the left thigh. (Feeback)

Early production A3J-1 (BuNo 147856) wearing flashy flight test scheme during Special Weapons Trials at Kirtland AFB, New Mexico, in 1962. Aircraft hugs its shadow executing a high-speed run-in prior to pitching up for a low-level loft delivery. (Mike Machat painting)

Heads-Up

The Pilot's Projected Display Indicator (PPDI) was one of the first heads-up displays (HUD) to be fitted to an operational aircraft. Almost all of today's aircraft have HUDs. Besides flight data, imagery from the radar and the TV camera were displayed on the back-seater's radar scope and the PPDI. Probably the least successful innovation was Terrain Avoidance (TA). TA is a most desirable feature for all-weather low-level attack capability, but it was ahead of its time in the Vigilante because of the lack of advanced digital computer technology.

"TA was demonstrated a couple of times while we were at NAS Sanford. Preparing the aircraft for flight required several tech reps, and 8 to 10 hours for alignment, to ensure that the system would have a chance to operate as advertised. In other words, the most advanced capability was theoretically provided, but the technology still had to be developed to provide the reliability to make the system routinely operable in a real-world situation for all normal missions."[4]

When the Vigilante's mission became reconnaissance and no longer had the requirement to fly hugging the ground, the complex and hard-to-maintain system was removed, giving the pilot one of the most unobstructed forward views of any military aircraft.

First Flights

The first prototype YA3J was rolled out of the Columbus plant on 16 May 1958. There was little doubt of its name; "Vigilante" was painted on the nose in large florid, black lettering. The radome was black. No one could have foreseen that after a successful 21-year career and 156 aircraft, the last Vigilante noses would also be black.

NAA test pilot Dick Wenzel had the honor of the first flight on 31 August 1958 in BuNo 145157. The takeoff and the landing were made using manual control systems. Electric flight was engaged and tested at altitude. The planned supersonic run was canceled due to a radio failure. The YA3J did reach 0.92 Mach and 35,000 feet.

The only uncomfortable incident was on descent when the windscreen frosted over. The canopy defrost system worked but took 5 minutes to clear a view and "produced an uncomfortably high cockpit temperature and head buffeting." The conclusions paragraph from the report reads: "The only major deficiency revealed within the scope of the flying performed on this flight was flap-horizontal stabilizer buffet. Lateral control effectiveness will require further evaluation. Although a number of malfunctions were encountered, none were critical."[5]

The second Vigilante, BuNo 145158, completed 49 test flights but then crashed after a fire erupted in the nose wheel well of the aircraft. NAA test pilot, Zeke Hopkins, ejected successfully. Because this aircraft was heavily instrumented, it dealt a severe blow to the program. The cause was attributed to a hydraulic leak in the wheel well, which was ignited by the battery installed there. Ironically, the battery was not a production feature of the aircraft but was installed to provide power only for the instrumentation package located in the rear cockpit.[6]

The initial run of nine A3J-1s and the surviving prototype were turned over to the navy for evaluation trials.

Bob Elder, as Director of Flight Test at Patuxent River during the Vigilante's initial testing, was the first military pilot to fly the Vigilante, a YA3J-1. He recalled, "Among the several advanced technologies of the period, the Vigilante incorporated an early form of fly-by-wire flight control system. Both the longitudinal and lateral flight control systems used electric signaling for normal operation with mechanical backup preloaded to actuate automatically should the electrical system fail, and it did, or at least the fly-by-wire longitudinal system did, at an altitude of about 200 feet, immediately after my first takeoff.

Late stage of NAA assembly line where the tracks for the cradle end. The Vigilante now has landing gear and can be rolled on its own. A second assembly line is on the other side of the factory. (NAA)

"During reversion to manual, a full nose-down pitch command was pulsed to the horizontal stabilator and the ensuing recovery was best described as a steeplechase through the sagebrush, chasing jack-rabbits and trailing a dense plume of dust for several miles across the desert shades of the F-16! Fortunately, no harm, no foul, but hardly a confidence builder."[7]

A problem that came up early in development was the failure of the longeron attachment fitting, the barrel nut, located just aft of the BN cockpit. This fitting provided structural continuity between the forward section of the aircraft and the after section starting just aft of the engine intakes. The first failure occurred during drop test at about 17 ft/sec when trying to meet the specification of 21 ft/sec. The forward section of the plane sheared off as if someone had hit it with a guillotine.

"After a fix was developed and repairs made, drop tests recommenced. I was present at the drop test when the next failure occurred at about 19 ft/sec, and saw the tail resting on the safety support straps provided under the empennage, and the nose sitting on the floor. I can still remember John Shepherd, the Attack Design Class Desk Officer at the time, coming to Columbus and laying down the law—the program was in serious trouble—and telling North American to 'fix the plane—or else.'

"An improved barrel nut was developed, which was to ensure the integrity of the upper longeron so that it would meet its specification requirements. The resulting Airframe Service Change was to be installed as soon as possible but it was not at that time considered a safety of flight item."[8]

Airplanes were left unpainted and coated with an anti-corrosive (which crews called "S**t-brindle-brown) until factory check flights were completed. The Columbus factory is directly below. (Turner)

Tests, Demos, and Showing Off

One of the best ways to garner publicity for a new airplane is to set records with it. The navy put famous aviatrix Jacqueline Cochrane in the back cockpit of an A3J to make her the first woman to fly faster than twice the speed of sound.[9]

A more significant record was set on 13 December 1960 when an A3J-1 flew to 91,451 feet carrying payload of 1,000 kilograms (2,204 pounds), setting a world record. The crew from NATC Patuxent River was pilot CDR Leroy Heath and bombardier-navigator LT Larry Monroe. The feat was made possible by using fuel cans as "payload," which were weighed by official observers before being loaded in the Vigilante's linear bomb bay.

Larry Monroe

Larry Monroe was on the ground floor of the BN profession. He enlisted during World War II and was a Torpedoman in the Pacific before changing to aviation electronics in 1947. As a new First Class Petty Officer (AT-1), he was at NOTS China Lake in 1948 and worked on *Project Atlas*; the forerunner of the system that was used in Vigilantes.

After graduating with distinction from Officer Candidate School (OCS), ENS Monroe was in two AJ Savage squadrons and an A3D training unit; he was the R&D project officer for the systems in both the A3D and A3J before going on to VAH-7, the first squadron to deploy. Monroe was the first navy bombardier-navigator to fly the Vigilante with the ASB-12, first to drop a bomb with the system, and first to go Mach 2+.

Record Runs

The navy's new A3J aircraft was tested and evaluated at Patuxent River Test Center, Maryland. CDR Heath and LT Monroe pushed the experimental A3J to incredible new limits. The aviators performed three test flights at Patuxent River prior to the record attempts at Edwards AFB. On one test flight, they climbed to 80,000 feet over the Atlantic, which meant they had (unofficially) broken the previous record (69,000 feet). However, at peak altitude, CDR Heath made an adjustment of the nose and wing, which sent them into inertial coupling because the air was so thin at that altitude that there was no resistance, and they started tumbling end over end on all three axes. Legend has it that the cockpit recording was pretty colorful. They finally regained control at 12,000 feet.

That experience prepared them for the record flight, where everything was going great until the fire warning lights came on. They decided to come out of afterburner, shut down both engines, and zoom climb from there. When they reached the record altitude (91,450.8 feet), the plane nosed over and they again tumbled around all three axes. This time, they made no adjustments, knowing that the aircraft would eventually right itself when it reached denser air and they could relight the engines. It also meant a 70,000-foot free fall![10]

Although not a record, Bob Elder wrote of an early public display of the Vigilante:

I had received approval to stop at Andrews [during their annual air show] en route from North American, Columbus in May of '59 with the first Patuxent River flight test aircraft, A3J-1 BuNo 145159, specifically for static display only.

Now static display may be better than nothing, but not much! In fact, the thought of that sleek new bird roosting on the ramp while the show went on was depressing to me. So much so that I decided

Early version of rear cockpit side console. The round knob controls the navigation system and was changed to a more ergonomic vertical handle. The flip-down shelf, upper left, gave the BN a flat place to work. The warning flag is in the alternate twist-and-pull ejection handle with the padded leg retractor in front.

to test the water with DCNO (Air) VADM Robert B. Pirie. Hoping for a mellow response, I placed the phone call to his quarters the evening before the show, along about the cocktail hour. Approval was granted, with some constraints.

Unfortunately, my performance the next day neither lasted very long nor did much to credit my confidence, or the Admiral's decision. Every aircraft manufacturer seems to have an Achilles' heel, and with North American Aviation it was wheel well doors or panels. Shedding one or more seemed to be a necessity in the developmental test history of a number of its airplanes. I acquired that test point shortly after takeoff, a rather sporty chandelle reentry to a burner pass down the runway on the deck—all out—streaming parts down the runway and along the flight path!

Not all of them, however, as the right main wheel well door buried itself about three feet deep into the leading edge of the stabilator, none of which did anything to improve the aerodynamics or control qualities of the airplane, or my morale.

Following a somewhat gimpy trip from Andrews 50 or so miles south to Patuxent, I made an uneventful landing and filled out the not-so-uneventful reports. The rest of the day and night were spent uncomfortably wondering where the substantial number of missing parts had impacted along my route of flight.

Sunday morning early, having scanned the *Washington Post*, happily with negative results, and hoping it had all gone away, I

A3J with test markings hooked to a tug on a carrier (probably the USS Saratoga) on an elevator lowered to the hangar deck. Nose, wings, and tail are folded. (NNAM)

received a phone call from an air force major, who, with family and friends [had] gathered at home watching the air show, while roasting hot dogs and the like. [They] last saw the barbeque disappear in a trailing stream of burning charcoal! Miraculously, no one was injured.

A new barbeque, a bag of charcoal, a generous supply of steaks, and an understanding fellow pilot ended what could have been an otherwise more distasteful incident."[11]

1961 Grand Tour, Salon international de l'aéronautique et de l'espace de Paris

Did you say two weeks in Paris? Where do I [LT H.L. "Larry" Monroe] sign up?

That was my immediate response when I learned of the navy's plan to send an A3J [Vigilante] and F4H [Phantom II] to the 1961 International Air Salon in Paris. It had all the earmarks of a lot of good flying with a great liberty town thrown in as a bonus.

I had visions of We Three (that's the "J-Bird" [A3J], John Moore, and I) leisurely winging on our Great Circle across the broad Atlantic, nonchalantly plugging into a tanker and then thrilling the eager crowds as we taxied in at Le Bourget Airport in the prettiest airplane in the world.

The A3J, F4H, S2F (Tracker), and HSS-2 (Sea King) helicopter (three of these aircraft held world speed and altitude records at the time) were then being evaluated at Patuxent River and going to the show. The Marines provided a GV-1 Hercules for air refueling the jets en route. The HSS-2 was shipped, the "Stoof"[12] flew.

The route was not to be a quick nonstop Great Circle, but two Great Circles intersecting in the Azores where we were to RON [Remian Over Night]. But surprise came when I learned that I wasn't going to have my "Boon to Bombardiers," the automatic navigation system, to do all the work for me. [It was unspecified as to why he did not have the ASB-12 inertial navigation system. Unavailable or security?] No sextant, no omni, no "bird dog," no radar, not even a drift sight.

My navigation was really great up to Boston, but that's where the TACAN ended and my "wet finger"/compass [Dead Reckoning] DR began. We were to rendezvous with our GV-1 tanker 110 miles southeast of Argentia so our great circle track kept us just outside of range of the few TACAN stations on Nova Scotia and Newfoundland. I never really appreciated the AFCS [Automatic Flight Control System] in the A3J until now. It was holding heading to a gnat's eyebrow, and I thought the altimeter was stuck, we were so steady.

The Phantom chose the right side fuel drogue so the Vigilante took the left. During refueling, Heath and MSgt Carl Mayers, Radar Operator (RIO) in the Phantom, compared their navigation calculations. *It's comforting to have another head checking your computation when you're playing with 28 degrees of variation and 70 to 100 knots of wind. It could spoil your whole day if you happened to apply that variation as east instead of west.*

As we taxied in at Lajes, the air force tower operator called and asked, "852 what type aircraft is that?"

"This is the Alpha Three Juliet, a Vigilante."

"Roger, 852. 819, what type of aircraft are you?"

MSgt Myers answered in his best Inner Sanctum voice, "Tower, 819—this—is—the—Phantom."

The S2F had left Patuxent with a two-day head start, spent the night in Argentia before tackling the 1,300-mile leg to the Azores. As the jets landed in Lajes, the slow-flying Stoof was already there.

After passing our position report to Santa Maria and rogering for a "guesstimate" for the Paris FIR [Flight Identification Region], they bid us adieu as we climbed to 39,000 and headed for the Lido.

I really tried to comply with the rules. I called France Control until I was sounding like a broken record, trying to report entering the Paris FIR, but no joy. We went feet dry, right on the nose, just south of Brest, but I still couldn't raise France Control. By now I was glad John was the pilot and I was the BN. He would get stuck with the flight violation.

France Control finally came up and cleared them direct to Le Bourget. *Not one cross word about our missing reports!*

As we taxied into the static display area, who was the first to greet us? The crew of that hot-rod S2F!

We didn't realize how busy we'd be [the two weeks at the show]. Brief, debrief, critique, stand by the airplane, answer questions, practice flying for the air show, tape a radio broadcast, and meet the press.

There was another type [of spectator] with slide rules, note pads, super-duper cameras, and even binoculars, outside the roped-off area standing on tiptoe, lying on the ground, straining in all directions to study every available detail.[13]

The last day of the show, four plane divisions of A4Ds, F8Us, and A3Ds from Air Wing 8 on the *Forrestal* (CVA-59) were scheduled to do a fly-by. The navy liaison officer bet the air force representative a barrel of beer that the flight would arrive exactly on time, to the minute. He won the bet.

All the aircraft then spent a full week performing demonstrations in England and Germany before heading back across the Atlantic. *We were bucking 100 knots on the nose from Lajes to Argentia. We rendezvoused with the GV 300 miles at sea, out of reach of any and all navigation fixes. We arrived in Argentia on the prettiest VFR [Visual Flight Rules] day the natives had seen in quite a while. Both jets were still in an up status and only needed routine servicing for the last leg to Pax the following morning.*

The big liberty turned out to be a total of two days off between 20 May and 16 June.[14]

Presidential Question

When the A3J-1 and the USS *Kitty Hawk* (CVA-63) were new, Ed Gillespie flew a Vigilante to NAS North Island for a presidential visit to the aircraft carrier. As he said, "The aircraft was unfortunately hoisted aboard, so I didn't get a trap out of it, but it was still a thrill to stand by the navy's newest when the president of the United States came by."

To make it look special, NAA had Ed's name painted below the cockpit Navy style, "LT Ed Gillespie USNR."

Most aircraft being tested have high-visibility paint applied in simple, geometric patterns. The sleek lines of the Vigilante seem to have inspired painters as seen on this A3J, BuNo 147857, at the NAS Pensacola air show celebrating the 50th anniversary of Naval Aviation. The pulchritudinous young women are candidates for the title of "Miss Fiftieth." The caption in Naval Aviation News *August 1961 notes that the winner is seventh from the right.*

The Vigilante wasn't the only airplane on display. There were Crusaders (F8U), a Skyray (F4D), Skywarriors (A3D), Demons (F3H), and others. As President Eisenhower toured around, he stopped at the Vigilante, looked it over, turned to his naval aide, and said, "I thought this airplane was one of our newest types."

"Yes, Mr. President, it certainly is," replied the aide.

"Well then," asked Ike, "why are the goddamn reserves flying it?"

How Do You Get In?

Several navy carrier aircraft had cockpits that were high off the deck either because of the attitude required for catapulting or clearance for hanging ordnance, yet they did not have steps for entering the cockpit. The F3H Demon, F7U Cutlass, A-4 Skyhawk, and RA-5C Vigilante all required special boarding ladders. (The black-painted indexes on the cockpit edges at the canopy seam of the Vigilante showed where to hang the ladder.) The ladders were fine on board ship or at home base, but what did the crew do at cross-country stops or diverts to non-navy bases?

Before shutting down the engines and losing hydraulic pressure, the pilot had to remember to trim as far nose down as possible. This put the trailing edge of the big horizontal stabilizer at its lowest position. Then when the crew came back to the airplane, they opened both canopies with switches on the side of the nose, walked back to the tail, and (with skill worthy of an acrobat) jumped, pulled, and turned themselves onto the stabilizer. This was difficult without torso harness, life preserver, survival vest, hard hat, map bag, and G-suit getting in the way.

Once up, it was easy to stand, take a short step onto the relatively flat fuselage, and walk forward to the RAN's canopy, grasp the edge for stability while inching forward on the narrow sill on the cockpit edge. The RAN could then step into his cockpit. The poor pilot had still to grasp the edge of the back cockpit with one hand, reach forward to his own canopy with the other and take a giant stride to get his left foot on his canopy sill, pause spread-eagle 9 feet off the ground, and hop-shift his weight forward. Not a whole lot of fun on a windy, rainy night.

The view at the start of the climb to the cockpits (which would have been opened). Display airplane at NNAM, Pensacola, with late-model ECM antennas in a "beaver tail" fairing and the usually unpainted tail cone, gray and white.

Sonic Booms

The navy loaned NASA A3J/A-5A BuNo 147858 for simulation studies for the then-ongoing American supersonic transport (SST). The flights from the Dryden Center at Edwards AFB also studied sonic booms and noise pollution. The year-long research program ended in 1963, making BuNo 147858 one of a handful of Vigilantes to fly as an A-5A and the last to be converted to an RA-5C.

Next Model

Experience showed that improvements were needed in fuel capacity and low-speed handling and were made in the early 1960s; the resulting aircraft was the A3J-2/A-5B. An added fuel tank on top of the fuselage and an additional weapons pylon on each wing were the obvious external differences. Bleed air for BLC now came from the leading-edge droops, effectively "blowing" the entire wing instead of just the flaps. Production was begun even as the first squadrons were making their first deployments with Vigilantes.

Only two A-5Bs were delivered to the navy before two events complicated the identification of the Vigilante. First, North American Aviation (NAA) merged with Rockwell Corporation to become North American Rockwell (NAR). Second, the Department of Defense redesignated all aircraft to a unified system. The basic A3J became the A-5.

A3J-1 (BuNo 146694) at NAS Miramar. The third Vigilante built, this airplane crashed at Port Columbus in September 1963. (THA)

Prototype A3J-2/A-5A modified from A3J-1. The added fuel tank and subsequent modification to the fuselage is obvious because the changed area has not been painted.

Demonstration of the wide variety of weapons and stores the Vigilante could carry as an attack bomber. Front row: unguided rockets with launching pods, large and small Bullpup missiles. Middle area: low-drag Mark80 series conventional bombs and a multiple ejector rack (MER). Nearest the airplane: dispensers and small practice bombs. Back row: droppable fuel tanks and nuclear bombs carried on wing stations. The four wing stations indicate that it probably is an A3J-2/A-5B posed to show the adaptability of the Vigilante. (NNAM)

Chapter 3

VIGILANTE AT SEA

The sixth Vigilante built being hoisted aboard the USS Saratoga (CV-60) in July 1960 prior to the first carrier trials. The tail has the chevron marking of the Pax River test center and the NAA "Advertising" logo and name on the nose. Wings and tail are folded and the radome is raised. Civilian workers (NAA tech reps) are near the canopy and on top of the wing. (NNAM)

The Vigilante went to sea for the first time during the week of 25 July 1960, aboard the USS *Saratoga* (CVA-60). Fourteen successful launches and arrested landings were made by pilots from NATC Patuxent River, and no major problems were discovered. Later tests evaluated the A3J at higher gross weights and reduced wind over the deck to establish minimum catapult end speeds.[1] At the conclusion of these carrier qualification tests, North American's new twinjet thoroughbred officially became a carrier-based US Navy aircraft.

In June 1961, four Vigilantes went to VAH-3 in Sanford, Florida, to train crews and maintainers. "Heavy Three" had been the RAG

for the A3D, and the transition was a natural. (A-3 training eventually went solely to VAH-123 at NAS Whidbey Island in Washington state.) The men in the back cockpits were BNs and many were enlisted men until, in 1962, "No more enlisted BNs" was decreed and many former chiefs and petty officers rapidly became ensigns. The pilots were all second tour, mostly from A3D squadrons, which meant they were senior lieutenants or lieutenant-commanders.

As A3J-1s were delivered from the North American factory in Columbus, Ohio, two more squadrons transitioned from the A3D: the VAH-7 *Peacemakers* and the VAH-1 *Smoking Tigers*.

RVAH-3 patch on a G-2 leather flight jacket. Call-sign was Drake, *and nickname was* Dragons, *although it was rarely used and usually simply called, "The RAG."*

any major handling problems. One evolution was to move the aircraft from the flight deck to the hangar deck. The number-2 flight deck elevator was too small to lower the full length of the Vigilante, so the radome had to be raised.

Once at the hangar deck level, the radome had to be put back down again and the upper portion of the vertical tail had to be folded because of the low overhead of the *Roosevelt's* hangar deck. The limited size and height of Midway-class hangar decks determined the impracticality of ever operating the Vigilante routinely from the Midway class.[2] However, this did not preclude running carrier qualifications, as the aircraft remained on the flight deck. Both VAH-7 (1962) and VAH-1 (1963) did CarQual (CQ) periods on the *Roosevelt.*

VAH-7 *Peacemakers*

Previously an A3D squadron, VAH-7 transitioned to the Vigilante beginning August 1961 using VAH-3 aircraft and their own as they arrived. The *Peacemakers* were operational by January 1962 and carrier qualified on the *Roosevelt* the same month.

During CarQuals on the *Roosevelt*, operating out of Mayport, Florida, CDR Bud Gear hit the ramp on his first night landing attempt and the aircraft fell off the angle for the first fleet loss of a Vigilante. CDR Gear was slated to be CO of VAH-7 and his loss was a shock to all of Heavy Attack.[3]

Assigned to CVW-6, VAH-7 became the first squadron to deploy with the Vigilante when it took a dozen A3Js on board the USS *Enterprise* (CVAN-65) for the ship's and aircraft's first extended time at sea. The planned stay in the Mediterranean was cut short when the Cuban Missile Crisis broke in October 1962. VAH-7 was placed in standby at Sanford, but did not fly any missions directly related to Cuba.

"After the return of VAH-7 to Sanford, the Cuban Missile Crisis erupted, and the *Enterprise* and the Air Group were ordered to Cuban waters. VAH-7 had not yet unpacked its maintenance cruise boxes and had to prepare to go back to Norfolk. All personnel, except pilots and BNs of those aircraft scheduled to fly to the *Enterprise* from Sanford, were flown back to Norfolk for loading aboard.

"*Enterprise* deployed to Cuban waters and on Sunday morning, shortly after arriving on station, just before noon, we were all called into the ready room and were told that an augmented squadron of Marine A-4s was to come aboard, so the Vigilante recovery was canceled. It was determined that the Vigi's range could well encompass Cuba from Sanford, if needed.

VAH-7 flight crew with A-5A Vigilante on the flight deck of the USS Enterprise *(CVAN-65). The torso harnesses and flotation devices are the type that could also be worn over the MkIV pressure suit. G-suits were sometimes not worn depending on the mission. The orange cotton flight suits were standard in the US Navy until the war in Vietnam.*

Small Boat

There was an early evaluation of operating from the Midway class of aircraft carriers. A couple of A-5s were loaded on board the USS *Franklin D. Roosevelt* (CVA-42) at Mayport, Florida, to determine

Two A-5As of VAH-1 on the USS Franklin D. Roosevelt (CVA-42) in May 1963 while carrier qualifying in the new airplanes. VAH-7 had done CQ on the same ship the year before. The low height of the hangar deck is not a problem during CQ as there is no reason for the Vigilantes to go there. The VF-74 F-4 Phantom is not part of the ship's assigned air wing; the A-4 Skyhawk and F-8 Crusaders are. (NNAM)

"The XO [Executive Officer] pointed a finger at me and said, 'George, you got it,' and I had the enviable (sic) task of off-loading all personnel and gear by C-1A Carrier on Board Delivery (COD aircraft) and getting them back to Sanford."[4]

The Mediterranean deployment resumed in February 1963 and lasted for seven months when the *Enterprise* was relieved by the USS *Independence* (CVA-62) with VAH-1 on board—the only other squadron to deploy with A3J/A-5A.

"Just a week or two before the *Enterprise* cruise was scheduled to get underway, LCDR George Jessen and his BN, LT William Blakemore, while preflighting a Vigi, noticed that the nose section had an unusual droop. They reported the condition to maintenance, and further inspection revealed a failed barrel nut. As a result, installation of the improved barrel nut became an urgent action that had to be completed before VAH-7 went to sea.

"The Airframe Change kits, which were already in development from the last drop test failure, were delivered to NAS Sanford without delay. A contractor team came down to Sanford from North American Aviation with the newly designed barrel nuts and one or two special torque wrenches. All 12 of VAH-7's Vigis needed the change, so a 24-hour round-the-clock program was set up in each hangar.

"Because one of the critical items was the specially designed torque wrench, the Wing Commander, CAPT Joe Tully, established a 'Junior Officer Watch' to maintain accountability of the torque wrench. And woe to the 'watch' if he did not know where it was when needed. Once, when one of the torque wrenches failed, the ever-dependable NAS Sanford Aircraft Intermediate Maintenance Department (AIMD) manufactured a replacement on-site to meet the NAA specifications. Timing was close, and as I recall, one or two of the aircraft had to be recovered after the *Enterprise* left Norfolk, not so much as a result of the barrel nuts, but for last-minute maintenance actions that were delayed because of their installation."[5]

After a half year at home, the *Peacemakers* headed out, again on the *Enterprise*.

While in the Mediterranean, attack aircraft squadrons were

Vigilante of VAH-7 launching from the bow catapult and F8U Crusader of VF-62 off the waist catapult of the USS Enterprise *(CVAN-65) during the ship's initial time at sea in 1962. The other fighter squadron on board flew F4H Phantoms. The ship is at high speed to provide wind to aid the launches. (THA)*

1962 To Cuba . . . Almost

The RA-5C's first opportunity to go into harm's way came before the airplane was even accepted by the navy.

On 13 October 1962, high-flying U-2 airplanes first photographed ballistic missile sites under construction in Cuba. Although the event was kept quiet, two weeks later one of the high-flying American spy planes was shot down.

Late that same day, John Fosness, then Vigilante Program Manager at NAA, received a call from the Pentagon at his home. The question asked was, "Could the two prototype RA-5C's have the test instrumentation removed and be reconfigured with advanced RA-5C electronic countermeasures along with the basic cameras?"

He replied, yes, and was stunned when his high-ranking caller told him they were wanted for deployment in 24 hours.

Fosness immediately began calling his people. The problem was, it was a Saturday evening and many of the engineers and technicians were not at home, but scattered around Columbus,

Ohio. He remembers talking to many babysitters and luckily reaching two groups at parties. By midnight, more than 100 had been assembled and given their rather formidable task.

The airplanes were ready on time. The pair of Vigilantes may not have looked the best—cosmetics such as paint had a low priority—but they were operational with cameras and side-looking radar ready to extend the surveillance of Cuba and the surrounding seas. Plus, they had the correct ECM equipment to defeat the newest Soviet radars.

Although held in readiness for two weeks, the prototype RA-5Cs were not used. As the crisis eased, Fosness convinced the navy that such things as accurate fuel consumption figures for the new model would be good to have and the two Vigilantes had their instrumentation reinstalled and resumed development tests.

This rush job was not the Vigilante's last involvement with Cuba.

Test firing of HS-1 ejection seat. The stabilizing plate has extended and the drogue parachute is at the end of its lanyard, but not yet open. The early seats provided a good escape if the airplane was going above 100 knots while on the ground. This was later improved to a zero-zero capability.

VAH-7 A3J/A-5A an instant before trapping on the USS Enterprise (CVAN-65) in 1962. Fuel drop tank on wing pylon. BN's window is closed, possibly because Vigilante is being flown solo for CQ. BuNo 149277 was later converted to RA-5C. Tail stripes are dark blue with white stars. (NNAM)

Pachyderm

Fighter pilots, of course, tended to look down on the big bomber, comparing it to an elephant, though apparently at least as much for the wild sounds made by the Vigilante's twin J79s when they were throttled up or down during landing approach, with jokers suggesting that the beast sounded like an elephant in heat. Leroy Heath, back in fleet service as XO of VAH-7, picked up the comparison and ran with it, naming his Vigilante the Passionate Pachyderm. He also bought a windup toy elephant, painted the Pachyderm's aircraft number "701" on its side, and took to setting it on strolls across the closed-circuit TV camera that gave the ready rooms a view of carrier-deck landings.[6]

Excerpts from The Elephant Coloring Book *prepared by a pair of VF-33 lieutenant fighter pilots, Norm Gandia and Dick Truly[7]. Why is this funny?*
• **The sound of the J79 engines from inside the long intake ducts of the Vigilante were compared to an elephant in heat and a nickname was born.**
• **PIO is Pilot Induced Oscillation; reference to the Vigilante's pitch sensitivity.**
• **The only bombs dropped while deployed were 25-pound Mk76 practice bombs.**
• **LCDRs (O-4) wear a gold leaf. Being the assistant line division officer is far, far below his rank, a situation the result of only second-tour pilots being assigned to VAH.**
• **The BN cockpit was claustrophobic and the BN had no control over the airplane. It took a special type of courage to ride back there, especially landing aboard ship, and doubly so at night. (THA)**

VAH-7 VIGI'S

I AM AN A3J-1 ELEPHANT. I AM THE NEWEST ADDITION TO THE NATION'S ARSENAL. COLOR ME PIO GREY. COSTING ONLY .MILLIONS OF TAXPAYER'S DOLLARS, I CAN BE USED EQUALLY WELL IN AIR SHOWS OR AS A BOOKEND. THIS IS MY WEAPON: . COLOR IT MK 76 RED. IT COSTS , COLOR THE PENNIES COPPER.

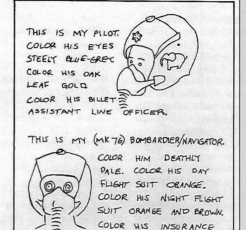

THIS IS MY PILOT. COLOR HIS EYES STEELY BLUE-GREY. COLOR HIS OAK LEAF GOLD. COLOR HIS BILLET ASSISTANT LINE OFFICER.

THIS IS MY (MK 76) BOMBARDIER/NAVIGATOR. COLOR HIM DEATHLY PALE. COLOR HIS DAY FLIGHT SUIT ORANGE. COLOR HIS NIGHT FLIGHT SUIT ORANGE AND BROWN. COLOR HIS INSURANCE POLICY REVOKED.

Excerpts from "THE ELEPHANT COLORING BOOK" by Norm Gandia and Dick Truly (now a shuttle pilot) when they were VF-33 J.O.'s during the first Vigilante deployment. Former Vigi personnel are offered equal space for rebuttals.

This large decal was placed on RVAH-7 aircraft. Squadron callsign was Flare and nickname was Peacemakers.

assigned contingency missions according to the national Single Integrated Operational Plan (SIOP), which would be executed in the event of a nuclear war. Individual pilots and BNs in the Vigilante and Skywarrior squadrons would be given a target folder with routes and timing on which they were regularly briefed. Dave Sharp of VAH-7 remembered, "As I recall, only one squadron ever dropped a bomb from the tunnel on an ORI [Operational Readiness Inspection] exercise. Believe it was VAH-1. It worked, but the CEP [Circular Error Probability] was huge. Thus, all future planning used wing loads. In fact, on my cruise, our assigned route was two bombs, drop one, shut down one engine, drop the second, go out into the Black Sea, eject, and a destroyer would pick us up. No S---!"[8]

In May 1964, pilot LCDR J. Chapdelaine and bombardier-navigator Petty Officer C. Stringer launched in their A-5A, BuNo 148931, for a dual mission as duty tanker and for practice bombing. The weather was calm, moderate sea state, with a fresh breeze. Chapdelaine began a high-angle loft maneuver using a smoke light as the target. After passing approximately the vertical position, he noted unusual rolling and yawing tendencies and selected maximum afterburner.

As the nose passed through the horizon, he attempted to roll upright, but the Vigilante entered uncontrolled flight. Unsuccessful at attempts to recover, the crew ejected after passing an indicated altitude of 2,500 feet, hitting the water about 4 miles from the carrier. A plane guard destroyer rescued Chapdelaine and a Kaman Seasprite, from Helicopter Utility Squadron 2 Det 65, flying the starboard plane guard position, retrieved Stringer.[9]

LSO Games

"[CDR Norm Gandia] thought it would be 'instructional' to have the LSO perspective of A-5 ops. He draws on his experiences aboard the USS *Enterprise* during VAH-7's initial A-5 deployment in the 1960s to demonstrate what he characterizes as 'the expertise and humor required of all involved in bringing the A-5 back aboard.' Names have not been changed to protect the innocent, but expletives have been deleted to keep us off the Chaplain's hit list [say that one carefully!].

"Pick up your paddles, Norm, and tell 'em the story."

"While a few of us were cross-qualified to wave the Elephant, night recoveries were almost always attended to by the then-eminently able Heavy 7 LSO, 'Deacon' Bakke, now CAPT, USN.[10]

"Launches then were large and recoveries long, with the *Elephants* last but certainly not least! This recovery order meant that Deacon could man the platform, then sit and snooze for 20 minutes or so until his first patient approached.

"As a recovery drew to conclusion, the atmosphere got a little tense in anticipation of the last participants. So much so that usually, when the first A-5 was still miles out, Deacon would be implored to take over. He always rose to the occasion—literally.

"A typical instance would have the controlling LSO yelling over his shoulder at the recumbent Deacon: 'A-5 at 5 miles!'

"Deacon would then hurl his large economy-sized body to the vertical (and to the physical detriment of us normal humans) with a 'Roger . . . power, Power, POWER!'"[11]

After five months operating in the Mediterranean, and without going back to the States, the *Enterprise* was joined by the cruiser USS *Long Beach* (CGN-9) and frigate USS *Bainbridge* (DLGN-25), loaded sufficient aviation fuel, parts, and provisions to last the journey,

VAH-7 A-5A runout after arrested landing on the USS Enterprise. *The hook runner is going to make sure the cable has dropped off the tailhook. Farther up the deck, a plane director is ready to signal the Vigilante out of the landing area. This photograph was published in the* Virginian Pilot *newspaper. (NNAM)*

LTJG Dave Sharp (left) and LCDR Jack Tuttle (right) with an unknown flight surgeon on deck of the USS Enterprise *after being rescued by helicopter after ejecting from their A3J/A-5A Vigilante off the coast of Brazil in 1964. (Sharp)*

VAH-7 A-5A dumping fuel; the drop tank is on the right wing. White area inside pilot's canopy is the opaque, plastic shield that could be pulled down to avoid flash blindness from a nuclear blast. Later converted to an RA-5C, BuNo 148932 was destroyed in the Forrestal *fire. (NNAM)*

and began an all-nuclear-powered task force around-the-world cruise. *Operation Sea Orbit* was a statement of American technical achievement similar to that of the coal-burning *Great White Fleet* of 1907–1909.

En route, Task Force One (TF-1) performed "Underway calls," where VIPs were flown to the carrier, greeted with all due ceremony to witness a demonstration by Air Wing 6, and flown back ashore. Typically, TF-1 progressed 100 miles during that time.

Underway calls were made at Rabat, Morocco; Dakar, Senegal; Freetown, Sierra Leone; Monrovia, Liberia; Abidjan, Ivory Coast; Capetown, South Africa; and Mombasa, Kenya, before the first port calls at Karachi, Pakistan, and Sydney, Australia. The Task Force crossed the South Pacific and rounded Cape Horn before underway visits off Buenos Aires, Argentina; Montevideo, Uruguay; and a port call in Rio de Janeiro, Brazil.

On 27 September 1964, the *Enterprise* sent up the mixed formation of 40 airplanes for a flyover of Recife, Brazil. Another airplane in the formation reported seeing hydraulic fluid from A3J BuNo 147863. The pilot, LCDR Jack Tuttle, dropped the ram-air turbine for emergency power, but with the fluid gone, he moved the stick only twice and the controls froze. He and his bombardier-navigator, LTJG Dave Sharp, ejected and were soon back on the *Enterprise* flight deck.

Dave Sharp voluntarily worked in the TV studio on the *Enterprise*, as it had been his college major. Since he may have been on the last flight of the long cruise, the photomates in the studio loaned him their handheld cameras to take on the flight. When Sharp submitted a reimbursement claim for three Pentax and two Canon cameras, the navy challenged whether he was trying to pull a fast one.

After Recife, the ships stopped at San Juan, Puerto Rico, before returning to Norfolk, Virginia. Task Force One had spent 65 days deployed, with 57 of them at sea, and steamed 30,216 miles in total without replenishment. *Sea Orbit* ended 3 October 1964.

VAH-7 returned to NAS Sanford and began the transition to the RA-5C. One year later, now designated RVAH-7, the squadron again rode the *Enterprise* around Cape Horn—west this time—as the carrier moved to its new homeport at NAS Alameda, California.

VAH-1 *Peacemakers*

The *Smoking Tigers* of VAH-1 were the second Vigilante fleet squadron. Chief Petty Officer Colin "Pem" Pemberton was teamed with pilot LCDR Jim Bell. A few weeks after they began flying together, their Vigilante (BuNo 151616) had hydraulic problems; first the rudder quit.

"Flying without a rudder was like trying to fly a bathtub," said Bell. Then the main system died and the backup pump would not engage. At 3,500 feet, Pem had the dubious distinction of being one of the few enlisted men who went for a "Rocket ride." They were picked up by a helicopter and taken back to NAS Sanford.

VAH-1 went to sea in the USS *Independence* (CVA-62) with 12 A-5As (the redesignation now in effect) as high-altitude, supersonic bombers.

For VAH-1, the deployment did not begin well. While conducting Air Ops during the Atlantic crossing, and out of divert field range, when the Bell/Pemberton team made six "OK" passes, all resulting in hook skips because the tailhook had a bad snubber and was bouncing over all the wires. Since they were between Bermuda and the Azores, the decision was made to trap them in the barricade, although the Vigilante had not yet been certified for that procedure.

Bell remembered, "Pem was the greatest! He calmly said, 'It's gonna be okay, Jim. We'll be telling our grandkids about this.'" This was the first barricade engagement of the A-5 and it was relatively successful with most of the damage restricted to the starboard leading-edge flaps and starboard intake.[12]

"When we deployed on the *Independence*, however, we had only four or five tech reps, and there was no real logistics analysis made for spares based on projected failure rates. If we started out with six of our twelve aircraft flyable in the morning, we would feel fortunate to have three flyable aircraft when night operations began. The maintenance crew was very capable, but we could only work with

A-5As of VAH-1 parked on the USS Independence in 1962. Vigilantes were frequently parked in alternating directions to reduce the space needed. The aircraft parked nose-in, pushed onto the deck by a tractor. The BN in 603 and both the pilot and BN in 607 are wearing MkIV full-pressure suits. These side numbers are unusually large and painted farther back than the later standard. Vigilantes came from the factory with a wavy demarcation line between gray and white on the fuselage. Names below the cockpits on the right sides of the A-5As are flight crew; those on the left sides are enlisted men. Weapons pylons are empty. BuNos 149295 and 149299 were later converted to RA-5Cs. And I flew them both in RVAH-3. (NNAM)

what we had. Fortunately many of the 'down' systems were not necessarily a 'mission ready' requirement, so that a safely flyable aircraft might have several 'up' squawks.

"The technology may have been there, but the reliability was not. As a result, failure rates of the more sophisticated systems exceeded the spares provided. In fact, failure rates of some of the more basic parts, like nosewheels, hydraulic actuators, and flight control components, were not available as spares; consequently maintenance experienced a high Aircraft Out of Commission for Parts (AOCP) rate."[13]

Returning to NAS Sanford from the Mediterranean in March 1964, the *Smoking Tigers* transitioned to the RA-5C and as RVAH-1 went on the second Vigilante combat cruise on the *Independence* for that ship's only combat deployment.

VAH/RVAH-3

The squadron that became the training center for all Vigilantes began as an operational A3D-1 Skywarrior squadron of Heavy Attack Wing ONE and deployed to the Mediterranean in 1957. When VAH-3 arrived at NAS Sanford in June 1958, it was merged

A3J being loaded from pier to lowered elevator; a normal procedure to ensure that all airplanes were on board before a deployment. (USN)

A-5A on catapult launch from the USS Independence (CVA-62) as part of CVW-11 (AG). The plane guard helicopter is a Kaman HU2K Sea Sprite. (NNAM)

Smoking Tiger embroidered patch. Mushroom-shaped smoke represented the nuclear delivery mission. The patch and name remained after the attack mission ceased. Callsign was Comanche Trail. (Carlton)

The first barricade engagement of an A-5; the procedure had not yet been approved. The crew was LCDR Bell and Chief Petty Officer Pemberton of VAH-1 on the USS Independence (CVA-62). Damage to the Vigilante was minor. (NNAM)

with the Heavy Attack Training Unit (HATULANT) and became the Heavy Attack Replacement Training Squadron, RAG, for the Atlantic Fleet. Its new mission included the "Basic Readiness Qualification" of all replacement flight crews and maintenance support personnel within HATWING ONE.

To fulfill this task, VAH-3 received six A3D-2T (TA-3B)[14] aircraft that had been specifically designed and built as bombardier-navigator airborne trainers. These "School room Skywarriors" replaced the bomb bay with space for training stations, which had repeater scopes for the ASB-1 bombing and navigation system. One station had complete system controls with the master scope.

"In the cockpit, there were two seats, but only the left had flight controls. In the back, there was one radar station on the right side and four seats on the left, one for the instructor and three for students. During the flight, students rotated through the radar station and the instructor stood beside it.

"An interesting side note, one of the pilots had a little trick he would play on the students from time to time. Even though Douglas Aircraft claimed the plane could not do a roll, he not only could roll it, but could do a perfect 1G roll that couldn't be felt in the back. Of course, that would completely wipe out the radar presentation. He would wait until everyone had had a turn on the scope.

"No weapons on board, but we did do radar bomb scoring on the range in Jacksonville. There was a tone that was turned on and automatically went off when the 'bombs away' button was pressed. The ground station would use the aircraft position, altitude, and the wind speed to calculate the accuracy."[15]

"As new RANs, we had to draw what we anticipated radar returns would look like . . . in our case, Jacksonville, from various directions.

The windows in the fuselage indicate that this was a trainer version of the Douglas Skywarrior at NAS Sanford. With repeater radar scopes, the TA-3B made an effective trainer for BNs. GJ tail code and orange stripe were on all the types of aircraft assigned to VAH/RVAH-3. (USN)

F9F-8T (TF-9J) Cougar used in the RAG for instrument (trainee was in the back seat under a canvas hood) and bomb delivery training (trainee was in front). The Cougar is carrying four practice bombs. TF-9s were in use in the Advanced Training Command until the late 1960s.

In flight, we'd compare our predictions with actual returns. The instructor would stand beside us while we navigated using the radar scope. I remember a night trainer over the city, my first time seeing bejeweled city lights out the window as the jet turned hard for the next leg."[16]

In the event of a bailout, a bar was above the entry hatch and the riders in the fuselage instructed to grab it with their arms crossed, so as they jumped they twisted and went down the slide facing aft.

The number of A-3s assigned was reduced over the life of RVAH-3.

As the RAG, VAH-3 also had four Grumman F9F-8T/TF-9J two-place Cougars for pilot instrument currency and bomb delivery training. The Cougars were later replaced by Douglas TA-4 Skyhawks.

An oddity among the jets on the flight line was a single R4D/C-47 (officially a "Skytrain" but unofficially, and popularly, a "Gooney Bird"), which was used for visual navigation training and utility transport. Eventually, only its utility mission endured. RVAH-3 had a Gooney until 1969 (by then a C-117 Super Gooney).

With the new A3J/A-5A Vigilante arriving, training facilities were expanded, the curriculum revised, and the squadron's organizational structure adjusted. There were 18 courses, totaling some 14,000 instructional hours—a 50-percent increase.

On 16 June 1961, the first four A3J-1 (A-5A) aircraft were received, and replacement flight crew and a maintenance on-the-job training commenced. VAH-3 worked closely with North American Aviation Corporation to implement the innovative Fleet Introduction Program (FIP); contractor support in the form of technical training, spare parts, and maintenance. Assistance was usual during the test and development phase, but this was new on the fleet level. A key role in the FIP was contractor tech reps assigned to both the RAG and deployable squadrons.

At the beginning of 1962, VAH-3 was assigned the following aircraft: one R4D-7 (TC-47K), four F9F-8T (TF-9J), six A3D-1, (TA-3B), 12 A3D-1 (A-3A), and 8 A3J-1 (A-5A).

A-3 training continued until 1964 when Skywarrior training was transferred to VAH-123 at NAS Whidbey Island. Unlike most types of navy aircraft, the A-5 and A-3 were single based and supported both the Atlantic and Pacific fleets. Along with all their bomber versions of the A-3, VAH-3 transferred two of its TA-3Bs.

As late as 1965, there were A-5As in the RAG, now RVAH-3. They were used throughout the syllabus, including bomb drops. "I was there when Heavy 3 still had a couple of A models, and we did a little bit of laydown bombing up at Lake George using the small 'beer can' bombs. The target there was an old landing craft with three rings of pilings around it.

"I remember one day when a fisherman was tied up to the inner ring. The controllers wouldn't clear us live on the range, so we made a couple of LOW passes over him. He moved to the outer ring, and they cleared us to drop. He was right on the runout heading and, somehow, I dropped the first bomb on that ring instead of the bull's-eye. I don't know how that could have happened because the next five were all right on target. After that first run, the fisherman took off as fast as his boat would run."[17]

Gooney Goofs

VAH/RVAH-3 had a R4D/C-47 in its mix of aircraft. The slow-flying round-engine propeller-driven transport was useful in ferrying parts, mechanics, and crews. The qualified pilots were senior types left over from the AJ Savage or even the P2V. Because most C-47 flying was at odd hours or on weekends, they decided to check out the junior pilots coming into the Vigilante program.

The first lieutenant to try smacked the wing of the tail-wheel transport into a hangar while taxiing. Jerry Coffey[18] was next. While practicing with one engine shut down, he let the airspeed bleed off and the C-47 flopped over and entered a spin over Daytona Beach.

On the ground, the senior petty officer, who was the plane captain and was on all flights, swore he would quit, "If we keep trying to check out them lootenants."

Douglas R4D assigned to VAH-3 in Sanford. Besides training BNs in navigation, the venerable Gooney carried mechanics and parts to rescue broken A3Ds and A3Js as well as other logistic missions. This photograph was taken on Eleuthra Island, Bahamas, circa 1961. The R4D/C-47 was later replaced by a C-117 Super Gooney and stayed in RVAH-3 until 1969. (R. Winter)

The biggest frustration in going through a RAG is aircraft availability. RVAH-3 may have been worse than others due to the complexity and newness of the Vigilante. The first flight in the syllabus was not a flight, but a high-speed taxi on the runway. The pilot lit the afterburners, accelerated to between 80 and 100 knots depending on runway length, pulled the throttles back to idle, and braked to a stop.

Bob Johnson[19] had spent a long day waiting for an "up" airplane for his Fam-1 [taxi]. He was finally assigned an A-5A tanker with a full load of gas. He roared down the runway in afterburner, pulled the throttles back to the stops, used heavy braking to be slow enough to turn off the runway, and had to keep applying brakes to control his taxi speed. As he neared the fire station, the crash crew came running out and signaled him to stop because smoke was pouring off the wheels.

The A3J/A-5A had an intermediate stop that was above idle to decrease engine acceleration time in the event of a wave-off. The combination of a heavy airplane, a down-sloping runway, and being above idle thrust resulted in hot brakes. The syllabus "flight" was considered complete.

A-5 Bravo

With the cost of the A3J/A-5A worrying the US Congress, North American was quick to promote the improvements for its

Pilot and BN wearing Goodrich MkIV full-pressure suits ready for flight with torso harnesses and flotation gear. A television scanner inside its glass blister is between their heads. The complex sensor (pitot) probe on the nose is at the top. (R. Williams)

second-generation Vigilante. An accelerated production rate along with the tapering off of bombing system development allowed North American to claim a revised unit production cost slightly less than $5 million. At the same time, the Joint Chiefs of Staff reached a somewhat acrimonious accord that air force bombers and missiles and the navy's submarine-launched Polaris ICBM would assume the nuclear deterrent mission. This meant naval aviation would be biased toward conventional tactical responsibilities.

For the Vigilante, it was a chance to correct shortcomings in the original design. The navy had also removed the zero-wind launch requirement, which made optimizing the Vigilante simpler.

RA-5C during testing in landing configuration with a full set of 400-gallon fuel tanks on the removable wing stations. (NNAM)

More Fuel

Increasing fuel capacity by adding fuel tanks on the top side of the fuselage, sometimes referred to as the "Top Cap Mod," required a major redesign of the upper fuselage and relatively minor changes to the canopies. The change in profile became the most obvious difference between the early model and the B and C versions. (This also began a ceaseless debate as to which was a better-looking airplane: the sleek but slab-sided A3J or the curvaceous but bulky Bravos and Charlies.) The added fuel tanks gave the Vigilante almost twice the internal fuel as its high-speed twin-engine competitor, the F-4 Phantom II.

Slow Is Better

The ability to go fast is an asset in combat, but for landing on ships, slower is better. The wing leading-edge droops became ducting for engine bleed air to flow across the entire wing, not only across the flaps as on the A3J, for boundary layer control. High-pressure air was tapped off the final engine compressor stage. Air supply for the BLC system came from between backflow check valves and the primary heat exchangers. This meant that when the flaps were lowered, activating BLC, the air to cockpit air conditioners was greatly reduced. The noticeable rise in temperature was the only way a BN could tell that the flaps had extended.

The flaps were larger, and travel was extended to a full 50 degrees, versus 40. These changes reduced the Vigilante's approach speed and made carrier landings safer. Since the maximum gross takeoff weight increased

In afterburner, the J79 used gas so fast that there was no fuel-flow gauge. To figure how fast the fuel was being burned, you multiplied the fuel flow for the basic engine (there was gauge for that) by three if up high and by five if at low altitude. Or you could simply measure the dropping fuel quantity with the sweep second hand on the clock. (Carlton)

by 60 percent to 80,000 pounds, improved wheel brakes were installed.

Production

The 18 airframes remaining on the original contract for 52 Vigilantes were built as the dramatically reconfigured A3J-2/A-5B. The first, BuNo 149300, following conventional ground and taxi tests, flew in April 1962.

When the requirement for a reconnaissance version came, the 18 A3J-2s were too far along in the production process to be reasonably reconfigured to reconnaissance and were completed to A-5B standard.

Only two were delivered to the navy under that designation. Another 4 of the 18 count batch were delivered as A-5CLs (also called YA-5CL), nicknamed "Cleos." Lacking reconnaissance systems, they were used by VAH-3 as interim trainers for the RA-5C during late 1963 and early 1964 prior to receipt of fully configured reconnaissance airplanes. The remaining 12 A-5Bs were retained at Columbus as undelivered, pending a decision concerning their conversion to a RA-5C standard.

Conversion of all 18 A-5B aircraft eventually took place alongside aircraft purpose built to RA-5C specifications. Following conversion, they retained their original bureau numbers and gained an additional factory C number.

This Vigilante was transferred to RVAH-9 and lost after a touch-and-go landing on the Ranger when the engine exploded in January 1966.

Designations

The US Navy used letter and number designations. Y is for a prototype. A is for the major role of Attack. The number is the number of types by the company. Companies were indicated by a letter, and J is for North American Aviation, which built the Savage AJ (ones are left out) and the A2J (a turboprop version of the Savage) before the Vigilante. The dash number is model/version of the type. Final letter indicates a special purpose, for example P means Photography.

Supposedly, at a Pentagon briefing, Secretary of Defense Robert S. McNamara was confused and pointedly asked why there were two A-3s (A3D Skywarrior and A3J Vigilante). He then decreed a unified, and simpler, system for all US military aircraft in which a prefix letter indicated a special purpose. As the older airplane, the A3D kept being an A-3, while the A3J became the A-5 (Douglas had the A4D/A-4)[20].

A difficulty in the conversion was contracts were let some time before the aircraft were produced. Aircraft made in the early 1960s may have had previous designations the pilots and mechanics never heard of.

- YA3J-1: 2 prototypes, 1 crashed
- A3J-1/A-5A: 52 contracted, 34 delivered
- A3J-2/A-5B: 18 completed, 2 delivered to the US Navy
- YA3J-3/A-5C: 4 converted from A-5B
- A3J-3P/RA-5C: definitive reconnaissance version

Chapter 4

"R" IS FOR RECONNAISSANCE

the plane came into use. The scouts were equipped with guns so they could pursue and shoot down the enemy's observation craft before they could see and report what was happening on the ground. The age of aerial combat had begun.

Cameras at Sea

Navies adapted carrier aircraft to carry cameras. Multiple-crew airplanes could use handheld cameras, which had the disadvantage of being unstable. Fighter airplanes had the advantage of higher speed over the targets. For propeller aircraft, the cameras were mounted in the fuselage and operated remotely by the pilot, who did not have a viewfinder but did have his wing guns . . . just in case. When jets became the photo ships, nose guns and cannons were replaced

Salmson 2.A2 of the US Air Service 91st Aero Squadron. The observer has a large and bulky aerial camera, typical of the era. In 1912, the Royal Flying Corps discovered that vertical photos taken with 60-percent overlap could be used to create a three-dimensional effect when viewed with a stereoscope. This perception of depth aided greatly in interpreting aerial images. (Wikipedia)

Photographer with handheld camera in rear cockpit of Curtiss SB2C Helldiver during World War II. The aircraft's two 30-caliber machine guns are stowed below the rear decking. (USN)

Cameras went aloft soon after the invention of the airplane. The first use of airplanes in war was to find out what the enemy was doing. Hence, the term "Scouts" was used for the light machines that ventured forth in 1914. Far better than verbal reports from a pilot, who was busy just keeping his "aeroplane" upright, were aerial photographs. Specialized cameras were soon developed, and larger airplanes that could carry an additional crewmember to aim and work the cameras without having to fly by cameras, leading to the cynical expression that, on a mission, the pilots were, "Alone, unarmed, and unafraid."[1]

US Navy photographic squadrons were designated with the letter P added to the basic designation (e.g., VAP, VFP). The change to R for Reconnaissance was recognition of the additional capabilities of the Vigilante; night flasher pods, side-looking radar (SLR), electronic emitter location (PECM), and, later, infrared (IR) mapping. Heavy attack squadrons, VAH, which transitioned to the Vigilante, became RVAH. The aircraft itself added the R to become RA-5. BNs became RANs.

What Now?

When in late 1961, naval aviation was not included in the new Nuclear Triad—heavy bombers, intercontinental ballistic missiles, Polaris submarines—the Vigilante lost its primary reason for existence. However, newly appointed secretary of defense Robert S. McNamara recognized a long-standing and legitimate need for a navy fleet reconnaissance capability and ordered the Vigilante be kept in production. After being granted approval by the tri-service Darrow Tactical Reconnaissance Board, a contract was generated for more aircraft under the existing model designator as it had the payload capacity to accommodate side-looking airborne radar and the numerous optical sensors specified for the navy's reconnaissance mission.[2]

North American Aviation was a step ahead and was already working on a reconnaissance version before the last A-5A came off the line. The A-5B provided the ideal vehicle for the added range and sensor-carrying capacity for what became the RA-5C. The first two RA-5Cs began as an A-5B and an A-5A. The first purpose-built RA-5C was actually the third to fly. It did so on 3 June 1962.

Just as the Vigilante was created as a complete system, so it was when the conversion to reconnaissance took place. Photography used a wide variety of cameras in interchangeable modules. High-powered flasher pods gave a night photo capability, side-looking radar worked in any weather, and an electronic

Fully restored F2H-2P Photo-Banshee at the NNAM with three types of aerial cameras. The nose was lengthened from the fighter version and could hold up to six cameras. The Photo-Banshee and the photo version of the Panther, F9F-2P, were the US Navy's and Marines' primary reconnaissance aircraft during the Korean War. Each white camera silhouette on the fuselage represents a combat photo mission. (Stafford)

The two airplanes that provided aerial photography for US Navy and Marines over three decades. The Grumman F9F-8P Cougar was in use from the mid-1950s until replaced by the F8U Crusader. VFP-62 (pictured) gained prominence during the Cuban Crisis of 1962. (Obrien)

RA-5C configured with distinctive canoe containing side-looking radar antennas and camera modules. The glass-covered ports for the cameras are the dark squares. The dark opening on the fuselage is the defensive chaff/flare dispenser. (Carlton)

for the systems and information required for full utilization of the data obtained from the reconnaissance systems. This data is complementary since, by comparison, more information can be obtained than would be possible using any single system."

Reconnaissance Systems

The range of cameras that could fit into the Vigilante's modules included a range of focal lengths, stabilized cameras, night-specialized cameras, and panoramic cameras.

Cameras are categorized by focal length. The longer the focal length, the greater the magnification. However, the longer the focal length, the narrower the field of view. What intelligence is required and at what altitudes the airplane will fly determine what the optimum cameras will be.

data-gathering system that gave a tactical capability previously only available from specialized aircraft, and all the systems had digital data recording.

The Navy Intelligence Processing System (NIPS) was created to process all this information. The primary segment of NIPS on board ships was the Integrated Operational Intelligence Center (IOIC). The concept was to have simultaneous strips of photographic images on a light table, side-looking radar imagery, and the PECM tape side by side with the digital data system, providing input as to what was being looked at. NIPS training was conducted at a new facility called NIPSTRAFAC (Naval Intelligence Processing System Training Facility).

From the NATOPS Manual, introduction to Section VIII, Reconnaissance Systems:

> "The data obtained is utilized during post mission analysis for future mission planning. Systems providing reconnaissance data collection capabilities of the photographic systems, side looking radar system, infrared system, and passive electronic countermeasures system. Digital data system provides control signals

Aerial cameras need to correct for the speed of flight. The problem is analogous to taking a picture of a race car. With a standard camera, the solution is to move the camera keeping the car centered, accepting the blurred background as a unavoidable penalty. With the aerial camera, the solution is to move the film to keep the desired object in focus. The speed the film must travel is a factor of the airplane's speed over the ground (Vg) and its height (H). Charts are available for determining the Vg/H for use in mission planning. In the RA-5C, Vg/H (sometimes shown as V/H) correction is computed by air-data and inertial-navigation inputs.

To monitor the system, and correct if necessary, the RAN has moving bars superimposed on the optical view finder. If all is well, the lighted bars move along the screen as fast as an object on the ground. "I *always* monitored the grid lines and would override if the auto systems failed; the intel product would be crap if this were not done, especially at our mission speeds and altitudes."[3]

Rather than a dilating, round aperture, the aerial camera uses a focal plane shutter for exposure control. The width of focal plane shutter gap governs how much light reaches the film; essentially, an f-stop.

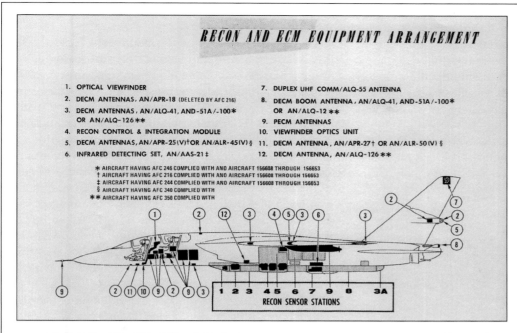

RECON AND ECM EQUIPMENT ARRANGEMENT

1. OPTICAL VIEWFINDER
2. DECM ANTENNAS, AN/APR-18 (DELETED BY AFC 216)
3. DECM ANTENNAS, AN/ALQ-41, AND-51A/-100* OR AN/ALQ-126**
4. RECON CONTROL & INTEGRATION MODULE
5. DECM ANTENNAS, AN/APR-25 (V)†OR AN/ALR-45(V) §
6. INFRARED DETECTING SET, AN/AAS-21‡

7. DUPLEX UHF COMM/ALQ-55 ANTENNA
8. DECM BOOM ANTENNA, AN/ALQ-41, AND-51A/-100* OR AN/ALQ-12**
9. PECM ANTENNAS
10. VIEWFINDER OPTICS UNIT
11. DECM ANTENNA, AN/APR-27† OR AN/ALR-50 (V) §
12. DECM ANTENNA, AN/ALQ-126**

* AIRCRAFT HAVING AFC 246 COMPLIED WITH AND AIRCRAFT 156608 THROUGH 156653
† AIRCRAFT HAVING AFC 216 COMPLIED WITH AND AIRCRAFT 156608 THROUGH 156653
‡ AIRCRAFT HAVING AFC 244 COMPLIED WITH AND AIRCRAFT 156608 THROUGH 156653
§ AIRCRAFT HAVING AFC 340 COMPLIED WITH
** AIRCRAFT HAVING AFC 350 COMPLIED WITH

RECON SENSOR STATIONS

1 2 3 4 5 6 7 8 9 8 3A

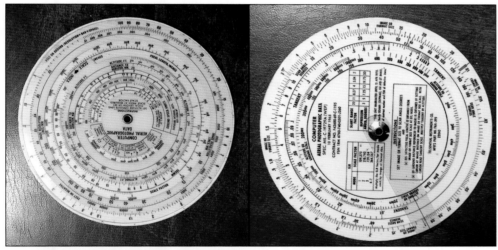

COMPUTER, AERIAL PHOTOGRAPHIC DATA
The factors entered or derived on the computer include: Ground coverage, feet on negative, resolution: lines/mm, feet on ground, distance to horizon, exposure interval, focal length, ground speed, scan angle, slant range factor, and format size. Instructions on one side include: "GD (GROUND DISTANCE REFERENCED TO NADIR) IS OBTAINED BY SETTING CURSOR AT IMAGE DISTANCE ON IMAGE OR FORMAT SIZE SCALE. WITH CURSOR READ TANGENT SCALE. MULTIPLY TANGENT BY ALTITUDE."

- *"I vaguely remember it. I don't believe I ever used it in the cockpit. I think it was mainly a planning tool to determine what altitude was needed to get a desired amount of ground overage with a certain focal-length camera. Just another example of how primitive things were back then when slide rules were the high-tech method of computing."—Jim Owen*
- *"Never used at all by the true pros. We just had a precision 'feel' for that kind of s**t." —"Buffalo" Brem*

General arrangement diagram from NATOPS Manual: DECM is Defensive Electronic Counter-Measures, PECM is Passive Electronic Counter-Measures, AFC is Air Frame Change (method for updating equipment).
Recon Sensor Stations:

1. *Forward oblique 6-inch camera (used for recreating flight track as well as imagery)*
2. *Vertical camera station for either 1.75-inch or 6-inch (normal) cameras*
3. *PECM antennas*
4. *Three types of interchangeable modules*
   4-1: (oblique cameras)
   1.75-inch at 52 degree depression angle
   3-inch at vertical, 37.5, or 52 degrees
   6-inch at 5, 19.75, 37.5, or 52 degrees
   12-inch at 19.75 degrees
   4-2: 3-inch or 18-inch panoramic cameras
   4-3: (vertical cameras) 1.75-, 3-, 6-, or 12-inch
5. *PECM electronic control module*
6. *PECM canister (in bomb bay tunnel)*
7. *Infrared mapping scanner*
8. *Side-looking radar*
9. *Flasher pod*

Serial Frame

Still (serial frame) cameras are basically alike and differentiated by their focal lengths. All received signals from the Data Converter to control Image Motion Compensation (IMC), stabilization, and input for the data matrix block. Stabilization limits are narrow (between 5 and 10 degrees in pitch, and roll) and designed to compensate for aircraft motion when level. Camera mount angles give coverage when maneuvering.

There are two sizes of serial-frame film cassettes: large and small. A large cassette with 4.3-mil film has 350 feet of film for 840 frames. The configuration of the camera module determines whether a large cassette will fit. Film may be standard black-and-white, color negative, color transparency, or infrared sensitive.

A certain malfunction of the Data Converter caused all of the film to run through the camera in just a few minutes without recording any images.

Right oblique serial camera in module-4.

Panoramic

The main camera module, Number 4, could take either a 3-inch panoramic camera for low altitudes or a huge 18-inch pan camera for high altitudes. Both were marvels of sophistication using spinning prisms to sweep from horizon to horizon in alternating and overlapping frames. They also used film at a prodigious rate.

Its film canister contained 2,500 feet of film (5 inches wide) and was so heavy that a moving counterweight was needed to keep the system balanced as the film moved through the camera. Each image was almost 4 feet long (44.1 inches) and 4.5 inches wide. A full canister could take 535 images. RANs had to be careful to take only as many images as necessary. While the whole RA-5C was called the "14 million dollar Kodak," the 18-inch pan was known as the "million dollar Brownie." It did, however, have incredible capabilities.

RAN Dave Sharp saw this firsthand. "Coming back to Key West down the center of Florida one day, we [don't recall the pilot] were mentioning how clear the day was. You could make out each coast as clearly as if you were standing on a sand dune at the coast. Got a call later from intel to come up and look at

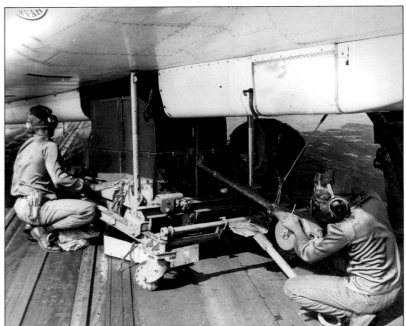

Photomates loading module-4 using a hand-cranked winch. The modules had specialized dollies for moving around the ship. (USN)

Forward oblique camera port. The compartment swung down on the forward hinge for access to the 6-inch camera. The opening for the vertical camera in module-2 is farther aft.

the film. We had been at about 20,000 feet. Clearly, near Orlando, you could make out a tennis ball on a court below."[4]

Fragility

Production of the 18-inch pan camera was so precise that the two spinning prisms and the lens chain had to be formed from the same pour of glass. Because of these optics, the pan camera required a preheat of five hours. If the RAN missed locking the camera for a cat shot or trap, a prism sometimes hit airplane structure and chipped. The repair required a change of all the glass in the optic chain—not cheap.

Viewfinder

The view itself is purely optical. A series of lenses and mirrors (optic relays) in tubes go from a wide-angle lens behind a quartz window flush on the underside of the fuselage—just below the pilot's seat—to the glass viewing screen on the RAN's main panel. The system is sealed and pressurized with dry nitrogen. The field of view is 5 degrees aft of nadir to 80 degrees forward and 85 degrees laterally.

Two reticles appear on the viewfinder screen. The first reticle is a nonadjustable, fixed field displaying drift angle and coverage boundaries. The other reticle is automatically or manually positioned to correspond to the aircraft's flight path.

A traveling VH grid, indicating exposure interval, expands and moves downward, disappearing at nadir. The track line moves to the

CRT scope for radar and television on left, optical viewfinder on right, navigation readouts in the middle. Table has cutout to install radar warning scope. Upper panel has flight instruments, warning lights, and SLR monitor. (Creager)

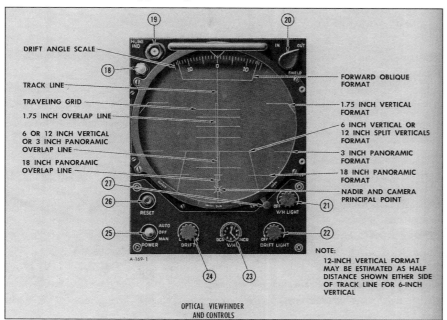

Optical viewfinder diagram. Two keys that are not labeled on the viewfinder panel are 27 (Polaroid Filter Lever) and 18 (Pressurization Fitting). The shield in/out is left over from the nuclear bombing mission. (NATOPS Manual)

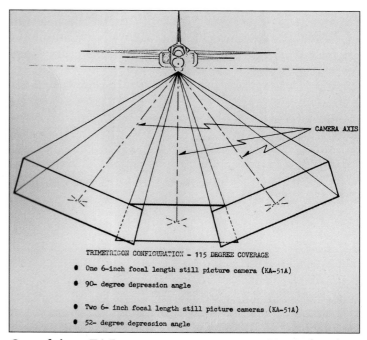

One of three Tri-Fan camera arrangements. Vertical and oblique cameras have 6-inch focal lengths. At 5,000 feet, the coverage is 1.7 miles on either side of the centerline. A 3-inch vertical and pair of 6-inch obliques gives 146 degrees of coverage. A 1.75-inch camera in the vertical station gives 180-degree Tri-Fan coverage, which is horizon to horizon. (CRAW-1 Capabilities Presentation)

calibrated drift angle. During a photo run, the RAN monitors the track and VH grid, adjusting them manually if necessary.

Until later, there was no mechanical means to check whether oblique cameras were centered on the assigned road, river, or coastline. So an oblique camera sight was improvised. Pilots carried a grease pencil. If the installed cameras were mounted at 37.5 degrees, en route to the target area the pilot rolled to 37.5 degrees (hah!) on the attitude gyro and drew a line on the canopy along the horizon. This grease pencil line indicated whether the Vigilante was too close or too far for optimum coverage.

The RAN could pass control of the oblique cameras to the pilot who fired them with the trigger on the control stick. That was useful for taking pictures of specific objects, such as ships or aircraft.

For air-to-air photos, IMC was turned off (i.e., no relative motion), which meant that Vg/H = 0.

Side-Looking Radar AN/APD-7

Most of the canoe was filled with the 13-foot-long side-looking radar (SLR) antennas. SLR images were recorded on a continuous strip of film with data matrix blocks at intervals. The SLR could sweep both sides of the flight path or left or right. The RAN had a small scope to monitor SLR operation. "I turned on the SLR over Oak Ridge, Tennes-

The SLR had a high enough resolution to show the outline of an aircraft carrier, as this enlargement shows. (Conrad)

NAME COASTAL SEG C-13   CTY VN
COORD 17591ON 1062910E   BE 0617-C9044
MSN YT 71/082/N/2152   DATE 23 MAR 71
POS SLR   FRAME   SP 1

The "Canoe" with camera modules, SLR section, and IR panel added. The warning flag was attached to the safety pin for the nosewheel door. (San Diego Museum)

SLR imagery of the coast of North Vietnam. The dark line is the path of the Vigilante. Radar is independent of weather or daylight. WBLC stands for water-borne logistics craft, a catchall phrase.

see, one day and almost had to classify the image since a lot showed up on film that was not on the charts. The AI took care of it."[5]

Flashers

For night photography, flasher pods could be hung on either one or both wings. The pod had three strobe lamps, powered by the air stream, which generated 3 million candlepower in a 43-degree cone of illumination. The flasher pods could be set to flash either together or alternately, depending on the altitude and speed of the aircraft. The alternate mode gave each pod more time to recharge and therefore a brighter flash. The maximum usable altitude was 3,500 feet above the ground. A strap-on unit was used on deck to provide power and shielding for testing the flasher pod. The NATOPS manual warned, (because of the 2,600 volt capacitors), "Do not touch for 10 minutes after power off" and "Flasher can inflict PERMANENT BLINDNESS."[6]

An advantage of the flashers over explosive photo flares was that they could cover stretches of road or coastline and not just a point target. However, an inherent problem in combat was that dust and humidity made the flashes visible, even from well outside the illumination cone. Ground gunners saw a series of regularly spaced flashes of light revealing not only the Vigilante's location but also its speed.

From pilot's notes, the technique for a point target, which could not be over flown, was "800 feet abeam, 45 degrees bank, 300 knots, low-altitude camera mode."

"GG [Gary Gretter] and I only used the flashers one time in North Vietnam. I believe the target was just above the DMZ, a suspected supply dump. I turned the flashers on at the target and almost immediately the tracers were going all around us. GG shouted,

A remarkable picture of a Vigilante at night taken by another Vigi. Bob Kuhlke and Al Wattay were flying night training missions, saw each other and arranged to cross with a 500-foot separation. The instantaneous photo flash stopped the motion of the airplane, but, in a night setting, the shutter was open and recorded the wingtip lights as lines. (Wattay)

'Turn 'em off, turn 'em off!' as I frantically fumbled for the switch, which was located near the canopy switch. We didn't get any photos of the target, nor did we fly anymore Night Flasher missions."[7]

PECM

The Passive Electronic Counter Measures (PECM) system was misnamed. More correctly, it was a passive, electronic emitter locator and analyzer. Any "counter measure" came later when the enemy emitter was electronically jammed or physically attacked.

PECM was a sophisticated and complex system. Flat-panel antennas embedded in the fuselage sides below the aft cockpit picked up the emitter's frequency band, pulse rate frequency, and other characteristics and correlated them with data from the ASB-12. Emitter source characteristics and bearing, time of recording, navigational data, and status were recorded on tape for analysis by intelligence personnel. A tape was ground adjustable to record for 56 or 112 minutes. One

Photo flasher pod on wing of RVAH-12 RA-5C during maintenance (left J79 engine is removed and engine bay doors open). The small access doors on the pod were closed in operation. (Gehrig)

of the Air Intelligence officers (AIO) assigned to a reconnaissance squadron was a PECM specialist.

A factor in the use of PECM was the weight of the unit—more than a ton. Not only did it replace a 295-gallon bomb bay fuel can but it also added to the airplane's weight—a significant item when landing aboard an aircraft carrier. PECM-equipped Vigilantes at maximum

This picture was taken to show an RVAH-6 aircraft having the squadron's nose flash being painted. Two PECM antennas can be made out on the fuselage. A close look at a Vigilante shows rectangular antenna panels scattered along the fuselage sides. However, because the panels are painted the same as the rest of the aircraft, they are not usually noticeable. Additional antennas are in the wing leading edges, apparent as dielectric material in the stainless steel. All Vigilantes had the antennas so the PECM "can" could be installed as needed.

"Peck-'Em"

For pilots, PECM missions were usually dull. For RANs, they were busy; besides all their usual duties, they kept a log noting geographical coordinates from the ASB-12 as backup to the automatic system. Pilots engaged the autopilot and read off TACAN bearings and distances just to have something to do. There were moments, however.

A frequent night mission for the Vigilante was a radar-locating PECM track. The "Blue Track" ran safely off the coast of North Vietnam, north then south, while the "Black Track" was over Laos roughly parallel to the western border of North Vietnam and over the Ho Chi Minh Trail. To get accurate bearings from radars, the Vigilante had to be straight and level. The Vietnamese defenders knew this.

All the way north, the Radar Alert and Warning equipment (ALQ) threat-warning systems was quiet with only an occasional beep from a search radar, but when the RA-5C banked to turn back south at the end of the run, the ALQ warning system lit up with orange strobes, flashing lights, warbling tones—every indication of tracking antiaircraft guns and imminent surface-to-air missile (SAM) launch, giving the crew a shot of adrenalin. The thrill was brief because as soon as the wings went level, the tracking and fire-control radars went quiet. The North Vietnam Air Defense Force had tested their equipment.

One night on the Black Track over Laos, a crew from RVAH-6 had excitement of another kind. Air force B-52s were effectively, if inefficiently, carpet-bombing North Vietnamese army and Viet Cong storage and troop areas in South Vietnam, Cambodia, and Laos. Each bomber dropped eighty-four 500-pound and twenty-four 750-pound bombs; the B-52s flew in cells of three. The 324 bombs with a combined weight of 90 tons from one cell created utter devastation in mile-wide swaths. The massive bomb drops were called "Arc Light." As a precaution before bombs away, announcements were made over the radio on guard channel, which all friendly aircraft monitored.

I was flying blissfully along on a Black Track when guard channel blared, "Arc Light, Arc Light, coordinates north seventeen twenty-two, east one oh six zero five [estimate after the fact, not the sort of information one remembers], Arc Light, Arc Light." I did not pay much attention because Arc Light warnings came frequently.

Moments later, my back-seater, LCDR "Bull" Davis, announced in a voice pitched higher than his normal cool, "We're there!" I looked up over my shoulder and there were the black silhouettes of six B-52s. I lit the afterburners, rolled, pulled, and dived fast to get out of the way. Safely away, we looked back to see explosion after explosion rippling through the jungle—so close together they formed a solid carpet of flame and fire.

Photo flash picture of aircraft carrier taken at night. The automatic code matrix block is in the upper right corner. The added block on the lower left has the same information embedded in the matrix block. As the reliability of the automatic system decreased, the added written data from the RAN's navigation log became standard. (Johnson)

landing weight had 2,000 pounds less fuel than airplanes without it—especially critical at night at sea.

"On Seven's [RVAH-7] return from Vietnam, they wanted to get as much equipment flown off as possible. The XO and I had an airplane with an 18-inch pan camera, two flasher pods, and the PECM package. That gave us a cat weight of around 80,000 pounds. Not an experience that I would like to repeat very often."[8]

"Really did NOT like PECM missions. Accuracy of the PECM data collected was directly proportional to navigation data logs the RAN had to take. Missions were high-altitude, long, straight legs. I don't recall position data logging requirements, but it was a handful to do. Actually, I don't even want to try and remember this. This was the only recon system I operated that I never was able to see the results. All others, I saw and self-evaluated every image I took. PECM . . . have no idea if any of it was good or not."[9]

Digital Data System

A data converter took inputs from the bomb directing set (ASB-12), air data system, and flight reference set and supplied data to each camera, the side-looking radar, and the PECM, where video amplifiers controlled cathode-ray tubes that printed the data matrices on film. These blocks of data were read to align the images from the sensors.

Fixed Data (set prior to the flight)
• Date
• Sortie number
• Sensor identification

Variable Data

• Barometric altitude	• Pitch	• Radar Altitude
• Heading	• Time	• Bomb/nav mode
• Drift	• Latitude	
• Roll	• Longitude	

Resolution Test Targets

With the importance of the camera to the Vigi's mission, use of resolution targets became necessary. The targets had been used since the 1950s and were simplicity itself. A pattern of white and black bars were painted on the ground—some aircraft carriers had a resolution target painted on an open deck in the superstructure—arranged in elements and groups. Each element was made up of equally spaced bars: three horizontal and three vertical. Groups consisted of elements of diminishing size. The effective resolution limit of a camera system was found by examining an image of the resolution target. The element where either the horizontal or vertical lines were not indistinct marked the effectiveness of that camera. The targets were

DO YOU SHOOT THE RESOLUTION TARGET ON EVERY MISSION ??

THE SHADOW DO!!

A typical RVAH squadron in 1972 had three AIOs: head intel, photo intel, and an electronic evaluator with a senior CTT that assisted with PECM. It also had three PTs and six PHs who worked for a PH warrant officer. Over time, squadrons became smaller.

Film processing and interpretation in IOIC was time consuming and required great talent from PTs and PHs to get correct. Film was unloaded painted at most military airfields that had reconnaissance aircraft and definitely at Vigilante bases. from the Vigilante and brought to the IOIC photo lab, where machines processed the silver-based film. PHs needed to ensure

Special People

The mission of the reconnaissance squadrons required the assignment of both officer and enlisted specialists. While one was the norm in other navy squadrons, there were up to three Air Intelligence Officer (AIO) in a RVAH squadron. At times a Warrant Officer Photographers Mate replaced one of the AIOs.

The enlisted ratings[10] in an RVAH squadron included:

- Photographers Mates (PH), obviously, did the processing of the film in IOIC and loading/unloading cameras in the planes.
- Photographic Interpreters (PT), who became Intelligence Specialists (IS) in the mid-1970s, studied the film and reported items of interest.
- Aviation Electronic Technicians (AT) and Radarmen (RD) (later replaced with CTTs, Cryptologic Technicians, Technical) and Data Processors (DP) collected, analyzed, and provided electronic intelligence.

Photo Interpreters using a stereoscope on a light table. Most analysis was done looking at negative film before printing.

Mission to Cubi Point

Jerry Gehrig and Jim "Pirate" Pirotte joined the already-deployed world-famous *Savage Sons of Sanford* in Atsugi, Japan, as the USS *Ranger* was in the shipyard undergoing repairs to its machinery. The carrier finally went to sea, but after only a short period of operations, a fire broke out in the arresting gear spaces, and word went out that there would be no flying for a couple of days.

The *Savage* officers headed to their rooms and broke out the secret stashes of adult beverages. The partying went on until the wee hours of the morning.

At 0630, the squadron duty officer called each of the flight crews and told them to be in IOIC in 30 minutes for a meeting with the CO. A request from 7th Fleet had come in tasking RVAH-5 to map the perimeter of Danang Airfield to see where the Viet Cong were holed up and lobbing mortars rounds onto the airfield. The *Ranger*'s arresting gear may have been down, but the catapults were working just fine. The two new, and junior, squadron members were to plan and fly the mission.

They were to launch, refuel from A-3 tankers before and after the mapping runs, and deliver the film to Cubi Point. The mission took almost four hours.

"On the way to Cubi, being unsuccessful in contacting the Air Force, Air Defense Identification Zone (ADIZ) gurus, and having a terrible headache, I suggested to the Pirate that we turn off our Identify Friend or Foe (IFF) transponder and go into afterburner to outrun any interceptors that may come after us. He agreed and we reached 0.95 Mach before slowing down and asking, 'Cubi tower, this is *Old Kentucky* 605, request VFR entry to land on runway three-zero.'

"The tower came back and said, '*Old Kentucky* 605, permission granted, but who is that F-101 on your right wing?'

"We looked over and saw a Philippine Air force F-101 Voodoo and thought we were in deep trouble. We didn't say a thing, got the film developed, and never heard a word about our successful evasion of the Philippine Air Defense Zone."[13]

---

that processing time and chemicals were correct or the processing would be a bust. For interpretation, PTs used portable light tables, not the huge auto-interpretation machines as originally intended, as they rarely worked. The coded navigation matrix block also almost never worked well. Therefore, PTs relied heavily on RAN debriefs with cockpit charts and tracks to find targets of interest or that were tasked to write up the reports.

PTs typically worked all night on the ship to process the results of the three or four Vigilante missions each day over North Vietnam with a full complement of cameras. The 18-inch pan camera was especially difficult because there was so much film to go through. "I remember PTs knee-deep in film most of the nights on the line in Vietnam, finding targets, writing reports, and sleeping days. They did a wonderful job with little recognition."[11]

Analyzing PECM tapes using the bulky computers in IOIC also required considerable effort. The tapes were processed to specifically identify radar attributes of interest and were selective in identifying specific emitters. The electronic evaluator AIO worked with the data processors to ensure that the appropriate analysis was based upon the tasking. This could be varied for emitter type, attributes, and/or area of search. In Vietnam, most tasking was to find SA2 missile sites, and the associated early warning and acquisition radars to ensure an updated SAM order of battle (OOB).

"Sometimes I asked the DPs to make multiple processing runs of the tapes to ensure that we understood details of the tasked emitters needed to write up the reports and send to higher headquarters. The CTT and I spent considerable time reading and plotting OOB reports to associate and identify changes to what we found on the tapes. It

was a great mission when we identified SAM or early warning (EW) radar movements, which they did frequently in NVN [North Vietnam], moving their equipment to pre-developed sites at night to prepare for attacking incoming sorties next day."[12]

Special Training

During the Vietnam Era, most Air Intelligence Officers were commissioned upon completion of Aviation Officer Candidate School (AOCS) in Pensacola, Florida. AOCS was 11 weeks of physical and military training under the loving supervision of Marine drill instructors plus classroom instruction in aviation, navy regulations, and history. Future AIOs underwent the same training as those cadets who went on to pilot or flight officer training. AOCS was followed by a five-week navigation course, also at Pensacola.

The Armed Forces Air Intelligence Training Center (AFAITC) was at Lowry Air Force Base in Denver, Colorado. Students there were a mix of air force officers, former Marine Corps and navy enlisted who had worked in intelligence-related fields and were now LDOs or warrant officers, and Pensacola graduates. Other specialized schools—some so hush-hush that the course titles were classified—followed for many, depending on their next assignment.

As part of the complete reconnaissance system that included the RA-5C, North American Rockwell combined its air, surface, and sub-surface systems into a single IOIC. These centers were put on board aircraft carriers as well as amphibious control (LCC) and helicopter assault (LHA) ships. Training for all personnel in NIPS had its inception as a department within RVAH-3 in the mid-1960s at NAS Sanford, Florida.

In July 1969, NIPSTRAFAC was commissioned as a separate command within Reconnaissance Wing-1 at NAS Albany, Georgia. As before, NIPSTRAFAC's primary mission was to train officers and enlisted personnel for duty in or associated with the Naval Intelligence Processing System, including CV, CVN, LCC, and LHA Intelligence Centers.

The NIPSTRAFAC curriculum was divided into 17 separate courses of instruction, which were from 1 to 38 weeks in length. Periodically, special maintenance courses were offered to update fleet personnel as new equipment was added to the NIPS system.

The second mission was to provide operational and training support to Commander, Reconnaissance Attack Wing One, and the RA-5C Vigilante squadrons based at NAS Albany and, later, NAS Key West. In a two-year period, the photographic department processed 980,000 feet of black-and-white film and 69,000 feet of color film. Also processed were more than 88,000 black-and-white prints and 41,000 color prints. More than 3,600 Troy ounces of silver (247 pounds!) was recovered from used photographic solutions.[14]

A third mission was to conduct navy-wide testing and evaluation of NIPS software and hardware programs and photographic-related equipment. (NIPSTRAFAC did the testing and evaluation of the NIPS-15 EA-6B Grumman Prowler Software package.)

Picture of the Month

In 1969, the Picture of the Month Award was established "to honor the squadron best exemplifying excellence in aerial imagery." Each squadron submitted one to five entries each month to Commander Reconnaissance Attack Wing-1. The entries were "judged on the basis of their applicability to tactical targeting and intelligence exploitation, image sharpness, sensitometric exposure, and code-matrix-block accuracy and readability." After the AAS-21 came, infrared imagery was allowed. Entries consisted of a select print, an original or duplicate negative (positive color transparencies were acceptable), and an information sheet with administrative and intelligence data.

Competition among the squadrons was high with all hands taking an interest. Even while deployed, amid the hundreds of exposures viewed from assigned missions, sailors and officers would spot a likely submission and pull it for consideration. Most were of assigned targets, but a particularly interesting subject was submitted just for something different. (I once took an air-to-air oblique of the Goodyear blimp. It didn't have a chance. There was no time to set the Vg/H and the usual zero setting wouldn't have worked anyway because of the closure speed. The result was what we called a "fuzzygram," but a Mach 2 jet alongside a blimp?)

Because it was an unusual subject, a photo of an AV-8A Harrier was submitted. The photo did not win but was used on the front page of the Key West newspaper. NAS Key West held its 1974 air show the same day as the offshore power boat races. A Vigilante took off in the morning and took pictures of the Harrier on its way to perform a dockside demonstration and the racing boats far out in the Gulf of Mexico. By the afternoon, that RA-5C was on static display with large prints on easels of the photographs taken mere hours before; a demonstration of tactical reconnaissance capabilities.

Bomb Derby

"Delivery of the first twin-jet RA-5C aircraft to Sanford in December brought a new mission to Heavy Attack Wing ONE and a liberal flavoring of reconnaissance to the Tenth Annual Bombing Derby. Both VAH-5 and VAH-3 will enter three RA-5Cs in all scored events except Event VI (A-5/A-3/A-4 Loft Bombing). In Event II, RA-5C flight crews will substitute photo missions for loft bombing deliveries. The blending of the RA-5C's dual capabilities will be demonstrated in Event III as RA-5C entries make two low-level bomb deliveries and two low-altitude, 600-mph photographic runs on the same 1-hour flight. Opposing the versatile aircraft will be A-5A Vigilantes from VAH-1 and A-3B Skywarriors from VAH-9, VAH-11, and VAH-11 Detachment Eight."[15]

Yankee Team

By 1964, US military action in Southeast Asia included Yankee Team missions over Laos. Reconnaissance flights by both the US Air Force and US Navy were of increasing importance in fighting the Pathet Lao. Significantly, the first navy aircraft shot down, in what became the Vietnam War, was on a reconnaissance mission. On 4 June, an RF-8A Photo-Crusader from VFP-63 on the USS *Kitty Hawk* (CVA-63) was shot down near the Plain of Jars in Laos.[16] The next day, a second navy aircraft was lost, an F-8 Crusader escorting another RF-8 on a photo mission.

In August, NVN torpedo boats attacked US destroyers in the Tonkin Gulf. Retaliatory raids into North Vietnam, *Operation Pierce Arrow*, were ordered.

Back at NAS Sanford, Florida, the first RA-5C squadrons were preparing for the new model Vigilantes' first deployments: RVAH-9 on the *Saratoga* (CVA-60) to the Mediterranean and RVAH-5 on *Ranger* (CVA-61) to WestPac (the Western Pacific) and what became the all-too-familiar spot in the Tonkin Gulf called Yankee Station.

NAME: _HARRIER_ BE/IR: _NONE_

COORD: _KEY WEST, FLORIDA_ CTY: _US_ ALT: _10,000'_

MSN: _611_ DATE: _09 NOV 74_

SENSOR: _KA-51A_ FL: _6"_ FRAME: _N/A_

PRODUCED BY NAVY _LCDR POWELL / LTJG PARR_

VMA-542 AV-8A Harrier over Key West.

The hash marks below the camera stencil represent combat reconnaissance missions. The mechanics are preparing the aircraft for its next flight, the pilot's helmet is on top of the ejection seat while he completes his walk-around inspection. The reddish rubber compound is an at-sea repair to the windscreen sealant.

RA-5C of the Checkertails of RVAH-11 has an empty module-4 and engine bay doors open. This photo was taken from stores ship USS Wichita (AOR-1) during underway replenishment of the USS Constellation (CVA-64) in the South China Sea in December 1971.

The owl represented the squadron's all-weather capability. Callsign and nickname were both Hooter. Frequently heard at beginning or end of radio transmissions was, "Hoot, hoot!"

Chapter 5

FRESHMAN TERM

Vigilante of RVAH-6 heading to the safety of the Tonkin Gulf, going "feet wet." (Illustration by David Schweitzer, 2palettes.com)

Originally, "feet wet" had a rather innocent meaning: to do something for the first time, such as putting your feet into the water before going for a swim. However, in the jargon of combat in Southeast Asia, it took on an entirely new meaning. Feet wet represented safety. It meant you had flown across the coastline into the safety of the Tonkin Gulf in the event of a bailout and rescue. This new meaning of feet wet began in 1964 in both senses of the term for North American's RA-5C Vigilante.

Feet Wet

Already designated as the Vigilante training squadron (RAG), VAH-3 received A-5Cs in June 1963 to begin conversion to the RA-5C, which began arriving in December of that year. Redesignation to RVAH-3 followed. RVAH-5 also had its first Vigilantes, RA-5Cs, in 1963. The early months of 1964 had RVAH-3, RVAH-5, and RVAH-9 (its first Vigilantes came in April), adapting to the reconnaissance mission in RA-5Cs. Both VAH-1 and VAH-7 with A-5As were on deployment to the Mediterranean. US destroyers were attacked in August and Operation Pierce Arrow when air strikes into North Vietnam began. Congress passed the Tonkin Gulf Resolution, and America was at war in all but name.

Savage Sons

The squadron claims the longest history of those that flew the Vigilante.[1] Established in 1948, VC-5 was known then as the *Grim*

Following the tradition that CAG flew "Double Nuts" (side number 300) aircraft, RVAH-3 dedicated BuNo 156609 to the reconnaissance wing commander: GJ300, Roman "I" and "COMRECONATKWING-1" on the nose, multiple colors on the tail stripes representing each squadron. Angle of photo and reflections on canopy indicate that this was taken with a handheld camera. In RVAH-12, in 1973, LCDR Fowler and LTJG Dipadova ejected from this aircraft when a fuel can tore out on the catapult shot. (NNAM)

When RVAH-5 deployed in the USS Ranger in 1965 it was the first time the RA-5C saw combat. The detachable pod on the starboard wing was a night flasher that generated light strobes of 3 million candlepower for night photography. (Wells)

Brand-new Vigilante in RVAH-5 with the wavy demarcation between gray and white. (Wells)

The Mushmouth lingered on as a Kilroy-like face peering over the arrow on the tail.

Reapers, and flew the P2V-3C until 1950 when they received AJ-1 Savages. When the squadron moved to NAS Sanford in 1955, they adopted *The Savage Sons of Sanford* for their aircraft and new home base and changed their insignia. Redesignated VAH-5, they flew A3D Skywarriors until transitioning to RA-5Cs in 1963. Deploying in the USS *Ranger* (CVA-61) in August 1963, the *Savage Sons* became the first to fly the Vigilante in combat.

Hooters

VC-9 was established in January 1953 with a mix of airplanes before getting AJ-1 Savages. The owl's-head insignia meant that they were capable of attack at night, in any weather. Becoming VAH-9 and flying A3Ds, the Hoot Owls made five consecutive deployments to the Mediterranean on the *Saratoga* (CVA-60). During the transi-

In this photo dated 5 April 1966, BuNo 149280 of RVAH-9 is over a cloud-topped mountain. Probably Mount Fujiyama, as all squadrons had we-were-there pictures taken when the carriers were in Japan. This aircraft was lost at sea while in the RAG in September 1969.

RVAH-9 on the USS Saratoga in 1965 before deploying to Southeast Asia. Nosewheel door is open and the bath tub down for access to the avionics rack. Owl-head insignia was prominent on the fuselage along with dark green tail bands, which Hooter aircraft kept for the squadron's entire existence. (Mark Johnson)

tion to the RA-5C and preparations for their next cruise, the crew of LCDR Smith and ADJC Carolyers ejected from BuNo 149308 at NAS Sanford. Their sixth consecutive deployment on the *Saratoga* began in November 1964. With a new type of airplane, going to the Mediterranean on a familiar aircraft carrier, and not being shot at, made life a bit easier.

Welcome to the War

The air war in Vietnam was unlike World War II or Korea. Many tactics carried over, but more did not. Commanders of air wings, captains of ships, embarked admirals and their staffs all had to find what worked best in those first months. Despite contradictory and politically driven directives from Washington, able and intelligent officers were able to get the job done.

There was as steep a learning curve for Vigilante squadrons in Vietnam as there was for all US forces in the modern world of radar-guided antiaircraft artillery (AAA), SAMs, and electronic warfare. One of the first lessons was that no matter how fast you were flying, low was bad because every peasant soldier with a rifle could shoot up to 3,000 feet. And even if you were fast, a well-thrown rock would do as much damage as a bullet.

Indicative of the high risks to come is the graduating class of the RVAH-3 RAG in December 1965. Back Row (left to right): Petty Officer Chick Winship (instructor), LCDR Tom Kolstad (RVAH-6 shot down, KIA), LT Giles Norrington (RVAH-1 shot down, POW), LT Jerry Coffey (RVAH-13 shot down, POW), CAPT Fowler (Wing Commander), CDR Charlie Smith (CO RVAH-6), LCDR Jim Thompson (RVAH-6 shot down, rescued), LCDR Greg Davidson (RVAH-7). Front Row (left to right): ENS Gunder Creager (RVAH-5), ENS Bill Klenert (RVAH-6 shot down, KIA), LCDR O.B. McGuire (RVAH-6), CDR B.B. Brown (RAG, RVAH-3, CO), LTJG Bob Hanson (RVAH-13 shot down, KIA), ENS Dick Tangeman (RVAH-1 shot down, POW), LTJG Gary Parten (RVAH-6 shot down, rescued). (Creager)

Photomate (PH) working on the film canisters for the forward oblique camera in a lowered module-1. (Sharp)

RVAH-5 was in Hawaii as scheduled on the USS *Ranger* (CVA-61) during the Tonkin Gulf incident. Because of it, their training was cut short and they arrived on-the-line in mid-September. Unsure of the effectiveness and reliability of the new and unproven aircraft, CVW-9 had a detachment of VFP-63 RF-8 Crusaders assigned as insurance. Cooperation between the "Light Photo" and "Heavy

Recce" units was excellent with photographers mates and related intelligence ratings sharing watches and work in the new IOIC. After this deployment, only a Vigilante squadron was assigned to the big deck carriers and the RF-8s to the smaller carriers: 27 Charlies and Midway class.

There was also an official reluctance to send the expensive (approximately $14 million in 1960s' money) and advanced technology (airplane, ECM, and reconnaissance systems) Vigilante into high-risk areas, so the RA-5C was initially restricted to flights over South Vietnam and Laos. By 1965, the restriction was lifted and the RVAH-5 *Savage Sons* flew the first RA-5C missions over North Vietnam.

LCDR Donald Beard and LTJG Brian Cronin crashed in BuNo 149306 (the first Vigilante produced as an RA-5C and not a conversion) on a reconnaissance run in South Vietnam on 9 December 1964. The most junior pilot in RVAH-5, LT Jim Pirotte, was lowered by helicopter sling into the jungle to investigate. Although the exact cause was not determined, it was considered a combat loss—the first of 23 Vigilantes to be downed.

Next Up

Unlike RVAH-5, *The Smoking Tigers* were already flying Vigis; they had completed a successful Mediterranean deployment in the USS *Independence* (CVA-62) with A3J/A-5As. However, with the change of mission, less than half the flight crews were bomber qualified.

The deployment was unusual in several ways. The ship and Air Wing 7 were part of the Atlantic Fleet, RVAH-1 was only the second RA-5C squadron in combat, the McDonnell F-4B Phantom was new to the fleet, and Grumman's A-6A Intruder, with an associated electrically fused bomb problem, was on its first deployment. With the program of contractor support for new and complex aircraft, all three types had teams from the manufacturers assisting and advising the sailors in maintaining what were no longer "airplanes" but "weapons systems."

The *Independence*'s route to war took ship and air wing from Norfolk, Virginia, around Africa, across the

Vigilantes of RVAH-1, Smoking Tigers, on the USS Independence in 1965. The three cans of the fuel "train" with the tail cone can be seen beyond the first RA-5C. Nose numbers were light blue to go with the markings applied at the factory. (Woodul)

RA-5C on the Independence's number-2 catapult an instant before being shot during CVW-7's flyoff on returning to the United States in December 1965. Flaps are full down; launch bridle and hold-back bar hooked up. Empty pylon on starboard wing. RVAH-1 earned the Tonkin Gulf Yacht Club crest painted below the cockpits. (NNAM)

Nam Dinh POL storage BDA after an air strike in 1965. A 6-inch vertical camera from 1,500 feet. The enlargement (on right) is from the approximately 5-square-inch original (left). A good, clear data matrix block is in the lower left corner. (CRAW-1 Briefing Book)

Indian Ocean, and into a port visit to Singapore before sailing into the Tonkin Gulf.[2]

Rolling Thunder

Operation Rolling Thunder began on the first day of March 1965 and was intended to force North Vietnam to negotiate a settlement through a campaign of air strikes of increasing intensity. What targets could be hit and which areas were off limits was determined in Washington, DC. The specific targets that required a major effort were on the A-list. A is Alpha in the phonetic alphabet so attack missions using a large number of airplanes from an air wing became known as Alpha Strikes. For the reconnaissance squadrons, RF-8 and RA-5C, pre- and post-Alpha strike (BDA, Bomb Damage Assessment) photography became a major mission. During cyclic operations, route (roads, trails, waterways, railroads) reconnaissance was the equivalent of attack aircraft doing armed reconnaissance. Technically, reconnaissance missions into the North were called *Blue Trees*.[3]

In addition, the RA-5C used SLR to make and update radar maps of Vietnam. The new A-6A Intruders used these to plan their

RVAH-12 had the advantage of making their first deployment in 1966 aboard the USS Saratoga to the Mediterranean. They kept a SIOP commitment while deployed and practiced bomb delivery. A practice bomb dispenser is on the right wing. Sixth Fleet operations were overshadowed by action in Vietnam, but were an important phase of the Cold War. (THA)

night and all-weather attacks. Each RVAH squadron also had one or two aircraft PECM capable and ran tracks along the borders of North Vietnam to locate enemy search and fire control radars.

One month after the start of Operation Rolling Thunder, in April, RVAH-5 turned over what they had learned to the RVAH-1 *Smoking Tigers* who had arrived in the Tonkin Gulf aboard the USS *Independence* for that Atlantic Fleet carrier's only time in combat.

The navy's presence escalated; by the end of 1965 RVAH-1 in *the Independence*, RVAH-7 in the *Enterprise* (CVAN-65), and RVAH-13 in the *Kitty Hawk* (CVA-63) were all on the line. RVAH-9 in *Ranger* replaced *Independence* when that ship began its long journey home. For the remainder of the Vietnam War, there was always two, usually three, and, briefly, four aircraft carriers deployed to Southeast Asia with RVAH squadrons on board.

Independence

The deployment did not begin well with three A-6 Intruders lost due to faulty bomb fusing in the first month. The maps used to program the A-6's navigation system were also discovered to be erroneous and the Vigilantes were given the task of photo-mapping Vietnam, North and South, to update the plat.

John Smittle was an Ensign RAN in RVAH-1 and remembers flying into the Tan Son Nhut air base with the squadron XO for a conference at the USAF reconnaissance center. (The USAF was still operating RF-101 Voodoos.) Even as a junior officer, he realized that air force insistence on centralized control of all intelligence would become a sore spot for the navy, as its information was usually out of date while on-the-spot intelligence from Vigilantes and IOIC was not considered "official."

RVAH-1 lost its commanding officer that same month. Returning from a reconnaissance mission over North Vietnam, the arresting gear was set incorrectly, the wire broke, and the RA-5C (BuNo 151619) went off the deck into the water. There was no time to eject and the pilot, CDR Valentin Matula, and RAN, LT Carl Gronquist, were killed on impact. Because of the aircraft's size and weight, arresting gear and catapults worked at maximum limits. Incorrect settings remained a problem throughout the Vigilante's career.

The *Peacemakers* were familiar with the *Enterprise*, having made the first Vigilante deployment on it as VAH-7 flying A3Js. After an interruption for the Cuban Missile Crisis, VAH-7 went back on board for more months in the Mediterranean and the around-the-world nuclear-powered demonstration voyage. On return to NAS Sanford after *Operation Sea Orbit*, the squadron transitioned to the RA-5C and was redesignated as RVAH-7.

On station, the *Enterprise* and the *Independence* steamed side by side for a turnover of special equipment, unexpended ordnance, and most important, lessons learned.

By October 1965, the air war was hot. The first SAMs (SA-2) had been launched that summer and their locations were a high priority. The Vigilantes from RVAH-1 began searching for the distinctive six-sided launching sites. The first Vigilante shot down in North Vietnam had been searching for SA-2 sites and was near Hon Gai doing 650 knots when BuNo 151615 was hit in the tail by either an AAA or a SAM. After the flight controls failed the crew, LCDR James Bell, pilot, and LT "Duffy" Hutton, RAN, ejected and landed in the small islands off the coast. They both climbed into their survival rafts but were picked up by fishermen in sampans and became POWs.[4]

The next day, three F-4 Phantoms from the *Independence* were lost on an Alpha strike against the Thai Nguyen bridge north of Hanoi. The Vigilante covering the attack was unharmed.

RVAH-1 had taken six aircraft, but their losses were not replaced while deployed. They tried using flasher pods at night, but gave it up as a bad idea due to accuracy of the flak. As the North Vietnamese air defenses grew tougher, RVAH-1 used both 3- and 18-inch panoramic cameras to gain standoff distance.

Enterprise

The USS *Enterprise* (CVAN-65) had been home-ported in Norfolk, Virginia, across the James River from Newport News Shipbuilding Corporation, where the first nuclear-powered aircraft carrier had been built. In anticipation of the growing conflict in Southeast Asia, it was transferred to the Pacific Fleet and based in Alameda, California. The carrier went via the war zone and did not arrive at its new home port for nine months. For the ship's crew and men of Air Wing 9 (CVW-9), which included RVAH-7, this meant a long voyage east around Africa, across the Indian Ocean, and through the Straits of Malacca to the naval air station at Cubi Point in the Philippines. The time in port was short; supplies and ammunition were loaded and the *Enterprise* headed for the Tonkin Gulf and the newly designated spot in the ocean called Yankee Station.

Maps

Although the RA-5C had a sophisticated navigation system, pilots and RANs always had a map with course lines for the reconnaissance route drawn on it as a visual backup in case of ASB-12 failures.

"Flight planning applied all of our fine-art skills learned in grade school. We used scissors and glue to piece together our route from a 1:250,000-scale topographic map, colored markers, compass, protractor, and a template full of circles to determine our path over the ground turning at 600 knots. Known SA-2 missile sites were drawn with purple stars. The SA-2 threat circles were shown with purple circles. AAA had red dots. We plotted the actual mission in blue and our reconnaissance targets with a yellow highlighter. We carefully measured and double-checked our magnetic headings for each leg, and drew one-minute tick marks along the route, assuming 10 miles a minute at 600 knots."[5]

A junior RAN in RVAH-7 who flew with his CO made up his skipper's maps for him. As trips over North Vietnam became routine, the ensign RAN simply added another set of lines and headings rather than re-drawing the entire chart with AA and SAM envelopes. During a port visit in Japan, he bought a set of 24 colored pencils. Back on the line, he used a different color for each mission. When, after the tenth, he told his CO to, "follow the mauve line today," the commander crumpled the well-worn map, threw it over the side, and demanded a fresh one.[6]

What It Was Like: Launch

The hardest thing to do in a Vigilante was get in position for the catapult shot. The RA-5C used a bridle attached to two hooks under the intakes to launch, rather than the current nose-launch bar. This meant that the nose wheel had to go up and over the catapult shuttle, but not too far. The shuttle is shaped like a turtle shell with the end chopped off and slippery with an amalgam of jet fuel, condensed steam, and salt spray.

Taxi

The Vigilante had to be turned precisely from the deck onto the center of the catapult track. Because of the length of the fuselage, there was little distance to correct the lineup. At the shuttle the tolerances became even closer. Off the exact center of the hump, the nose gear could slip off the edge and cut the tire. You added power to get over, felt the wheel drop, and if not stopped in 2 inches, the holdback fitting in the tail cracked.

A good taxi director modified the standard signals and added lots of body English. He varied the speed and distance of his waving hands. His body leaned and twisted, shoulders dipped and head nodded with exact and subtle signals to the pilot. He could have become a ballet dancer or professional mime with the skills needed to launch a Vigilante.

Catapult

Once over the shuttle and with the launch bridle attached, the yellow-shirted director sweeps one hand low and forward, the other opens from a fist to splayed fingers. The below-the-waist signal is to the catapult crew, "Take tension." The high signal is to you, the pilot, "Release brakes." You drop your heels to the floor, but leave your toes on the rudders. Your left hand pushes the throttles to the detent for full military power. While the J79 engines spool up, you look over to the catapult officer, the "Shooter." He is waving his hand with two

Green-tailed RVAH-9 Vigilante on Saratoga's Catapult 4. The nose wheel has just gone over the shuttle. A pair of catapult crew are picking up the steel launch bridle while another is under the tail pulling down the attach fitting for the hold-back. The director in a yellow shirt has signaled a stop and hold brakes. Two squadron maintenance men in brown shirts and a safety inspector in a checkered white jersey are doing final checks. In 1965, flight deck personnel were not yet wearing flotation vests. (Mark Johnson)

What appears to be a dramatic black cloud is stack gas. Exhaust smoke from a carrier's boilers has been a problem since the beginning of carrier flying. What came out of the stacks was determined by the ship's engineers. Power changes meant readjusting the fuel-air ratio. Normal stack gas was almost invisible. (NNAM)

fingers up over his head. Eyes back in the cockpit to the engine gauges. RPM, temperatures, and pressures are all good.

The intercom to the back seat is hot. "Looks good. You ready?" The Shooter is flicking his hand from fist to fingers open to fist. Time for afterburner. You hear, "All-ready in back," from your RAN. Push the throttles past the detent as far forward as they go. Brace them there with your fingertips. To reach all the way to the cat grip could pull your shoulder off the seat back. Bad in case of ejection. Fast now; look at one tiny gauge with two needles—afterburner nozzle positions. They both swing around symmetrically. Too much time in burner could damage the sea water–cooled blast deflectors only feet behind the exhausts.

You tell your RAN and throw an exaggerated salute to the catapult officer. Drop right hand to the stick and brace your elbow on your thigh. Settle helmet solidly against headrest, check your back is straight. Your breathing shallows. You wait while the Vigilante quivers and roars with 36,000 pounds of thrust boiling the air around it.

The cat officer looks front and back in a final check, leans far forward, and touches his hand to the deck. At the edge of your vision, the sailor at the control console drops his hands from over his head and presses a large green button.

The catapult fires. The weight of your chest forces out a grunt. You strain your neck, trying to pull your head off the rest—if you succeed you will eject because something has gone wrong. Then, 70,000 pounds of airplane is being accelerated to 170 mph. As the Vigilante clears the deck, 3,000 pounds of hydraulic pressure in the nose gear extend the oleo strut hard enough to vibrate the nose and make the instrument panel blur—barely noticed in the day, moments of confused terror at night.

You can now lean forward, reach with your left hand to raise the landing gear lever, and pull the throttles back from afterburner to military power. Keep low, turn away from the carrier, accelerate, then climb and look around for your F-4 Phantom escort.

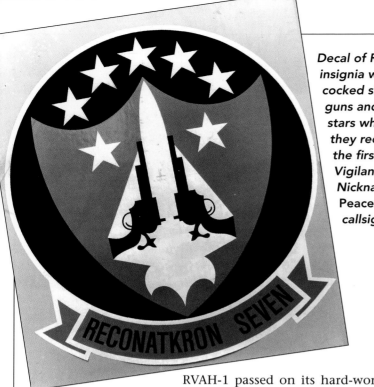

RVAH-1 passed on its hard-won knowledge to RVAH-7.

Enterprise began by operating down south from Dixie Station (a usual practice, as it gave newly arrived air wings a chance to adjust to combat flying and the pace of operations) and lost a Vigilante (BuNo 151633) in an area Navy airplanes rarely flew over; the far west coast of South Vietnam. The search was for "Wiblicks" (the fancy, official designation for boats, barges, sampans, etc. Water Borne Logistics Craft, WBLC) amid the coastal swamps.

The pilot, J. K. Sutor, was only a lieutenant and his RAN, G. B. Dresser, a JG. Flying 3,500 feet over the bay of Vinh Cay Duong, they felt a thump and their cockpits filled with smoke. The pilot killed the electric flight system and fought the controls until 10 miles over the Gulf of Siam the RA-5C became uncontrollable and they ejected. The nearest rescuer was an Army UH-1B Huey helicopter that was vectored to the crash site.

A sampan was approaching the survivors and, because its identity and intentions were unclear, the Huey pilot had the navy aircraft holding overhead fire a burst of 20mm cannon in front of the sampan to warn it off. As there was no hoist on the UH-1B, the pilot skillfully hovered with his landing skid on the water. First Sutor and then Dresser climbed into the helicopter and were flown to safety.

When they were returned to the ship several days later, CDR Ken Enney, the CO of RVAH-7, gave them a chewing out. It was bad enough, he said, that they were sent out looking for such insignificant targets, but to lose an expensive and sophisticated airplane while wandering around sightseeing was intolerable.[7]

LTJG Dave Sharp was in the back of a Vigilante heading north from Dixie Station and about to turn into Vietnam when the RA-5C did not turn the direction Sharp called for and the pilot, LCDR Jerry Chapdelaine, did not answer his increasingly frantic calls over the intercom. Sharp correctly guessed that his pilot was hypoxic from an oxygen system malfunction.

RVAH-7 Vigilante with flasher pod; NG was the tail code for CVW-9 in 1965. (THA)

"That's when I started calling him every name I could think of along with 'dive, dive, dive.' Then, when he did push over, I thought we wouldn't pull out.

"My call became 'pull-out, pull-out, pull-out, you SOB.' When he finally did, we kept going slower and slower, so I started yelling, 'power, power, power!' By this time we were at 8,000 feet and Jerry was beginning to sound normal.

"Apparently, when he attached his mask on climb-out it was not tight enough. When he started losing consciousness, he slumped forward and forced his mask on enough to keep him at a semi-conscious state. He later told me that all he could remember was hearing me call him various foul names, and he just wanted to catch me and kill me. I told him that I'd had a few similar thoughts about him myself."

Bats

VAH-13 was formed with A-3 Skywarriors in 1961 at NAS Sanford. As an all-weather attack squadron, they found an appropriate insignia in the spread wing bat on the Bacardi rum bottle[8], and their nickname was born, although the official callsign was *Flint River*. After completing cruises on *Kitty Hawk*, the *Bats* transitioned to the RA-5C and became RVAH-13 before again deploying on *Kitty Hawk*. Flying out of Sanford, BuNo 151821 crashed, killing the pilot, CDR Nolta, while the RAN, LTJG Paul Stokes, ejected successfully.[9]

RVAH-13 had a rough start to their first combat deployment. The Uong Bi thermal power station north of Haiphong had been the target for multiple air wing attacks, and two Vigilantes with F-4 Phan-

Based on the Bacardi rum label, the night-flying bat became the emblem, and nickname, of VAH, then RVAH-13. Official callsign was Flint River.

tom escorts were assigned to get BDA photographs. Visual and radio contact with *Flint River 604* (BuNo 151624) was lost. The area along the coast near Hon Gai was searched without finding any wreckage or sign of LCDR Guy Johnson or LTJG Lee Nordahl.

Only two days later, and three days before Christmas, *Flint River 603* (BuNo 151632) was after pre-strike photography of the railroad bridge at Hai Duong for the next day's strike. Flying at 3,000 feet between cloud layers, LTJG Glenn Daigle saw bursting AAA and heard hits on the Vigilante. The RA-5C went into gyrations and because the pilot, LCDR Max Lukenbach, was not answering the intercom, Daigle had to assume that his pilot had been hit and was unconscious or worse. There was an explosion and Daigle was ejected—he does not remember pulling the face curtain or alternate ejection handles.[10]

On 3 February 1966, LT Jerry Coffey was on a road reconnaissance between Vinh and Thanh Hoa when he was hit by AAA during a second pass over the same section of highway. Another hard-earned lesson for any aircraft in a hostile area was no multiple runs over the same target. Coffey headed for the water, but less than a mile offshore the Vigilante (BuNo 151625) broke apart and he and

1965, RVAH-13 RA-5C ready for night takeoff in full afterburner. The leading-edge drops are down and flaps lowered. (Edge-on to camera; partly obscuring "CVW-11") Note RVAH-13's Oriental-style tail letters. It was unusual to have both the ship's name on the tail as well as the air wing, here CVW-11 is indicated above pale-blue NAVY title. (NNAM)

Coffey was shot down three days after a 37-day bombing halt that President Johnson, at Secretary of Defense McNamara's urging, had declared ended. The halt did not work as hoped; the North Vietnamese did not begin negotiations and used the time to build up their air defenses to a formidable level. During the halt, pilots reported that at night the Ho Chi Minh Trail looked like the New Jersey Turnpike during rush hour.

Ranger

The USS *Ranger* was operating on Dixie Station for only the second day online when a RVAH-9 Vigilante (BuNo 149312) crashed after what should have been a routine touch-and-go landing on the ship. The starboard engine exploded when full throttle was applied and the airplane crashed into the sea with the loss of LCDR Charles Schoonover and ENS Hal Hollingsworth. It was the only RA-5C that the *Hooters* lost in two combat deployments.

The RVAH-9 Vigilante had been on a reconnaissance flight over South Vietnam before returning to the *Ranger*. One frustration in such incidents was that it would never be known if the airplane crashed because it had been hit by unseen and unfelt small arms fire that only took effect later in the flight.

After Vietnam, RVAH-5 did two Mediterranean cruises on Saratoga, *which made a port visit to Beirut where the Arabic keffiyehs and agals were purchased. Left to right standing: Top: CO Dearolph, XO Davidson, Butler, Gehrig, and flag holder Larry Hall. Bottom: Wally Sudal, Feeback, Bill Meyer, and John Bailey.*

LTJG Robert Hanson ejected. Coffey was hauled aboard a fishing boat and spent the next seven years as a POW. He had seen his RAN land in the water, but LTJG Hanson was never heard from again. The North Vietnamese later said that Hanson died and was buried on the beach.

A hard-earned lesson was to never fly above a cloud layer if there was the slightest chance of SAMs. The primary tactic to avoid the SA-2 was a diving, rolling turn toward the missile. Being above the clouds reduced the time available to spot and evade the SAM. There were crews who forgot or ignored this rule to their dismay.

On-the-Spot Intelligence

RVAH-13 was instrumental in one of the most effective strikes of the early air war. While most strikes on the Alpha target list were specified by Washington, local commanders were allowed to choose some targets, but they had to get permission. CAPT Martin D. "Red" Carmody was captain of the *Kitty Hawk* and an early supporter of the RA-5C. In April when a *Bat* Vigilante came back from a coastal reconnaissance run with photographs of a new, large, coal-loading complex near the port of Cam Pha, he saw an opportunity to hurt the enemy's war effort. The strike became a perfect example of how the capability of the IOIC should be used.

Timing was everything. In collusion with CTF-77

Chief-of-Staff CAPT "Jig Dog" Ramage, a squadron mate from World War II, *Kitty Hawk* launched a pre-dawn strike of eight F-4s with bombs and six A-6s, each with 6,000 pounds of bombs plus support aircraft. Captain Carmody sent the message that "unless otherwise directed" they were going to bomb the coal facility at a time of day when he knew the response in Washington would be slow. The ship's communication officer was carefully briefed to take his time delivering the reply when it came. The strike group had pulled off the target and the RVAH-13 Vigilante had gone in for BDA when the cease and desist message arrived . . . too late.

Three RVAH-5 aircraft on an airfield. Since there was a contingency requirement to have the large tanks available, installing four drop tanks to fly on the carrier at the beginning of a deployment was efficient. Once on board, the tanks were stored in the hangar deck overhead. (NNAM)

Four Big Tanks

Usually, the large drop tanks were taken from overhead storage and hung on the A-5s for the flight off the ship to home base. One crafty maintenance officer got permission to have the cumbersome tanks shipped back to NAS Sanford. When they arrived, he took the crating material home. His hobby was woodworking and he knew that in the Philippines, mahogany was used as commonly as pine was in the States.

Red, White, or Blue

The pattern for the carriers in the Tonkin Gulf was set with schedule designations as Red, White, or Blue. When there were three carriers available, as there usually was, one ship flew from midnight to noon (Red), another from 0600 to 1800 (White), and the third from noon to midnight (Blue). This gave each air wing/ship team a 12-hour flying period while providing double coverage during daylight hours.

Cyclic ops were the norm with aircraft launching and recovering every one-and-a-half hours. When Alpha strikes were called for, all aircraft were launched and recovered after the strike before either launching another Alpha or resuming a cyclic pattern. There were exceptions and variations because of the need to replenish food, fuel, and ordnance every six or seven days; the size of the carrier and composition of the embarked air wing; and carriers leaving the line for R&R in port or returning home.

Connie and the Fleurs

The USS *Constellation* (CVA-64) began its first war-time cruise in May 1966. On board was RVAH-6. The first CO of the *Fleurs* as a reconnaissance squadron was CDR C. R. "Screaming Charlie" Smith who claimed, "Tracers won't hurt you, they just bounce off." He led the squadron through an eventful deployment.[11]

Vigilante in the groove. Camouflaged airplane parked with tail over water. (THA)

Sewn on a flight jacket, the emblem of VAH/ RVAH-6 has a heraldic explanation: The blue is for the ocean, the trident is for sea power, Omega is for the ultimate, and the Fleur-de-lis has been the symbol of the sixth military unit since Napoleonic times, hence the nickname, Fleurs (or less flattering, the "Flowers of the Fleet"). The rather odd assigned callsign was Field Goal.

Bull and GG

LT "Bull" Davis was crewed with LT "GG" Gretter for the *Fleurs* first combat and first deployment in Vigilantes. During a mission to obtain the results of an air wing strike on the Dong Son petroleum storage site near Haiphong, they had a flight control malfunction and the RA-5C headed down. While Gretter handled the airplane, Davis kept the cameras running properly. Despite SAM near-misses and intensified flak because of their dangerously low altitude, they made it to feet wet safely, and with photographic intelligence that went beyond the intended coverage. A typical mission for the Vigilante.

Upside Down Over Haiphong

LCDR Art Skelly and his RAN, LTJG Joe Shevlin, survived one of the strangest events of the Vigilante's career. In 1980, then-Captain Skelly wrote:

"Of the 260 combat flights I flew in the Vigilante, the most unusual had to be with RVAH-6 in July of '66 aboard *Constellation*. One dark, overcast Sunday morning, we photographed an oil storage area that had been hit the previous night by A-6s. On our way out of the target area over downtown Haiphong, we took some severe AAA, automatic weapons fire, and SAMs. Tracers were crisscrossing over the canopy and the F-4 escort was going crazy calling out flak. I decided we had had enough, so I pulled up into a nearby thunderstorm to get away from the heaviest flak I had ever seen.

"It didn't work. Not only did we immediately encounter rain, hail, and lightning, but the tracers were streaking around us and there were bright flashes from lightning and exploding shells. I couldn't tell whether the turbulence was violent because of near misses or the storm. The attitude gyro didn't look quite right, but that was the least of my worries then. We soon popped out of the storm cell and I realized the gyro was correct—not only were we

Redrawn for The Hook by Jim Wogstad

"Do you think, Comrade, that Hanoi will believe it?"
from an original drawing by McMillan

Not long after the incident over Haiphong, LTJG Joe Shevlin had his canopy tear off on the catapult shot. LCDR Art Skelly heard a loud boom and looked in the mirror in time to seen the canopy sail past the tail. After the Mutt-and-Jeff exchange on the intercom, and dumping fuel, they landed back on the USS Constellation. *(Skelly)*

Cartoon that was drawn for the ship's paper after Skelly and Shevlin's inadvertent inverted flight over Haiphong. (THA)

upside down, but the F-4 was right there in position, also inverted!

"Joe recognized that the nose had fallen through and was telling me to pull out. I had rolled level and pulled hard because the water was awfully close. Joe said that the radar altimeter had gone to zero before we started to climb.

"There was a large merchant ship in front of us—turned out to be Chinese—and as we flew past, our escort Phantom called that a machine gun on the stern was firing *down* at us.

"Back on the ship, I had maintenance check the Vigi for overstress and battle damage. Despite some of the heaviest flak I had ever seen, there wasn't a single hole in the airplane!

"The guys in the ready room threatened to mount a Brownie on top of my hardhat for future maneuvers."

A fortnight later, this same crew was again over Haiphong when three large flashes of AAA exploded in front of their nose. LTJG Shevlin lost his radar and navigation system but got the photographs. Back on board the *Constellation*, a series of shrapnel holes were discovered from one side of the fuselage to the other inches in front of LCDR Skelly's feet.

High Speed

In August, LCDR Jim Thompson and his RAN, LTJG G. Parten, were on a road reconnaissance northwest of Vinh when triple-A opened up and the Vigilante (BuNo 149309) suddenly rolled. With only partial control, Thompson headed for the coast. The Phantom escort reported a fire in the wheel well area and sections of the left wing breaking off. When the nose pitched over, they both ejected at extremely high speed.

Thompson later said that time compression kicked in and when his eyes peered over the top of the windshield into the slipstream, he wanted to reverse-vector back into the cockpit. His ride was particularly violent and he was badly bruised with his flight suit in tatters. He landed in a marshy area close to the shore and, despite a dislocated shoulder, avoided capture by staying underwater in the reeds and breathing through a plastic tube he kept in his sock. A searching Vietnamese stepped on his leg, but must have thought it was a log as he moved off.

At nightfall, Thompson swam and drifted with the tide until far enough to sea for later pickup by a helicopter. LTJG Parten was rescued by a navy ship.

When flight surgeon Dr. "Hawkeye" Hughes asked Thompson, "Why the hell did you jump out at such a ridiculously high speed [since the survival curve of the seat asymptotically approached zero above 600 knots] coming out of Haiphong Harbor?"

"Well, Hawkeye, that's all the faster it would go."

Bad Day

22 October 1966 was a bad day. An F-4B Phantom of VF-161 was shot down north of Thanh Hoa. The next launch from the *Constellation* included a RVAH-6 Vigilante (BuNo 150830) and a Phantom for a Route Reconnaissance between Hanoi and Hai Duong. The escorting Phantom was hit by ground fire and began a turn back to the nearest coast. As the Vigilante turned to follow, the pilot, LCDR Thomas Kolstad, called a SAM launch. The crew of the F-4B lost sight of the RA-5C.

Nothing more was known about the Vigilante, Kolstad, or RAN LTJG William Kienert until a Vietnamese report said the aircraft had been shot down by an SA-2, the crew had ejected at a very low altitude, and both were killed.

One week later, the *Constellation* headed east and was home for Christmas. 1966 ended with only two RVAH squadrons on the line; RVAH-7 on the USS *Enterprise* and RVAH-13 on the USS *Kitty Hawk*. Both were unusual for staying with the same ship for consecutive deployments. (This happened only once more during the war.)

The most impressive flybys were flown in an arc around the spectators. (Carlton)

Green Airplanes

At this stage of the Vietnam War, the US Navy was concerned about increasing MiG activity and decided to try a camouflage that would make aircraft more difficult for high-flying enemy fighters to detect. All types of aircraft were painted. Four RVAH squadrons; 6, 11, 12, and 13 had Vigilantes painted with shades of green and brown on the upper surfaces. The patterns and colors varied depending on where the painting was done. RVAH-6 had its airplanes painted at the Overhaul and Repair Facility at NAS North Island in San Diego before embarking on the USS *Constellation*.

The green Vigilantes flew during the usual workups in Hawaii and during the trip to Japan and Subic Bay in the Philippines. After the first Tonkin Gulf line period, and the air

Example of experimental paint pattern used on RVAH-11 and -13 aircraft. The darker paint highlights the PECM antennas.

Freshly painted RVAH-6 Vigilante at NAS North Island in two shades of dark green, reduced-size insignia, and black lettering. Its belly was left in standard white.

Another Vigilante with the dark pattern; this with RVAH-11 whose vivid white and black checkerboard opposes the idea of camouflage. (THA)

wing's loss of an F-4 Phantom, an A-6 Intruder, and four A-4 Skyhawks—all to ground fire—the water-based camouflage paint was removed by sailors with solvent-soaked rags. RVAH-6 airplanes remained the standard gull-gray and white from then on. Despite the bad experiences of the *Constellation* squadrons, the camouflage idea was tried again later . . . with the same results.

"All Six's planes were overpainted at O&R [overhaul and repair] North Island prior to the cruise. After the first line period, the camouflage was removed. The finish was very rough, had almost a sandy feel, and it reduced the maximum air speed by 20 knots, or more. One thing the paint was good for was over-G inspections. Any loose fastener or loose panels showed up easily due to the colored paint being rubbed away.

"If I remember correctly, only the CO had prior combat flying experience from Korea and everyone else had to acquire the 'jinking' expertise. We could sure see where the spoiler/deflector had contacted the edges as they closed while the wings were bending. You can see that the star-and-bar insignia, side number, and BuNo on the vertical fin are much smaller than normal. I was told that was to distort distance indications for attacking pilots."[12]

Chapter 6

HARD TIMES: 1967–1968

Landing Signal Officers on their platform. Only the best could wave the Vigilante correctly. The controlling LSO, in white, is indulging in some body English. (USN)

If 1966 was a tough year, 1967 represented the peak of both air losses and the intensity of combat over North Vietnam. This applies to any statistic, be it the US Air Force, the Marine Corps, or the US Navy. Total US aircraft lost in 1967 increased to 635. For the Vigilante in particular, the jump was from four aircraft lost in 1966 to eight in 1967. These losses resulted from the intensity of the air war and the relentless grind of Operation Rolling Thunder.

The bombing halt, which President Johnson had decreed, began on 23 December 1966 and was like the intermission in a long drama, giving actors time to refresh. The North Vietnamese restocked their ammunition and installed new radars and many more lethal SAM sites. Halftime at a football game is probably a better analogy; when the break was over, both opponents returned to the fray with revised plans and renewed energy.

The rough box of white lines was drawn on the approximately 5-inch-square negative. The dark square is the area that was enlarged to show an NVN AAA site. A good, clear data matrix block is in the lower left corner. There were many similar sites throughout North Vietnam. (CRAW-1 Command Presentation)

The War: 1967

The New Year found *Kitty Hawk* (CVA-63) with the *Bats* of RVAH-13 and the *Enterprise* (CVN-65) with RVAH-7 in the Tonkin Gulf. The *Constellation* (CV-64) and the RVAH-12 *Speartips* joined them in March.

Part of the politics that permeated the war in Vietnam divided the North into six "Route Packages" with alternate navy and air force responsibility that became vaguer as time passed. The infamous Route Pack Six was subdivided into A and B, Hanoi and Haiphong.

BDA Run

The dust, dirt, and debris from 100 Mk82, 500-pound bombs was still settling back to the ground as the Vigilante began the photo run. The pilot had both afterburners blazing and lowered the nose to pick up more speed. In the rear cockpit, the RAN checked the film counters running down, image-motion bars tracking, inertial navigation readouts correct, all while watching the ALQ scope for radar lock-ons and missile launches. The Vigilante was doing 650 mph as the wings snapped level at the primary target. Inside the planned turn, the Phantom escort was in full afterburner trying to keep up.

The Vietnamese gunners who had not been injured in the attack had reloaded their weapons as fast as they could. They began to shoot as the RA-5C came over the target. The smaller guns tracked the fast-moving aircraft while an 87mm site put up a barrage of exploding shells where they hoped the Vigilante would be.

The Vigilante jinked left to throw off the track, avoid the burst, and get closer to one of the SAM sites that had been attacked. Tracers streaked the air, the ALQ screen was a mass of pulsing golden strobes, and missile lock warnings warbled in the crew's earphones. The RAN continued to monitor the reconnaissance and navigation systems as the airplane swerved and bounced. The RIO in the escorting Phantom called out gunfire when he saw it.

After long, breathless minutes, the two airplanes cleared the target area. The RAN moved a cursor handle, punched a button, said, "Follow steering." On the pilot's instrument panel a needle swung toward southeast, numbers showing the distance to their aircraft carrier spun up. They were still 40 miles from the safety of the Tonkin Gulf and remained in afterburner until off the coast and the report of "feet wet."

February 1967

CDR C. H. "Pinky" Jarvis and LTJG P. M. Artlip in RA-5C (BuNo 151623) were the *Enterprise*'s first loss during its second combat cruise with RVAH-7. The Vigilante and its Phantom escort were flying at 500 feet and 560 knots 30 miles northeast of Thanh Hoa when it ran into a heavy barrage of antiaircraft fire. Taking a major hit in the right wing, the Vigilante barely cleared the coast near the mouth of the Red River before Jarvis and Artlip ejected at high speed and were battered by the wind stream.

An E-2A Hawkeye coordinated the actions of four F-4B Phantoms, four A-1H Skyraiders, two SH-3 "Big Mother" helicopter as well as an Air Force HU-16 Albatross seaplane, and a navy destroyer in the large-scale SAR effort to save the pilot and RAN. A North Vietnamese patrol boat came along the coast at high speed in an attempt to snatch the airmen in the water. Without any other weapons, one of the Phantoms fired a Sparrow air-to-air missile at the enemy boat and damaged it, and it turned and fled. Jarvis was helped into the Albatross and Artlip hoisted into one of the Big Mothers.

The Prendergast Saga

On 9 March 1967, LTJG Frank Prendergast became the only American aviator to escape from capture in North Vietnam and in a way almost too incredible to be true.

Prendergast had gone through the RAG, RVAH-3, with LCDR Al Wattay and they continued as a tactical crew in RVAH-13. However, LT Jim "Bones" Morgan (a former enlisted BN and among the most decorated "Mustangs" in the Navy) had gone home on emergency leave so the *Bat*'s commanding officer, CDR Charles Putnam, needed a RAN. That afternoon, he chose LTJG Prendergast. The assigned mission was coastal reconnaissance. Usually flown at 3,000 to 5,000 feet and 2 to 3 miles displacement, CDR Putnam violated hard-learned rules about altitudes and cloud layers in a desire to get the tasked coverage.

Near Long Chau, 30 miles northwest of Thanh Hoa, CDR Putnam dove *Flint River 605* (BuNo 151627) to 350 feet less than a quarter-mile off the beach to start their run up the coastline. Hit by small-arms fire from the ground, the Vigilante burst into flames and became uncontrollable. Putnam initiated ejection for both crewmembers.

While it is most likely that CDR Putnam did not eject successfully, he was officially listed as missing-in-action based on a report from the escort aircraft that a Navy pilot may have been seen running from armed soldiers.

Prendergast landed in waist-deep water a couple of yards from the beach. He released his parachute, inflated the bright yellow life preserver around his waist, and fired all the tracer bullets from his .38 pistol into the air. A dozen soldiers waded out to him. Since their guns were pointed at him, Prendergast raised his hands in surrender. One soldier saw his navy-issue .38 revolver and took it. They began a slow, sloshy march toward the shore with Prendergast making the walk even slower by limping and acting dazed as to direction.

First, the escorting VF-213 *Black Lion* Phantom made passes and even fired Sparrow air-to-air missiles at the beach. When a pair of prowling A-1 Skyraiders from the USS *Ticonderoga* (CVA-14) arrived and began strafing with their 20mm cannon, most of the soldiers fled to the beach, leaving only their leader and one other with Prendergast.

Each time the airplanes came over, the North Vietnamese soldier with the submachine gun ducked under water out of fear of being hit. Prendergast saw the SH-3 rescue helicopter from HS-8 approaching and decided it was then or never.

The next time the soldier ducked, Prendergast pulled out a small .25 automatic pistol he kept in his flight suit and aimed at his guard. The guard pointed Prendergast's own revolver at him and pulled the trigger. Prendergast had counted correctly—the revolver had been emptied shooting tracers. There was a click as the hammer fell on an empty chamber. Prendergast shot him between the eyes with the small automatic.

When the second soldier came up, Prendergast knocked him in the head, threw his AK-47 submachine gun in the water, and headed for a nearby sandbar. The Vietnamese picked up his gun and began to shoot. On the sandbar, Prendergast bought more time by stopping and raising his hands. As the helo came closer, he wheeled, fired the pistol, and ran. The helicopter swooped broadside and the door gunner blasted the enemy soldier with a heavy M-61 machine gun.

LTJG Frank Prendergast of RVAH-13. The plane captain carries his helmet and nav bag to the cockpit. (Wattay)

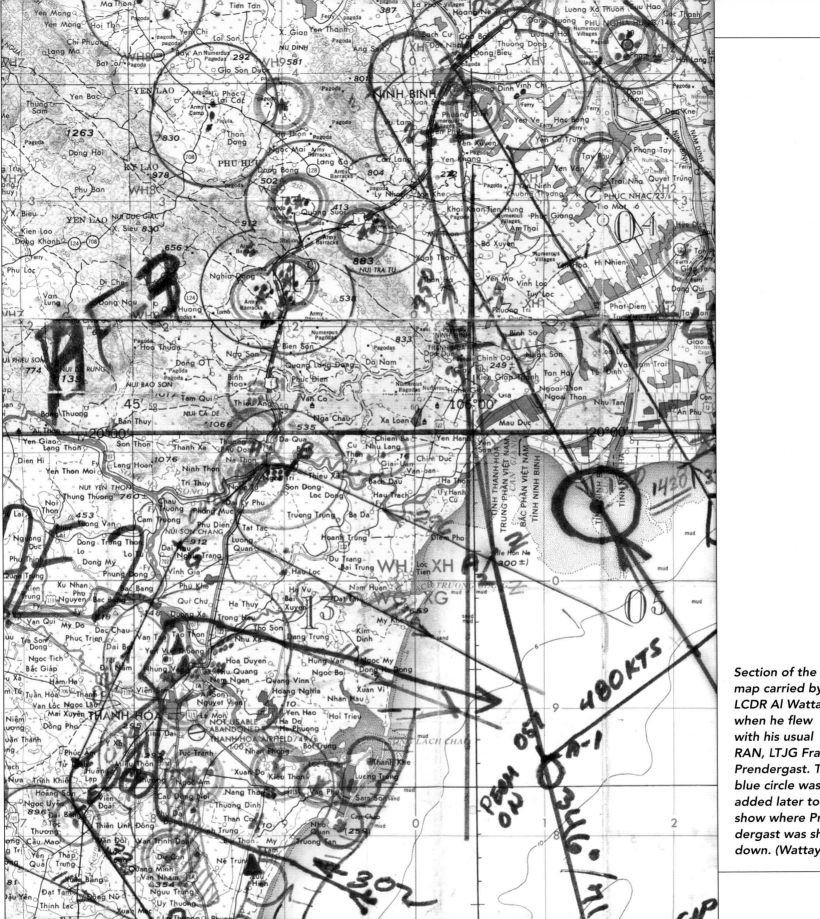

Section of the map carried by LCDR Al Wattay when he flew with his usual RAN, LTJG Frank Prendergast. The blue circle was added later to show where Prendergast was shot down. (Wattay)

Prendergast jumped in and was flown back to the *Kitty Hawk*. The Navy did not let him fly any more missions.[1]

Ho Chi Minh's Birthday

Six aircraft and 10 aircrew were lost over North Vietnam on 19 May 1967. It became the worst single day for US carriers on Yankee Station. The first navy attacks on targets in Hanoi itself were made hazardous because during the earlier bombing restrictions, defenders had had the opportunity to build up their numbers of AAA and SAMs.

That it was Chairman Ho Chi Minh's birthday may also have been a motivating factor for the North Vietnamese antiaircraft crews. The USS *Bon Homme Richard* (CVA-31) (an Essex class carrier that did not operate RA-5Cs) lost two F-8 Crusaders (and an A-4 the day before), the USS *Enterprise* with RVAH-7 on board lost an F-4 and an A-6 (and an A-4 the day before), and the USS *Kitty Hawk* lost another Phantom and a Vigilante from RVAH-13.

The RA-5C (BuNo 150826) was on a BDA run after the Air Wing 11 attack on the Van Dien military vehicle and SAM support depot near Hanoi—the same place the Phantom and Intruder had been shot down that morning. The Vigilante was hit on its initial turn over the city of Hanoi at 3,500 feet and 700 knots. It continued northwest in flames for 10 miles before LCDR James Griffin and LT Jack Walters ejected. Both were captured and died in captivity.

An indication of the aggressiveness of Air Wing 11 and the hazards of Rolling Thunder/Blue Tree missions was that RVAH-13 lost more Vigilantes in two deployments than any other RVAH squadron did for the rest of the war. LCDRs Ray Vehorn and Dick Daum were the only two airmen who survived both of those cruises.

Attack on the USS Liberty

Before and during the Six Day War in June 1967, US aircraft carriers deployed to the Mediterranean—including one transiting to Vietnam—stood by on alert awaiting developments. The war was three days old when word came to the USS *America* (CVA-66) that the USS *Liberty* (AGTR-5), an elaborate state-of-the art intelligence-gathering ship, had been attacked by both planes and ships with the attackers' identity unknown. The *Liberty* was in international waters off the Gaza Strip.

LCDR Ron Pollard was a pilot in RVAH-5. "The *America* launched an armed armada to go out to the *Liberty*. I flew the Vigilante with the group. I can still picture the setting. The sea was a complete glassy calm. The *Liberty* was listing slightly with many holes in all parts of the ship. Faint smoke was drifting out of it. After circling for a while, we were ordered back to the ship. Something like 40 sailors were killed and many injured. The survivors were under orders to never tell the facts of the attack. My film was unloaded and never seen by anyone on the ship.

"None of us could believe it when Israel declared that it was a mistake. The facts released in the last few years tell of a deliberate and brutal air attack and how [US President] Johnson covered it up for political reasons."

Even at the height of the Vietnam War there was always a RVAH squadron active in the Mediterranean. Here, an RVAH-1 Vigilante on board Saratoga *being directed onto a bow catapult.*

Downtown

Flight crews referred to Hanoi as "The Big H" and called missions there "going downtown." Singer Petula Clark was on the pop charts with the song "Downtown." Out on the carriers, fliers had a special set of lyrics:

When you're alone and you're a long way from home, you can always go — Downtown

But better yet be sure to stop at Kep, 'cause you can always go — Downtown.

Just listen to the rhythm of the crackling fifty sevens,
Listen to the Fansong as it scans into the heavens;
My, what a sight.
The flak is much brighter there; you can forget all your troubles,
forget all your cares, and go — Downtown, see all the flak in the sky;
Downtown, watch all the SAMs go by,
Downtown . . . everything's waiting for you.

Reportage

The first official SAM hunt had the RVAH-7 crew of Frank Hamrick and John Capewell bringing back photographs that revealed a camouflaged missile staging area near Hanoi. A major Alpha strike attacked it on 7 June. Squadron CO, CDR Philip Ryan, and his RAN, LTJG James Owen, flew the always-hazardous BDA mission. The Vigilante was hit on the bottom of its nose. In an article in the August 1967, issue of *Naval Aviation News*, Owen was quoted as saying, "Those AAA gunners were getting downright personal."

Jim Owen remembered, "The site was about 20 miles northwest of Hanoi. We were doing BDA. The gunners were not even aiming, they were shooting up the front edge of the smoke column from the bombs. Fortunately, Phil saw the tracers just in time and banked hard right so the AA round hit a glancing blow on the radar altimeter, which was located directly below the back seat. I still have a piece of it on a plaque on my wall.

"When we were hit, we were headed away from the beach and decided the best bet would be to get farther south before heading out. The hit took out my nav system and radar, so it was back to the pencil and dividers for navigation. We ran down along the Vietnam/Laos border to around Than Wa [sic] and then made a dash for the beach. When we went feet wet, there was a helo waiting for us. Fortunately, we didn't need it.

"That was the only time we got hit, but that was enough for me. When we got back to the ship, there was a freelance reporter there, and he is responsible for the story and the alleged quote, which I never said.

"The story appeared in my hometown newspaper the next day and, of course, my mother saw it and forwarded a copy in her next letter with the question 'What's going on over there?'

"The skipper did not tell his wife about it, but at a squadron party after we got back to the states, I let it slip, but without all the details. He died last year [2018] and his daughter sent me an email and mentioned it. I finally came clean and gave the family the whole story. It would have been interesting to know how he explained his Distinguished Flying Cross to them."[2]

Frank Hamrick said that the squadron, "Started with nine crews and ended with the same nine." He went back to the war the next year in RVAH-5.

Conflagration

Losses of a different kind came on 29 July when an errant Zuni rocket fired from an F-4 on the USS *Forrestal* (CVA-59) smashed into an armed and fueled Skyhawk. The massive fuel fire caused bombs to explode, which triggered more explosions around adjacent aircraft. Fuel tanks were ruptured and blazing jet fuel spread flames across the flight deck and down into the hangar bays; 134 sailors were killed, 161 injured, 21 aircraft of CVW-17 destroyed, 40 more damaged. RVAH-11 was wiped out with the total loss of three of their Vigilantes (BuNos 148932, 149284, and 149305) and two others needing overhaul from saltwater damage.

This checkerboard pattern was used from the time the squadron was flying A3D Skywarriors, hence the nickname Checkertails; *callsign was Glen Rock. RVAH-11 was the only squadron to have two insignia while an RVAH.*

Aft flight deck of Forrestal *with RVAH-11 aircraft parked in their usual spot behind the carrier's island. (USN via Dollarhide)*

Forrestal began its first, and what proved to be its only, deployment to Vietnam on 6 June 1967 (the same day a war started on the other side of the world). With the Suez Canal closed, *Forrestal* made a visit to Brazil and went around the Cape of Good Hope to get to the Philippines. Air Wing 17 had scarcely begun combat ops, four days with 150 missions, before the disaster.[3]

RVAH-11 had only recently transitioned from flying A-3 Skywarriors and was on its first Vigilante deployment. While others on the USS *Forrestal* could look forward to some well-deserved rest following their ordeal, the *Checkertails* started preparing for an immediate return to Southeast Asia. Arriving home at NAS Sanford, Florida, on 12 September 1967, the squadron spent the next three weeks com-

pletely reoutfitting in preparation for a return to sea, and on 6 October they departed Sanford to join Carrier Air Wing 11 and the USS *Kitty Hawk* in San Diego, California. Three weeks of operating off the coast of San Diego, two weeks back home at NAS Sanford, Florida, and the squadron was ready.[4] Starting with the quick two-month turnaround, the next months in Southeast Asia were among the toughest faced by any RVAH squadron.

From the time of the *Forrestal* fire at the end of July until RVAH-6 arrived on the *Ranger* (CVA-61) in early November, the navy's reconnaissance assets in the Tonkin Gulf were detachments of RF-8 Photo-Crusaders on *Coral Sea*, *Oriskany* and *Intrepid* and the Vigilantes of RVAH-12 on the *Constellation*.

Vigilantes of RVAH-11 burning on Forrestal *(a third RA-5C is under the flames). The nose of the airplane in the foreground has burned completely off and is on its side. (USN via Dollarhide)*

Speartips

The first unit commissioned as a Reconnaissance Attack Squadron from its inception was RVAH-12, which first made a seven-month deployment to the Mediterranean as part of CVW-3 in the USS *Saratoga* (CVA-60) in 1966.

Next, after a normal shakedown and Operational Readiness Exercises, RVAH-12 departed San Diego, California, as part of CVW-14 in the USS *Constellation* (CVA-64). The *Speartips* arrived on Yankee Station on 28 May 1967.

The *Speartips* lost two Vigilantes and their crews in August. On 13 August, BuNo 151634 was hit by AAA while doing 720 knots on a mission near Lang Son, in the extreme northeast of North Vietnam. The Vigilante was enveloped in flame and the tail section came apart. Both crewmembers were captured as soon as they touched down in their parachutes. LCDR Leo Hyatt and LTJG Wayne Goodermote were on their thirty-third mission. They were released together in 1973.

Four days later, Vigilante BuNo 149302 on a coastal reconnaissance crashed into the sea, killing the XO of RVAH-12, CDR Laurent

Coffee mug with RVAH-12 insignia, "a spear tip climbing into a blue sky at supersonic speed." The callsign and nickname of the squadron were both Speartip. (Sharp)

Dion, and his RAN, LTJG Charles Hom. There were insufficient facts to determine the exact cause, but the crash may have been another case of unnoticed small arms fire while on a mission, a frustration occurring throughout the war.

Fast Turn

RVAH-11 left San Diego on 18 November 67, after returning to NAS Sanford in September on board the *Kitty Hawk*. Following an Operational Readiness Inspection off the coast of Hawaii, the *Checkertails* arrived on Yankee Station on 23 December, to spend Christmas on-the-line. Because of heightened world tension and the greater demands placed on the navy during the *Pueblo* crisis, the ship conducted combat air operations for 62 consecutive days before a port visit in late February 1968.

Three more combat line periods followed with the squadron flying a record number of 518 combat reconnaissance sorties. Combat flight operations were completed on 1 June 1968, but then the squadron performed the major task of flying all its aircraft across the Pacific (TransPac) and on to its new home at NAS Albany, Georgia.

Arriving almost simultaneously due to the scrambled schedules following the *Forrestal* fire, RVAH-6 was on board *Ranger* for their second combat cruise.

On 16 December, *Fleur* CO, CDR C.C. Smith[5], and RAN, LT James Calhoun, flew over downtown Hanoi and confirmed the location of

Blue stripes with fleur-de-lis were the RVAH-6 markings for the 1966 deployment.

The RVAH-6 flash on the nose came and went throughout the squadron's life. This photo was taken in 1966. (NNAM)

the notorious "Hanoi Hilton" prisoner of war camp. The mission had special presidential approval as the area was on the no-fly list at the time.

"The tallest point in Hanoi was a radio tower, so the crew set their altimeter at 800 feet and flew over Hanoi at about 1,000 mph, probably breaking every window within a mile of the flight path. The cameras worked perfectly, and they got the information they were after. The crew was later awarded the Distinguished Flying Cross."[6] The photographs were used at the Paris peace talks.

Back Home

Three Vigilantes were lost during training flights in the RAG, RVAH-3, during 1967 (BuNos 149314, 149315, 151728). RA-5Cs made Grampaw Pettibone's column in *Naval Aviation News* twice that year. One of them was a misadventure that rated a "Jumping Jehosaphat!" and the other, a rare note of praise.

A replacement pilot (RP) with considerable experience in the A3J was on his first flight in an RA-5C with an instructor pilot flying chase in another RA-5C. The RP made an impromptu decision to take some air-to-air photos. Shooting obliques from the side went well, but when getting positioned for some vertical pictures, the Vigis collided top to bottom. There was only minor damage to the

instructor's airplane, but the RP and his RAN, thinking theirs was disintegrating, ejected.[7]

During CarQuals, a new pilot climbed into the cockpit while the RA-5C was being hot refueled. The RAN advised him that on the previous launch, the pilot had used 12 degrees of trim and experienced a slight settle. The new pilot set 13 degrees nose up and asked the RAN to remind him to drop the hook immediately to keep the bomb bay can fuel from transferring to keep the aircraft at the correct center of gravity (a Vigi idiosyncrasy).

Off the catapult, the pilot felt the aircraft settle, and the nose was below the horizon. At about 30 feet with the nose still low, he told the RAN to eject. The pilot took his hand off the throttles and reached for the left ejector handle while holding full back stick. He heard two explosions, saw the flash of the RAN's ejection in his mirror, and the nose moved up. (The other explosion was his tail hitting the water.) He decided not to eject and flew to a shore base. The RAN was recovered by the ship's helicopter.[8]

The War: 1968

The Northeast Monsoon swept in making visual bombing impossible for most of the first three months of 1968. The A-6 Intruders

RVAH squadrons flew into air stations serving the carriers prior to deployment to be hoisted aboard. BuNo 149287 of the Smoking Tigers *at NAS Alameda with engine doors open in 1968. This aircraft was lost in an accident at Albany in June 1969. (Lawson via NNAM)*

using their all-weather navigation and attack systems—and radar imagery from the Vigilante's SLR—flew single aircraft strikes into North Vietnam no matter the time of day or the weather. Four of the solitary Intruders were lost in 90 days. The *Enterprise* with the *Smoking Tigers* of RVAH-1 arrived in WestPac with the first of the year.

Double-A, Ess 21 Infrared

At night, initial attempts at photography with flasher pods proved to be unsuitable in combat. It was not because the imagery was bad, but because the pulses of bright light from the three million candle-power strobes made the Vigilante an easy target for antiaircraft gunners. As the number of guns in the country increased, night flasher missions became highly hazardous. Fortunately, the installation of the IR mapping sensor (designated AAS-21) beginning in 1968 made it unnecessary to use flashers to detect the heavy traffic moving southward in the darkness.

The IR sensor had the added advantage of being able to detect targets that photography could not. The AAS-21 recorded temperature differential and could "see through" vegetation that had been cut and put over trucks and storage as camouflage. The IR was run on all missions, supplemental in the day and primary at night.

RVAH-6 became the first squadron to receive the new AAS-21 IR mapping system. Airplanes were flown into NAS Atsugi, Japan, for installation of the new equip-

ment, which was eventually put in all RA-5Cs. The infrared mapper was a major improvement in the Vigilante's night capability. No longer were the hazardous flashers the only way to obtain imagery. The "double-A, ess 21" used liquid nitrogen to cool sensing crystals, which detected temperature differences. The system showed dead vegetation used as camouflage, found the hot engines of vehicles

IR scanner image of aircraft carrier. Hot areas are light colored, cooler areas dark. Flight deck is warm and catapult tracks hot. Aircraft are cool. The dark rectangles are the water-cooled jet blast deflectors. The smudge near the island is exhaust gas from the boilers. Time of day was a consideration in planning IR missions as there was a "cross-over" point where the subject and background were at the same temperature.

in the night, and even showed patterns of warmth where vehicles or airplanes had been parked.

In an amusing incident, early runs with the AAS-21 over the Ho Chi Minh Trail showed hot spots that intelligence officers and photo interpreters could not figure out. The hot spots turned out to be fresh elephant droppings.

Back in Albany, Georgia, while the system was still classified as secret, an unmarked old Beech 18 airplane arrived at the navy air station, had the system installed, and flew a series of night flights. Speculation ran wild.

The Twin Beech was being operated by the US Alcohol and Firearms Bureau. They were locating illicit whiskey stills in the hills of northern Georgia. Later, the Vigis themselves flew these "revenoo-er" searches.

Pueblo

On 23 January, the American surveillance ship the USS *Pueblo* was surrounded by North Korean patrol boats and forced to surrender. The USS *Ranger* with RVAH-6 at the end of their second line period and the *Enterprise* with RVAH-1 on a visit to Sasebo, Japan, were ordered to Korea. The *Fleurs* experienced the abrupt transition from a tropical flying environment to sub-freezing temperatures in the Sea of Japan. Both RVAH squadrons flew missions during the month that the carriers remained in Korean waters. The crews flew in bulky exposure suits and did a fair amount of night work. They operated off the North Korean coast, but overland only in South Korea. There was not enough winter clothing on board and flight deck crews wore what they could find. They looked like ragamuffins, but were less cold.

Screaming into the break for practice carrier landings at NAS Atsugi, Vigilante BuNo 148926 rolled past 90 degrees; Gene Campbell and Doug Cook (Lawrence deBoxtel's roommate) ejected into the cold waters of Tokyo Bay. The pilot never admitted that the most likely cause was that he may have inadvertently shut down the port engine.

Back on Yankee Station, RVAH-6 was tasked with a series of runs at twilight and 1,500-foot altitude along the coast of North Vietnam from the DMZ to Haiphong using SLR to look for Styx anti-ship missiles and boats before the battleship USS *Missouri* (BB-63) came in to shell the Thanh Hoa Bridge.

CO C. C. Smith made the first try and XO Ivan Lewis the next. They were both shot at by heavy 85mm antiaircraft guns. LCDR Herm Mueller with his RAN, LT Guthrie, flew the third mission in an exact repeat of the first two. Abeam Vinh, Mueller avoided a pair of SAMs. A third came at him while he was steeply banked and low. Knowing SA-2s came in twos, he pushed forward on the stick and the fourth SAM barely went over the Vigilante. Flak was heavy all through his maneuvering. Shaken, he aborted the remainder of the run and headed back to the *Ranger*.

LCDR DeBoxtel was assigned the fourth try. Wayne Mulholland said that there was no way he was going if they repeated the previous flight path, so they pretended to be a Shrike-carrying A-4

Box Bits

Here are some classic tales of naval aviation:

- Going through training in RVAH-3 at NAS Sanford in 1965, Larry "Box" deBoxtel chose Wayne "Tiny" Mulholland as his RAN, "Because he was a great big guy and would be useful if we ever jumped out." They stayed together as a crew and deployed in RVAH-6.

- The CAG (Commander of the Air Group) on Ranger was the F-4 escort pilot on a mission to Vinh Airfield. When ready for the pre-strike recce run, he called, "Cleared in, Box."
  DeBoxtel replied, "OK, CAG."
  Concerned about being identified by the enemy monitoring the radio, he said, "Don't call me CAG!"
  Instant reply, "Don't call me Box."
  "Fair enough."

- The USO troop with Bob Hope and songstress Barbara McNair were on board Ranger for a show. While McNair was on the LSO platform, she heard of the hazardous near miss that the returning Vigilante had over North Vietnam. Box handed her the radio and when LCDR Mueller called, "Field Goal 603, Vigilante, Ball," she replied, "C'mon home, baby, we're waiting for you."

- DeBoxtel was the junior pilot in RVAH-6 and had been sent to Cubi Point to pick up an airplane and fly it back to Yankee Station. While he and Mulholland were in the Philippines, Ranger sailed for Korea and they were told to go to NAS Atsugi in Japan. When they stopped in Kadena, Okinawa, it was already cold. Since their anti-exposure suits were on the ship, they drew flight jackets and thermal underwear from the USAF supply depot. (DeBoxtel wore the air force–style flight jacket with the orange liner for years afterward.)

- The legendary SR-71 Blackbird was then operating from Kadena AFB. The visiting Vigilante drew its usual oohs and aahs. One air force officer asked DeBoxtel what the airplane did. Box looked around to see who was near and whispered "It's the replacement for that," and pointed toward the Blackbird. The legend of the Vigilante grew.

RVAH-13's orange insignia partly hidden by wing rack. The Bats *used Oriental-style tail letters even when assigned to an East Coast carrier. The rectangle below cockpits was painted flat black where the maintenance chief wrote the launch weight in chalk for the catapult crew. When grease pencils became more common than chalk, the weight box was a black outline and the gloss-white paint was the writing surface.*

looking for missile radars. They stayed high and flew in figure-eights just off Haiphong Harbor. The fire-control radars locked-on when they headed away and shut down when they headed in. After several patterns, Mulholland turned off the IFF transponder, and deBoxtel put the RA-5C into a supersonic dive to 1,500 feet and headed south. They got the coverage and the Vigilante was not fired at.

RVAH-6 returned to the Gulf of Tonkin in late March and continued air operations over North Vietnam for two more line periods, returning to the United States at the end of May 1968.

Partial Halt

The devastating Tet Offensive had begun at the end of January and was dragging on. In another futile attempt to force a settlement, on 31 March, President Johnson declared an end to attacks north of the 19th parallel. This meant that Thanh Hoa and the infamous "Iron Triangle," Nam Dinh-Haiphong-Hanoi, was off-limits . . . again. The day was 1 April in Vietnam, and many thought the message was an April Fool's joke. The reaction of the flight crewmembers was mixed. On the one hand, they were no longer exposing themselves to the heaviest air defenses in history, but they also knew that the North Vietnamese would use the break—as they had done on earlier, shorter bombing pauses—to reequip and rearm.

The USS *America* (CVA-66) arrived in March with the *Bats* of RVAH-13 on board for that squadron's third consecutive combat deployment. Years before, an enterprising junior officer had obtained a stuffed fruit bat with obvious male genitalia. The 2-foot-high critter was in tune with the squadron crest and proudly displayed in the ready-room at sea and parties ashore. However, by 1968 the bat was becoming rotten and starting to stink. After due consideration, the officers decided to give the bat a last flight. Using helium balloons, the smelly bat was launched from the flight deck of the *America* in the Tonkin Gulf to drift west into the hands of the enemy . . . and possibly start a few rumors.

RVAH-5, callsign *Old Kentucky,* had made two cruises to the Mediterranean and returned to combat aboard the USS *Constellation* (CVA-64) in May.

"Gunder [Creager] and I were in RVAH-5 on the *Connie* when the bombing pause was announced in October 1968. The effective date of the bombing pause was 1 November, but reconnaissance flights were allowed. So my pilot, Tom Turpin, and I were the on-deck spare for the skipper for a recce flight on 1 November. Deacon Bakke's plane went down, so Tom and I were up.

"Canopies were down and taxiing to the cat when we were given the signal to stop and open the canopies. Up comes a ladder, and a captain in khakis climbs up to Tom, says a few words, and departs. We button up and proceed to the cat, and Tom tells me that that was the admiral's chief of staff, who informed us that no one cared if we got any pictures, they just wanted to know if we got

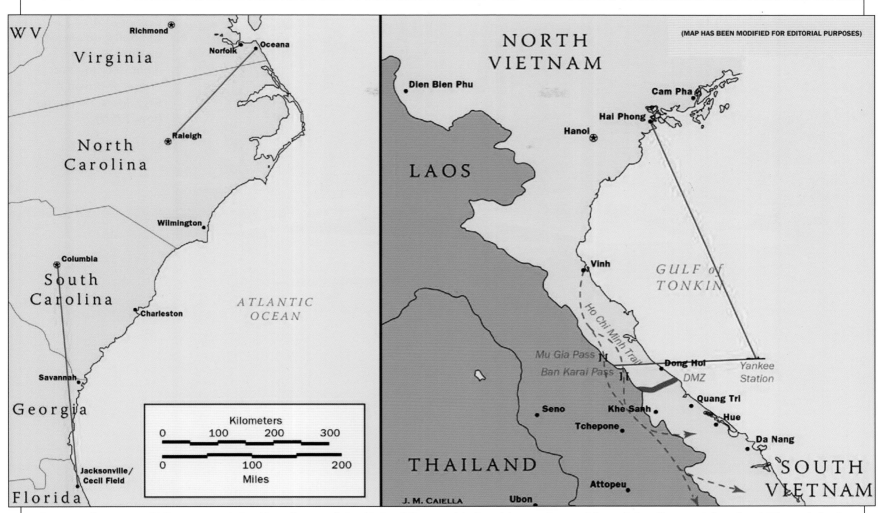

Same scale maps of Vietnam and the East Coast of the United States side by side to give an idea of the distances involved. The original was crudely done in 1967. Yankee Station to Haiphong is the same as flying from NAS Cecil Field (Jacksonville) to Columbia, South Carolina. NAS Oceana (Norfolk) to Raleigh, North Carolina, is the distance to cross near the DMZ to begin a reconnaissance route over Laos. (Jim Caiella, caiella.org)

shot at. To my knowledge, we were the first navy aircraft over the beach after the bombing pause, and no, we didn't see any tracers."[9]

Not a Church

In another example of the use of integral reconnaissance, AAS-21 infrared imagery had detected night-time truck traffic around the old cathedral in Vinh. A *Smoking Tiger* RA-5C made a surprise, fast, low photo pass at dawn. The processed film showed a missile transporter backed up to the nave, loading SA-2s into the cathedral. Vinh and the area surrounding the city were hot as the North Vietnamese had shifted defenses from the Iron Triangle.

CDR Paul Peck, CAG 9 aboard the *Enterprise*, used the intelligence that RVAH-1 brought back to good effect. CAG Peck grabbed the photograph while it was still wet and ran with it to the embarked admiral. A mini-alpha strike was ordered. The first bombs dropped caused secondary explosions, which went up to 8,000 feet. Flaming, falling debris ignited nearby buildings that also exploded.

It had been nine months since the *Enterprise* had lost an aircraft, but in May, *Comanche Trail 102* (BuNo 149278) of RVAH-1 was photographing Route 1A from 6,500 feet near Ha Tinh. As the escort described it, "The Vige burst into a huge fireball about twice the size of the aircraft and snap-rolled when the starboard wing came off." LT Giles Norrington and LT Dick Tangeman had been together since converting to the Vigilante in 1965 and had flown 22 missions over North Vietnam. Norrington and Tangeman managed to eject, but were injured and soon captured. They were released in March 1973.

One of RVAH-13's camouflaged aircraft on Kitty Hawk's flight deck in 1966. Propeller-driven A-1 Skyraiders are on the bow. (USN]

Hard Times Continue

Also in May, RVAH-11's *Glen Rock* 606 (BuNo 149283) was northwest of Vinh, close to the western border of the panhandle, and was hit by a 57mm burst—even 10,000 feet was not high enough to avoid the larger caliber AA guns. The Vigilante burst into flames and started to break up. The crew ejected. Two rescue beepers were heard and SAR aircraft headed for the area, but there was too much antiaircraft fire to continue the rescue attempt. Their capture was reported by Radio Hanoi. The pilot, CDR Charles James, was the executive officer of RVAH-11[10], the RAN was LCDR Vincent Monroe. James survived and was released in 1973, but Monroe died while a prisoner of the North Vietnamese.

Kitty Hawk and Air Wing 11 had lost eight aircraft in combat and another seven in accidents in 125 days online during their third Vietnam deployment. Twelve men were killed in action and three made prisoners of war.

New Phase

Between the March partial bombing halt and the end of Rolling Thunder in November, the US Navy lost 7 A-4s, 10 A-7s, 8 F-4s, 6 A-6s, and 2 RA-5Cs to enemy action. Reconnaissance flights continued.

On 25 November 1968, radar-guided antiaircraft guns tracked RVAH-5's *Old Kentucky* 113 (BuNo 149293) 2 miles northwest of Vinh as the pilot, CDR Ernest Stamm, jinked wildly at 550 knots in an attempt to throw off the gunners' aim, but the Vigilante was hit and exploded into four parts. The escorting Phantoms heard the tones of a Fan Song SAM radar on their ALQ gear so it was uncertain whether flak or a SA-2 destroyed the RA-5C. Two parachutes were seen, but neither Stamm, nor the RAN, LTJG Richard Thum, survived.

In 1968, two Vigis were lost during Sixth Fleet operations in the Mediterranean and a third during RAG training, depleting the inventory of RA-5Cs further. The size of deploying squadrons was reduced to five airplanes.

Stateside

"In mid-September 1968, the Pirate [Jim Pirotte] and I were assigned as instructors in RVAH-3. We were both due for refresher carrier landings and the squadron was getting ready to send some

Smoking Tiger *over one of the mountain passes on the Ho Chi Minh Trail. Frequent bombing has destroyed the vegetation.*

students out to Alameda to CarQual on the *Ranger*. So we took the maintenance detachment and got things ready for the students.

"The first day out to sea, as the ship prepared to bring the first Vigilante in, they used a tractor to pull out the number-1 wire to check it. They retracted the wire and with a 'clear deck,' Wes Wolf and Ken Kirby hit number-1, stretched it as far as it could go before it snapped and the plane (BuNo 149280) dribbled off the angle. It went into the water completely intact, popped back out and drifted along the port side of the ship. As we looked down, we could see two empty cockpits, and later found only a helmet. As it turned out, the wire had never been reset.

"The CarQual started on a pretty sour note. It was decided that we would need another plane. So someone brought one out directly from NARF Jax[11], and Jim and I got a COD ride into Alameda so we could bring it out to the ship. According to my log book, it was

149300. We had finished getting our refresher landings the week before when we had gone out to set everything up with the *Ranger*, so all we needed was a touch-and-go when we brought the replacement aboard.

"The flight from Alameda to the *Ranger* was uneventful and we had a typical picture-perfect Pirate landing. As we lifted and turned downwind, I heard what sounded like a compressor stall and asked Jim if he had any engine problems. He said everything looked fine. We dropped the hook, came around, and prepared to trap. Don't remember the LSO's grade, but it felt like an OK-3 to me—but we had a hook-skip. This time as we lifted and turned downwind the tower reported something streaming from the top of the aircraft.

"We made three more passes, each resulting in hook-ships. What had happened was a V-band coupling on a hot-air line behind my seat had not been properly torqued and had vibrated loose. The

RVAH-5 Vigilante on bow catapult of Constellation in 1968. Cat officer's upraised hand is flashing five fingers as a signal to go into after-burner.

escaping hot air ignited the fuel in the top cap fuel tank and blew a hole in the top of the fuselage. As we were tooling around the pattern, we were rapidly losing fuel and had no boundary layer control air, resulting in a flat approach.

"After it became apparent that we would not be able to get aboard, the ship began to rig the barricade, usually a 30- to 45-second evolution. It took them 2 minutes. When we finally arrested into the pliable nylon, we were both relieved, but not very complimentary of the flight deck's performance. I can't remember Jim's exact words, but I know they were 'choice.' The plane was torn up but would fly again."[12]

A standard reconnaissance flight topping off fuel before crossing the beach. KA-6 tanker (VA-165) giving fuel to RA-5C (RVAH-5) while F-4J Phantom (VF-96) awaits its turn.

New (uneven gray/ white border, pale blue NAVY and BuNo) RA-5C of RVAH-3 at NAS Sanford in April 1965. The dark emblem below the cockpit is unidentified. (NNAM)

Chapter 7

MASTER'S DEGREE: 1969–1972

Some 156-series Vigilantes of RVAH-1 after the flash marking on the nose was added. (Stark)

The end of the decade marked changes in the Vigilante world. The air war in Southeast Asia had calmed down; after 1 April 1968, bombing was restricted to below the 20th Parallel; by October, Operation Rolling Thunder was officially over. The last Vigilante lost in combat was in May 1968. The last new sensor, AAS-21, had been added to the recon suite and proven. Home base changed from Sanford, Florida, to Albany, Georgia.

Naval Flight Officers could become commanding officers. There was a subtle shift in the perception of, and the attitude of, the Vigilante community. Indicative of the change was the assignment of nugget pilots to RVAH squadrons.

Nugget Pilots

Nugget RANs—newly winged NFOs (previously NAOs)—had been common since the Vigilante had become operational, but there was a perception that, like the A-3, the A-5 was so difficult to fly that only experienced pilots were capable. The fearsome reputation and early high accident rate made the policy of only second-tour pilots seemingly obvious; this reputation was perpetuated by the natural human characteristic of pride.

"What airplane do you fly?"

"Vigilantes, the RA-5C."

"Wow, aren't they a hard airplane to fly, especially landing on a ship?"

"Yes, they are . . . but I can do it."

Five years of operations, including combat, had made Vigilante operations, if not routine, at least normal. There was always an attitude that a new "hot" type could not be handled by new pilots. Yet, in all cases, time proved this to be wrong. One era's frontline fighters became the next generation's advanced trainers. Even the propeller SNJ began in World War II as an advanced trainer (in the air force the "AT" in its AT-6 designation stood for advanced trainer), but by the 1950s became the primary trainer in which student pilots flew their first solo. The swept-wing TF-9J (F9F-8T) Cougar had been an advanced navy trainer since the mid-1950s. New pilots in the 1960s

Photograph sometimes titled "Shadow at the Ramp." (Carlton)

RVAH-3 RAG flight line at NAS Albany, TA-4 and row of RA-5Cs; both types share GJ tail letters. (Hoskin)

earned their wings in the navy's basic light-attack Douglas Skyhawk.

David "Skip" Jones was Nugget Number 1 reporting to RVAH-3 in October 1969. Bill Powell was Nugget Number 2 and John Carter, Nugget Number 3; although Carter claims to be the first. "Jim Parsons, North American's tech rep, did all he could to get Skip and myself trained. But then he took Skip on hunting trips and I slipped ahead in training."

All the Nuggets were products of the same training program. They flew T-34 Mentors at Saufley Field in Primary before going to NAS Meridian in Mississippi to fly the T-2 Buckeye for instruments and formation before going to Pensacola for CarQual. Advanced training was in TA-4J Skyhawks at Beeville or Kingsville in Texas where the syllabus added weapons delivery and combat tactics to their earlier skills. After another session of shipboard landings, they were awarded their navy wings.

First Skyhawks assigned to RVAH- 3 were TA-4Fs and painted in standard gray and white. (THA)

Vigilante on RVAH-3 flight line doing pre-taxi checks. Refueling probe extended. Plane captain on same type of ladder used for cockpit access climbing on top of intakes for checks. Next aircraft has CRAW-1's multi-colored tail. (Hoskin)

Jim "Flats" Flaherty's memories of his early days: "I had gotten my wings flying new TA-4s that had less than 10 hours on them. When I was told I was going to RVAH, I actually figured I was going to helos. On top of that, a Vigi had been at the base for a demo week before. On the S***Hot takeoff, the nose gear did not retract.

"I was sent to photo school in Pensacola with two other nuggets and a full commander who was transitioning from fighters. We went to the O'Club for lunch and he led us into the bar and told us nuggets we were rolling dice . . . for pitchers of Martinis.

"When I got to RVAH-7, the CO usually had me flying as a wingman. But then Dan Rowley (LCDR, RAN) arrived from the test center at Pax River and I was teamed with him for a month-long trip around the USA on camera tests. One time there was no boarding ladder. On my first try, I fell off and landed flat on my back on the ramp. It was an educational month.

"By the time we deployed to WestPac on *Kitty Hawk* (CVA-63), I was treated as a normal pilot."

With few exceptions, the nuggets made it through training and deployed in RVAH squadrons. Many received their baptism by fire during the intensity of Operation Linebacker. Some had exceptional careers.

Not that the nuggets with their brand-new wings were treated like experienced pilots while going through the RAG—there was hesitation, doubt, and reluctance to turn them loose. "Give them more flight time. Take it slow," was the attitude. Nuggets were encouraged to checkout in and fly RVAH-3's TA-4 Skyhawks. (The checkout never proved to be difficult, as they had recently flown the two-place Skyhawk for more than 100 hours in the Training Command.) Of course, there was added pressure on the nuggets to perform well. There were also moments of them suddenly realizing they were now the pilot in command. As one described it, "We were handed the keys to the TA-4s."

John Carter remembers a flight with the Reconnaissance Wing Commodore[1], CDR Ken Enney: "We took a TA-4 to Andrews AFB with me, brand new in Albany in 1969, in the back seat. On the transient line, he shut down, crawled out, said, 'Take 'er back to Albany,' and left. I was scared to death—planning, weather, air traffic control (ATC), filing, refueling. All in our nations' capitol and me with brand-new navy wings."

Eventually, 34 newly designated pilots[2] flew the Vigilantes between late 1969 and the community's end in 1979. While not formally grouped, several arrived within a couple of months, followed by a break before more were ordered in. The rumor was that the command wanted to make sure each batch made it through CarQuals before risking lives and airplanes for the next group. The first eight rated status as Guinea pigs.

The nuggets were frequently drafted to become LSOs. RAG LSO Larry DeBoxtel caught several nuggets while they were in class and asked what they were doing that evening. When they innocently replied they had no plans, Box said, "Meet me at 1500 in the parking lot." Next thing they knew, they were standing on the end of the Albany runway watching FCLP as LSOs under training.

Two Exceptions

The nuggets did have experienced RANs with them from their first familiarization flights all the way to CarQuals. Dave Vaupel (aka "Dr. Volcano") said, "It was ironic, as a back-seater, the longer you were in this business and the more experienced you became and survived, the more dangerous it became, because you were paired with younger and less experienced pilots." Vaupel had the bad luck to be with two of the nuggets who did not make it.

The nugget pilot had done fine during on his day landings. His first pass that night was a bolter during "pinky period," just after sunset, but had to bingo to NAS Miramar because of some problem the ship was having. After waiting, he came back out with Vaupel in his back seat after 2300. The LSO heard them check in at marshal, then got a call to switch his radio to the squadron tactical frequency, "Drake 3xx, Paddles, what's up?"

"We're not coming down. The kid just turned his wings in."[3]

The controlling LSO wrote, "Nugget pilot on CarQuals. Gent had an attitude problem and I probably shouldn't have taken him

Nuggets and RANs Who Did Well

From humble beginnings, great naval aviators are made. Here are a few of their journeys.

Nugget Pilots

Ken Carlton deployed in RVAH-14 then was a test pilot at Patuxent River. He had another tour in Vigilantes in RVAH-1 and after staff jobs and post-graduate school went back to the Test Center as commanding officer of the Test Pilot School and head of Strike Aircraft Test Division.

Jim "Flats" Flaherty deployed in RVAH-7 on *Kitty Hawk* and *Forrestal* (CVA-59), before going to RVAH-3 as an instructor and LSO. He trained in the F-14 Tomcat and went to VF-84, which was the first squadron equipped with TARPS (Tactical Airborne Reconnaissance Pod System). He was CO of F-14 squadron VF-211 and worked at the Safety Center before becoming commander of all the Atlantic Fleet Fighter Squadrons, ComFitWingOne.

Rob "Potsie" Weber deployed in RVAH-9[4] (with a memorable temporary assignment to RVAH-6 for LSO experience), before duty as LSO for TraWing 2 at NAS Kingsville. He transitioned to the Grumman A-6 Intruder, went to sea with VA-85, instructed in the A-6 RAG, VA-42, and deployed in *John F. Kennedy* (CVA-67) as CVW-3 Ops. Screened for command, he was XO and CO of VA-55 on *Coral Sea* (CVA-42) and led the Strike on Benina, Libya. Weber was administrative assistant to Secretary of the Navy John Lehman and commanded VA-42. He was executive officer of the USS *America* (CVA-66) and captain of the USS *White Plains* (AFS-4) before commanding the aircraft carrier *John F. Kennedy*.

Joe Dyer did his first sea tour in RVAH-1. After making two deployments on the USS *America*, he was a test pilot at Patuxent River for four years. He earned his master's degree at the Navy Post Graduate School and went to the Navy Weapons Center at China Lake. Dyer's next assignment was an interesting one: He headed the Navy Plant Representative Office in Melbourne, Australia. (The Australian Air Force was receiving FA-18 Hornets at that time.) A variety of flag officer assignments followed, culminating in Dyer commanding the entire Naval Systems Command as a three-star vice admiral.

RANs

Jim "Beaker" Stark served in two Vigilante squadrons (RVAH-1 and RVAH-7) and survived riding an RA-5C into the *Enterprise*'s (CVAN-65) catwalk before transitioning to the A-6 Intruder. He made five deployments in Intruders, including two as XO/CO of VA-65. He was the last CO of Naval Station Roosevelt Roads before retiring as a captain.

George Cannelos had an unusual military career. His only deployment was with RVAH-6 on the USS *America* during the frenetic days of Operation Linebacker II. His obligated service over, he went to school to earn a master's degree and found work in Anchorage, Alaska. Missing flying, he volunteered for the Navy Reserve and flew patrol planes from NAS Whidbey in Washington State. The commute for drill weekends was not easy, so when he learned the Alaska Air National Guard would accept him with no loss of rank, he went from being a navy lieutenant to an air force captain and flew with a C-130 Hercules squadron at Elmendorf AFB.

Mixing part-time and full-time with the ANG, he eventually became that squadron's commanding officer. After some staff positions, Cannelos was promoted to brigadier general in charge of the Alaska Air National Guard. In his office at Elmendorf, there was a very large photograph of LTJG Cannelos in flight gear by the island of the USS *America*. He believes he may have been the last Vigilante crewman on active duty.

William "Fox" Fallon made his nugget cruise in RVAH-5 on the *Constellation* (CVA-64) to Vietnam, then transitioned to the A-6 Intruder. He commanded VA-65, medium attack wing one, and Carrier Air Wing 8 during Desert Storm. In 24 years, he logged more than 1,300 carrier arrested landings and 4,800 flight hours in tactical jet aircraft. As an admiral, he commanded the T.R. Roosevelt Battle Group during NATO operations over Bosnia. A rarity for military officers, he had four assignments as a four-star officer, a navy full admiral. The last were as commander of the United States Central Command (CENTCOM), which covers the volatile Mideast. Fallon's leaving that position was a controversial issue.[5]

anyway. Pilots new to the Vigilante were teamed with experienced back-seaters, RANs from the RAG staff. 'Dr. Volcano' was with this kid. The A-5 did not have ailerons; it had spoilers for roll control.

"When you called for a lineup correction, you had to watch that the nose tweaked up to compensate for the drag. Day, steady deck, so no excuses. He drifts left, I call, 'Come right.' Spoilers open, nose comes down, and sets up a horrific sink-rate. 'Power, power! Wave-off,' and hit the lights. Too late, too slow.

"The Vigilante slams into the deck short of the Number 1 wire, bounces high, and traps on the Number 4. At the top of the arc, 'Dr. Volcano' ejects. Rocket-seat worked fine and a good chute, but he lands hard on the flight deck and is dragged into the nosewheel of the airplane he just punched out of.

"Went to see him in sickbay—he looked like the losing team in a football game—enough bruises for eleven men. His explanation for ejecting, 'I heard your power and wave-off calls and when we hit, I heard the airplane breaking apart.'"

Exodus

Vigilantes had been in Sanford since the first A3Js arrived in 1961. Add the pilots and BNs who had flown in the A3D and AJ and Sanford was their home since 1951. (Savage squadron VC-5 had named themselves the *Savage Sons of Sanford*. Clever alliteration as well as showing pride in their home base.) The air station was well set up with great facilities and a good location. The cost of living nearby was reasonable in the days before the mega-tourist attractions bloomed in central Florida.

But then, in 1968, came the exodus. The reason? Pure political "pork barrel." Although officially the move was a base realignment resulting from LBJ's Great Society program, the Vietnam War, and accompanying strains on the national budget. The USAF had closed Turner AFB in Albany, Georgia, which had a B-52 wing assigned to it. The powerful senator from Georgia (he was head of the Armed Services Committee) was not going to let all those jobs and money leave his state and ordered the navy to close Sanford and move the entire operation—lock, stock, and barrel—to Albany.

Turner AFB became NAS Albany. (The navy named its bases after a nearby town or city; the air force named them after individuals.) The navy operation and the air force operation differed in many ways, and buildings had to be modified. A warehouse with drive-in loading docks became the new quarters for RVAH-3. The former air force base did have all the necessary aviation support facilities: fuel supply and storage, public works, warehouses, maintenance shops, and hangars. Most important, there was a 12,000-foot-long runway—one of the longest in the world. Long enough for fully fueled Vigilantes to easily get airborne on hot-and-humid Georgia summer days. The reason for the extraordinary length was that Strategic Air Command (SAC) flew B-52 bombers and KC-135 tankers from the field.

As part of the transfer arrangement, the USAF continued keeping

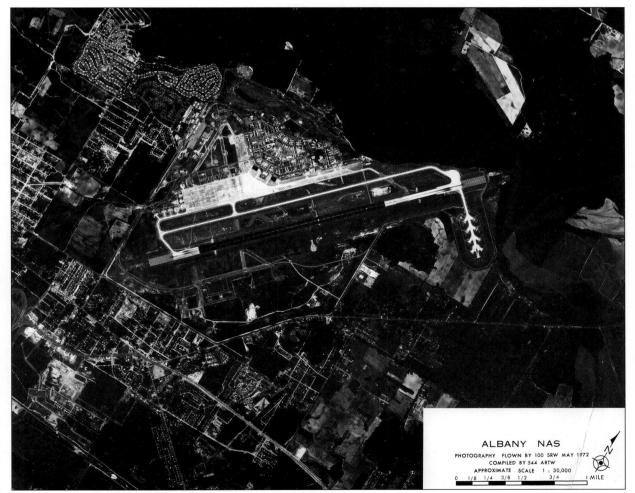

ALBANY NAS
PHOTOGRAPHY FLOWN BY 100 SRW MAY 1972
COMPILED BY 544 ARTW
APPROXIMATE SCALE 1 : 30,000
0 1/8 1/4 3/8 1/2   3/4   1 MILE

Aerial view of NAS Albany. Ironically, for the home of navy reconnaissance, this photograph was taken by USAF. The Flint River meanders through the dark area.

This photo of RVAH-14 Vigilante with flasher pod over NAS Albany was used on the cover of the city telephone directory. The long single runway, adjacent taxiway, vast ramp area, alert "Christmas Tree" pads for SAC aircraft, and Flint River are apparent. (USN via Carlton)

RVAH-3 Vigilante over NAS Albany. Buildings are all located in the angle between what had been the original crossing runways. (Cannelos)

one or two B-52s and their aerial tankers there as part of SAC's dispersal plan. A "tree" of revetments was at the far end of the runway with a command center and crew dormitory. The area was secret and security was tight. Most people on the base were only vaguely aware of the air force presence. USAF uniforms were seen occasionally at the base commissary and exchange. The theater on base had red lights that flashed when an alert was in progress and crews had to report to their restricted area.

On an irregular basis, a bomber and tanker took off on a mission. Whether the planes that landed were the same or replacements from a major SAC base was not known. The USAF would have been unhappy to learn the classified alert area was a favorite target for Vigilante cameras.

Military housing was relatively new and plentiful, so most families lived on base.

The Flint River ran past the air station's border and was available for recreation, although waterskiing was referred to as, "trolling for alligators."

One Runway Problem

The 12,000-foot runway was good except that it was the only one. Unlike Sanford with its three runways, if the Albany runway was blocked there was no other.

The test center at Patuxent River wanted some data on stopping distances and sent a test pilot to Albany. "The test pilot was me [Tom Myers]. It was a borrowed aircraft from either a squadron or the factory. At Pax, I mostly used the factory aircraft 156615. If we were going aboard the ship and a Vigilante squadron was on board at the time, we sometimes used one of their aircraft. Usually they didn't like that.

"The test was at touchdown, aero brake until the nose was on the ground, and then mash on the brakes as hard as you could and keep them there until the aircraft was fully stopped. The landing distance was documented and fans were put on the brakes to cool them.

"After some measured cooling, I took off for a second minimum landing test, extended upwind for more cooling, and made another

Publicity photograph of RAG aircraft placed in front of base operations building and control tower. (NNAM)

pass, with the same procedures. This time, when the fans were put on the wheels we spent 5 to 10 minutes cooling them and were about to do another flight. Upon adding power to taxi for takeoff, everyone realized the (brake) disks had melted together and the brakes were locked. The aircraft would not move.

"I even tried a little more power than usual to see if they would break loose. The tires didn't roll; they skidded. The fans were supposed to keep the disks cool enough so the tires wouldn't blow. It was good data on the ability to land, just not good to do it twice in a row. That's flight testing, folks.

"As I recall, the stacks were changed and we went home with what we had. The antiskid feature really worked well ONCE."[6]

The RAG's TA-4 had come back from a flight and with the test Vigilante on the downwind unwisely did a touch and go. When the Vigilante was stuck on the runway, it was too low on fuel to fly to another airfield, so the pilot chose to land on the parallel taxiway—as long as the runway, but less than half as wide. The landing was good, with no problems, but the pilot got a major ass-chewing.

Neighbors

I was at a "welcome to Albany" event and got talking to a city councilman. The gist of the conversation was, "Boy, are we glad to see the navy here. The air force sometimes took off as late as eight o'clock at night." I didn't tell him anything about FCLP and all-night bouncing.[7]

There was a low-level recce route out of NAS Albany that ran through the mountains of northern Georgia. There was also a small square on the charts away from civilization marked "factory." The building was a useful checkpoint.

North American Rocket Ride

October 1970 saw an ejection from *John F. Kennedy*. RAN Ralph Feeback, a former NEBN, tells of the aftermath of ejecting from an RA-5C Vigilante:

"E. O. Williams, then the CO of RVAH-14, and I were flying off *JFK* on our way home to NAS Albany. I felt something was wrong right after the cat shot, but he took what felt like minutes to tell me to eject, that our bird wouldn't fly single engine, so I got a little North American Rocket time. The helo soon snatched us out of the water and put us back on the ship. Since we were on our way to Albany, all of our clothes went down with the airplane (BuNo 151817).

"Down in sickbay we were issued a brandy or two and our backs were X-rayed, standard procedure after an ejection. The docs put our X-rays in big brown envelopes and told us to give them to our flight surgeon on return to Albany. The flight surgeon kept asking me how I felt, and I told him I was OK!

"We arrived in Norfolk the next morning. The maintenance troops had a C-130 scheduled to leave at 1530. They brought the skipper to the terminal, and he could hardly walk. This flight surgeon wanted him to stay in Norfolk, but he insisted on going home. This same doctor kept asking me how I felt. 'Fine,' I kept telling him. I had a couple of bruises, but a couple of rum and cokes took care of that. E.O. lay on the deck of the aircraft on the way home; you could tell he was hurting.

"After we landed at Albany, an ambulance picked up the CO. Meantime a couple of my shipmates insisted that we go to the O'Club. So, there I was in a dirty flight suit with my big, brown envelope with my X-ray. About 2000 HRS everyone was dancing and having a good time, when our squadron's flight surgeon's wife came to the bar and asked if I wanted to dance, I said 'Sure. And, hey, you just reminded me that I am supposed to give my X-ray to your husband.' I handed the envelope to her husband and she and I went on the dance floor.

"The next thing I knew, the lights were turned up bright, the music stopped, and I was being strapped into a back-board and loaded into the ambulance the Doc had called.

"In sickbay, they took more X-rays of my back. There was nothing wrong. Seems that on the ship they had put the CO's X-rays in my envelope. He had a couple of fractured vertebrae. No wonder he was hurting."

Then one day the NAS Ops Officer received a call from a gentleman who identified himself as the manager of a dynamite and explosives factory. "I don't mind y'all flyin' your jets overhead, but it ain't smart to startle any of my boys. Could you lemme know at least five minutes afore they come by."

Oops!

When Skyhawks were used in RVAH-3, instructor pilots might fly several times in the TA-4 before getting into a Vigi. It was not uncommon when starting taxi from the chocks for the airplane to stop because a slew of warning and caution lights came on. The nosewheel steering button in the Skyhawk was in the same place on the control stick as the "Kill" button in the Vigi. The embarrassed pilot simply had to reset Electric Flight and use the correct nosewheel steering button.

The dictated move was disruption of the worst kind. Homeowners lost thousands of dollars selling their houses. Kids were pulled out of school mid-term. Families were separated for months. Most difficult of all for families and men were those squadrons that were deployed when the move came. Try to imagine what moving would be like with Dad halfway across the world. For example:

- RVAH-6 had been on *Ranger* (CVA-61) since November 1967 on an arduous deployment to WestPac that included the diversion to the frigid waters off Korea. The squadron was the first to return to Albany and a squadron history says they were given, "a memorable welcome."
- RVAH-11 *Checkertails* also had a tough time. After a brief time on the *Forrestal* and its disastrous fire, there was a quick turn-around and they went back to seven months of combat on *Kitty Hawk*, returning to the new base in June 1968.
- RVAH-1 left aboard the *Enterprise* at the start of the year and, like RVAH-6, had been pulled off the line to go to Korea, before arriving in Albany in July.
- RVAH-13 *Bats* were among the last to depart from Sanford, flying to the *America* for that ship's first trip to Vietnam. The *Bats* came to Albany at the end of 1968.
- RVAH-5 and RVAH-7 also left Sanford before the closure, deploying on the *Constellation* to WestPac and the *Independence* (CVA-62) in the Mediterranean respectively. Both made the move to Albany in January 1969.

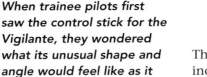

When trainee pilots first saw the control stick for the Vigilante, they wondered what its unusual shape and angle would feel like as it was much different than standard types. The unique NAA shape felt natural to hold and operate with the thumb. Electric Flight disconnect was the red button on left, nosewheel steering engage on the right side. The "coolie cap" set normal pitch and roll trim with the ridged wheel for pitch trim when Electric Flight was on. There was a trigger switch on the front of the stick. (This stick is mounted on a wood base as a memento)

NFO = CO

Early Vigilantes had Naval Aviation Officers (NAO) as crew. The career path for NAOs was haphazard until 1966, when the increasing numbers of Phantoms, Intruders, and Vigilantes as frontline aircraft led the navy to create the Naval Flight Officer program. NFOs rapidly proved their value. (There was mutual respect despite jibes about "I'd rather have 250 pounds of gas than a back-seater" and "Pilots are merely chauffeurs.") A new column appeared in flight log books; Mission Commander was added to Pilot and Aircrew. In early 1970, regulations were changed for command eligibility; NFOs were considered on the same basis as pilots.

Jerry Gehrig became the first NFO to command an RVAH squadron when he took over the RVAH-12 *Speartips* in December 1972. Gehrig began as a BN in A3D Skywarriors and made three Mediterranean deployments before joining RVAH-5 for the Vigilante's first combat deployment on the USS *Ranger*. He then went to the Test Center at Patuxent River. Screened for command, he joined RVAH-12 on the *Independence* as executive officer before fleeting up for a deployment on the *Constellation*. His last assignment was commanding officer of NAS Pax River.

Vigilante Meets the Blues

On a July weekend in 1972, there were airshows at both NAS Patuxent River and NAS Albany. An RA-5C Vigilante was configured with low-angle oblique cameras and color film (the setup used to take all those nifty photos for cruise books). The mission was to both fly in the show and afterward to accompany the Blue Angels en route to Albany. Unfortunately, Blue 2 was delayed and the resulting photos could not be released because there were only five aircraft; all official team pictures had to have four or six airplanes. Somehow, several 8x10 prints showed up at the O-Club reception that evening, which the team happily signed.

The unacceptable picture with signatures of the entire team, including the missing number-2 man.

RVAH NFO Commanding Officers		
Jerry Gehrig	RVAH-12	December 1972
Ron Queen	RVAH-13	October 1973
Al Perella	RVAH-9	May 1974
James Osborne	RVAH-7	December 1974
Jerry Henson	RVAH-5	October 1975
Dan Rowley	RVAH-6	January 1976
Dave Sharp	RVAH-7	February 1977
Al Frank	RVAH-6	May 1978

CarQuals

A setback for the new batch of RA-5Cs (156 series) came on 27 September 1970. Robert "Beef" Renner had served as the RAG LSO for almost three years so was well known and respected throughout the community. He was finally back in a fleet squadron. RVAH-1 was running routine CarQuals off California in preparation for deployment on the *Ranger*. Renner flew BuNo 156629 to what at first seemed a normal arrested landing.

Halfway through the run-out, one of the two attach points on the A-frame tailhook broke and the 50,000-pound airplane lurched to one side. The strain snapped the other attach point and the Vigilante went off the deck; too fast to stop, too slow to fly. The crew pulled the ejection handles, but were in every carrier pilot's nightmare—low, slow, and going down fast. LCDR Renner and his RAN, LT Max Joseph, both died in the sea.

All the Vigilantes, old and new, were restricted from shipboard operations. Extensive investigation discovered that the bearing where the hook frame attached to the fuselage did not have any provision for lubrication and the bearings were being stress-fractured. A procedure for lubricating the bearings was developed and the RA-5C was cleared to resume carrier operations.

Vigilante of RVAH-1 at NAS North Island before going aboard Ranger *in 1970.* Kitty Hawk *and RVAH-6's deployment to WestPac was at the same time and their aircraft frequently encountered one another over the Tonkin Gulf. BuNo 151618 was in RVAH-7 the next year and lost in combat with both CDR Polfer and LTJG Kernan becoming POWs.*

The new Vigilantes, which RVAH-1 on *Ranger* and RVAH-6 on *Kitty Hawk* took with them to the Tonkin Gulf, had the shiny factory paint scheme with a wavy demarcation line and lettering in pale blue.

Alameda

Sunday morning, when an instructor pilot and student RAN came to the transient line at NAS Alameda, they found fire trucks hosing down a huge puddle of fuel and hydraulic fluid under their Vigilante (BuNo 146695). Opening an access hatch on top, the fuselage showed an interior that looked as if a hand grenade had exploded.

A young sailor had gone out to get the airplane ready for its flight back to NAS Albany, but the canopies would not open. He asked the senior petty officer who told him the emergency flap air

bottle had probably bled down and to recharge it with nitrogen. The sailor took out the cart of gas bottles, opened an access panel on the belly, hooked up the line to the Schreader fitting, opened the valve, and heard a *whumph*!

The bellies of all airplanes are dirty; fluids leak down and mix with dirt thrown up from runways.[8] There was no labeling visible on the panel doors. He had hooked up to the valve for the hydraulic reservoir snubber, which used 300-psi air, and not the emergency flap bottle that took 3,000 psi.

Legitimate training missions that went crosscountry sometimes brought back items not obtainable at home base; Maine lobsters, for example. The RA-5C had an avionics bay up and behind the nose wheel well that could hold a fair amount of goodies. This crew had three cases of Coors beer[9] and lots of sourdough bread to take back to NAS Albany. Amazingly, a squadron TA-4 was there with an empty back seat. The RAN student got

A navy journalist in the port forward catwalk took this series of pictures. 1: The cans have come out and the jet fuel (JP-4) ignited by the afterburner. 2: Jet fuel burns rather than exploding like high-octane gasoline. The three tanks have the flames pushed downwind. 3: Each can weighed a ton and had 295 gallons of JP-4 in it. 4: The onboard fire truck and hose crew working to extinguish the blaze. (Sharp)

to go home right away. Because of space limits in the Skyhawk's ammo bay (tactical aircraft had some ingenious storage spots), there was no room for the third case and, ironically, the line guys got it. The RAN was a sight holding a bundle of loaves in his arms until the canopy was closed then shoving them down on consoles as the Skyhawk taxied out.

The overhaul facility at Alameda repaired BuNo 146695 and it returned to Albany for only one more year of flying before being scrapped.

Cans on Catapult

Dave Sharp wrote, "The pilot of the *Speartip* (RVAH-12) was the Skipper, John Huber. I was the RAN. To attest to the great capabilities of the Vige, we did not know what had occurred until I hit the 'check bomb bay fuel' item on the post takeoff checklist and John said, 'We haven't got any. Holy ____ look at the carrier!' and he rolled so I could see. We diverted to NAS Albany, checked our hydraulic/fuel lines, installed a new set of cans, and returned to the ship the next day. Loved that aircraft."

Speaking of the RA-5C "spitting" its tanks (that's what we called it), there were several such events. TINS: "Big Jim" Thompson, before he was CO of RVAH-6, was on a Vigilante RAG CarQual and during the flyoff, the first Vigilante spit its cans with ensuing flames in the cat. The carrier skipper called Thompson to the bridge as senior squadron officer on board and after ranting about getting the other RA-5Cs off, asked, "Are you certain that the remaining Vigis will not lose their fuel cans?"

Thompson looked the captain in the eye and in his deep Georgia accent said, "Cap'n, you put me in the first one off the cat, and I can absolutely guarantee it."

The main gate at NAS Albany in late 1972 when the closure was in progress. The airfield was never again used for aviation, with the concrete runway becoming the foundation of a large beer brewery. (Hoskin)

The insignia of Reconnaissance Attack Wing-1. Like many adopted mottos, the Latin meaning is imprecise. Officially, it was "Strength through leadership," although many sailors preferred, "Because we said so."

Volcano Hunting

A few weeks before Christmas 1971, the RVAH-6 squadron duty officer (SDOs were allowed to go home for the night) was amazed to get a call from the wing over normal telephone lines asking how many "up" IR mapping sets (the AAS-21 was still classified) the squadron had for "a mission down south." When the SDO reminded the staffer they were talking on an unsecured line, he laughed and said "Oh, nothing like that [Cuba], there's a volcano about to erupt in the Caribbean."

The next morning a *Fleur* Vigilante took off for NAS Roosevelt Roads in Puerto Rico, hot refueled, and took off again for Mount Soufriere on St. Vincent Island. On returning to Roosy

Test spray of three color stencils. Besides on the sides of the two Vigilantes, the logo went on toolboxes, ground equipment, and mechanics' T-shirts.

Roads, an indication of the importance of the mission was that the film was unloaded by the Base Photo Officer himself. The highly rated scientist in charge from the US Coast and Geodetic Survey talked to the flight crew about the capabilities of the AAS-21.

Concerned about security, they were reticent, but it turned out that the scientist knew more of the technical details of the equipment than they did. The mission tasking came all the way from the top levels of the Pentagon. Soufriere had all the characteristics of the volcanic eruption on Martinique, which had killed 1,680 people in 1902. *Project Volcano* was underway.

Another RA-5C followed the next day (BuNos 156624 and 156626 flew all the missions), and for the next three weeks flight crews rotated through and a detachment of maintenance personnel took care of two RA-5Cs.

A tholoidal plug of hot lava the size of a football field was rising through the crater lake in the mountain that had been quiescent for 100 years. The lake had turned from a benign blue to an ugly, boiling pea green.

Twice a day, a Vigilante launched and flew to the volcano. The old crater was irregularly shaped with one edge much higher than the other. A tropical cloud usually sat over the high ridge. The tactic the crews worked out was to fly low over the Caribbean and accelerate in afterburner to just under Mach 1, fly up the mountain slope 100 feet over the lush greenery, push forward on the stick, and go zero-G to level flight.

While the RAN monitored cameras and infrared, the pilot stared at a wall of solid rock coming at his nose at 300 knots.

BuNo 156626, moments after liftoff at NAS Roosevelt Roads on the end of Project Volcano. Afterburners on max, landing gear are up, flaps yet to be raised. RVAH- 6 in transition between Air Wing 11 (NH) and Air Wing 8 (AJ). Volcano project marking behind intake duct.

When the RAN called "Nadir!" the pilot pulled up at 4-Gs and went on instruments into the cloud. Once clear, they came around for another run, until after four to six such runs, the fuel remaining forced them to go back to Roosy Roads.

The missions inspired an evocative bit of prose from LTJG George Cannelos, a nugget RAN. Here is a sampling of stanzas from his "The Dawn Patrol":

- It isn't until you're running your alignment in the fuel pits that you realize something is terribly different. You watch your Alphas[10] rise and fall, and then it strikes home. It is the moon. The incredible, full white moon has transformed the jungle into a deep dark blue and has turned your instruments alive with an iridescent glow. An Alpha with a capital A and Homer just penned it.

- The Vigilante reaches altitude and the long, curving arc southward begins. Lights are turned off and radios silent and we slip helplessly into a feeling of peace and oneness with the world. Only the relentless, mysterious clicking of the present position counters tells you you're really plowing through the middle atmosphere at speeds the pirates of the Spanish Main never dreamed.

- One by one the islands slip away. Saint Croix, the Leeward's, Guadalupe, and Dominica. And far ahead resting patiently are the yellow strobes just waiting for the corner of Martinique to materialize under them. Sailing in our ship of steel, all the gems of old empire are ours.

- Visions of dragons and sea serpents are easily conjured up from the depths of the mind, and, literally, like knights wrapped in metal armor we seek battle with Vulcan, with Pele, goddess of fire.

- By day, the lake would be seen boiling—first an emerald green, then a drab, dirty yellow. Steam would be rising off the crater for thousands of feet. Mount Soufriere would be surrounded by lush green vegetation running down to touch the sea itself.

If the volcano began erupting and spewing rocks or lava, the damage would have as bad as AAA or SAM. Although the lava plug rose at more than 8 inches a day at the start, it slowed, and after three weeks the project was called off. As the flight crews said, "If Soufriere had erupted we'd all be famous . . . but it didn't."

Chapter 8

THERE WAS STILL A WAR ON:
1969–1972

Action in Vietnam had quieted with the end of Rolling Thunder in April 1968. While Vigilantes were central to the missions that sometimes went into North Vietnam, there were not many. Washington permitted limited recon flights into the north, Blue Trees, and allowed armed reaction if the reconnaissance plane was fired upon. Unspoken was the realization that the Vigilante was being used as bait. However, most missions were route reconnaissances along designated stretches of roads, trails, and waterways over Laos and South Vietnam with the attack birds blowing up large areas of jungle and the fighters boring holes in the sky. At night, Vigilante missions were of two types: route reconnaissance using the infrared mapping AAS-21 or a radar-locating PECM track. Flight

Quiet moment with RA-5C chained down near the forward starboard catapult.

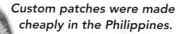

crews called the period the "Laotian Highway Patrol."

Deployment Interrupted

At the start of 1969, the USS *Enterprise* (CVAN-65) left Alameda, California, with Air Wing 9 and RVAH-6 on board. As usual for Pacific Fleet carriers, the ship and air wing trained around the Hawaiian Islands until the culminating ORI and departure for the war zone.

The first morning out of Pearl Harbor, hot exhaust from a jet-starter cooked off a missile and started a conflagration on the flight deck. The fire and explosions killed 27 men and destroyed 15 airplanes. That relatively few were killed and damage confined (unlike the *Forrestal* fire) was because the ship was at General Quarters as part of the training exercise: the ship's compartments were isolated, all hands in battle dress, firefighting and damage control parties were fully manned, and their equipment out and ready.

Besides the destruction from actual explosions and fire, many airplanes were ruined by saltwater from firefighting. Some had to have holes punched in them to drain the water. All of them were washed down with freshwater as soon as possible. Only one of RVAH-6's Vigilantes was damaged by shrapnel, but was repaired and flew four days later. Ironically, this airplane was shot down two months later.

Repairable and undamaged aircraft were craned onto barges and taken to NAS Barbers Point on Oahu. While the *Enterprise* was being repaired in Pearl Harbor, air wing training resumed. The schedule was relaxed with flying only Monday through Friday. The *Fleurs* of RVAH-6 mapped the entire Hawaiian Island chain and used their infrared sensors to locate a steam leak in downtown Honolulu. Announcements were made on radio and television to inform the public about what the low-flying Vigilantes were up to.

Tora, Tora, Tora

Sharing the airfield at Barbers Point were the replica Aichi Vals and Mitsubishi Zeroes (made from AT-6 Texans and Vultee BT-13 trainers in the best Hollywood tradition) used in filming the movie *Tora, Tora, Tora* about the 1941 attack on Pearl Harbor. The *Fleurs* with their photographic capability took many pictures of the mock Japanese airplanes, but, surprisingly, none are available today.

Yankee Station

RVAH-6 was back in the Tonkin Gulf on the last day of March. The first day back on the line, RA-5C (BuNo 150842) piloted by CDR Dan White, the squadron maintenance officer, with RAN LT Ramey Carpenter catapulted off but did not come back.

RVAH-6 Vigilante on waist cat. Twin fleur-de-lis on tail with NH for CVW-11. Early in 1970 deployment on Kitty Hawk, nose flash has not been added yet. This aircraft was later lost at sea in the last fatal crash of a Vigilante.

Field Goal 601 and its Phantom escort were flying northeast of Nakhon Phanom in Laos, and the RA-5C was in a steep turn at 5,000 feet and 420 knots when it burst into flames and fell apart. The large center section went into a flat spin. There were no ejections. The escort did not see any gunfire before the Vigilante exploded, but was fired on immediately afterward. (The remains of the crew were recovered and identified in 1997.)

Since there were official doubts that BuNo 150842 (the airplane damaged in the January fire) was a combat loss, an accident investigation was conducted. LCDR Larry deBoxtel had just become the new Safety Officer for RVAH-6. "The skipper ran us through a crash drill, all the reports and paperwork, during the transit. All I had to do for the crash was change names and numbers on the practice reports. We came up with some speculation on the cause: fuel tank explosion, overstress; but I'm convinced it was triple-A. They were on a second run over the target."

Korea Again

RVAH-6 had their first line period cut short when the North Koreans shot down an American unarmed EC-121 surveillance aircraft on 15 April and the squadron made an emergency run to the Sea of Japan for a second time. RVAH-9 aboard *Ranger* (the aircraft carrier the *Fleurs* had been on the previous time off Korea) joined them. The *Hooters* had been successfully operating off Vietnam since the end of November. Operations were much the same as before.

When the crisis subsided, *Ranger* headed east for home and transferred one of their Vigilantes to RVAH-6 to replace the one lost over Laos.

While the period off of Korea began badly due to maintenance problems, RVAH-6 recovered and gathered valuable intelligence before returning to Vietnam for a short second, and last line, period.

Vigilante portrait of USS Saratoga. *Squadron and IOIC emblems in left corner. (USN via Johnston)*

SA-2 GUIDELINE MISSILE FIRED AT AN RVAH-6 RA-5C DURING YE·71·060·N·3200 ON 1 MARCH 71

Many prints were made of this exposure from the vertical camera. At 35 feet long, SA-2s were called "Flying telephone poles." (USN via Conrad)

After White and Carpenter, the next combat loss was not until Operation Linebacker in 1972, but there were a dozen operational losses, seven at sea. The Vigilante was maintaining its fearsome reputation.

Scary Snapshot

One of the most remarkable photographs ever taken by a Vigilante happened accidentally on 1 March 1971. *Field Goal 602* was assigned a reconnaissance route that crossed over itself to get the tasked coverage of the Song Ca and a smaller river. The entire route was easily inside the SAM envelopes around Vinh.

At Vigilante speeds, LCDR Barry Gastrock and LT Emy Conrad were back over the river juncture at Hung Nghia heading south less than 4 minutes after crossing the same village westbound. AAA had only been sporadic and there had been no missile warnings when Conrad saw a flash in his viewfinder and yelled, "Pull up!"

Gastrock yanked hard. They heard a *whumpf* and were thrown against the seat straps. Speeding toward the coast, they watched for possible indications of damage to their Vigilante. There was none. At 600 knots, it did not take long to reach the waters of the Tonkin Gulf, and they soon went feet wet and headed back to *Kitty Hawk* for a routine recovery.

In the intelligence center, a photo-interpreter cranked the 6-inch-wide film from one massive spool to another across the lighted area of the viewing table and stopped. He called others to take a look. Soon that segment was cut out and positive image prints made. Perfectly framed in the vertical camera was an SA-2 missile still under boost. The crew was called to see the near miss. The best they could figure out was that since there was no terrain visible in the frame, the SAM passed under the RA-5C at the last target as Gastrock had banked hard to head for home.

Knowing the focal length of the camera and the size of an SA-2 warhead, the photogrammeters computed that the missile had passed 104 feet from the Vigilante's belly. No one knows why it did not detonate.

Fleurs Attract SAM Near Misses

One year later, "The SAM came a little past 5 minutes over the beach. We flew directly for the Than Hoa bridge first, tasked to get photos of the bridge from southwest and east. We got our photos and turned northwest to record any activity on Highway 119, turned northeast to run up Highway 124, finally turned southeast, still following Highway 128.

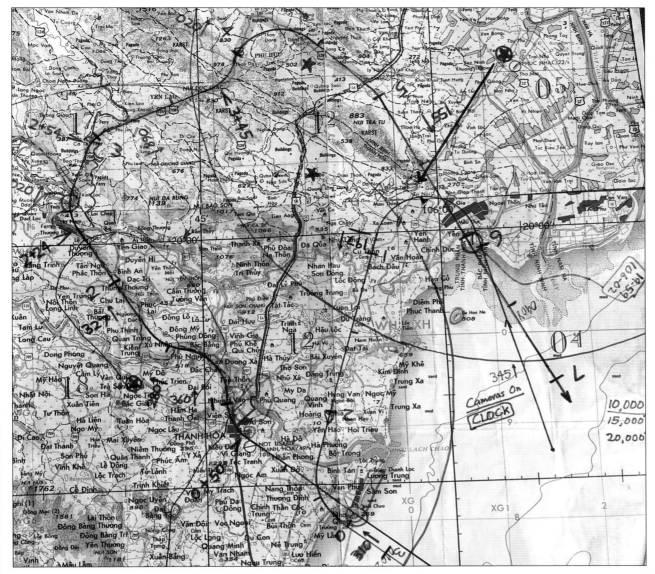

Section of chart used by LTJG George Cannelos of RVAH-6 during a 1972 route reconnaissance beginning at Thanh Hoa. The black arrow was recently added to show the path of a SAM near miss. The two distinctive rivers at upper right defined an area known to flight crews as "The Hourglass." (Cannelos)

turning past the 90-degree position heard a ball call and looked frantically for the SLUF (slang for A-7 Corsair), which should have been in front of him. When he couldn't see it, he took his own wave off. Minutes later, over *Kitty Hawk's* frequency, a voice said, "Hey Boss, you're not going to believe this; I'm on the wrong ship."

An RVAH-6 Vigilante was airborne, heard the wrong ship call and headed for the USS *Hancock* (CVA-19, a small-deck 27C Essex conversion) with cameras blazing. By the time the errant A-7 returned, there were 8x10 glossies in all the ready rooms, captain's bridge, flag bridge, etc., of a lone A-7 parked among a passel of A-4s and F-8s. The SLUF had been suitably decorated, and the pilot was awarded the nickname of "Trick."

Trolling at Quan Lang

In March "Protective Reaction" strikes were allowed. Stripped of political niceties, "Protective Reaction" was justification for attacks in North Vietnam. If a reconnaissance mission was shot at, US forces were allowed to "react" to "protect" the unarmed aircraft. The RVAH squadrons called it, "trolling for flak and SAMs with ourselves as bait."

"At 5+00 [minutes] we turned to heading 155 for the beach, mission tasking complete, but still a long minute away, when Phil [LCDR Pirafalo] yelled, 'Left window!'

"I looked out to see the SAM pass under and explode in a black-and-orange puffball explosion in the blue sky just off the right side. Launched, we believed, from a site plotted near the Phuc Nhac airfield. When it missed us, we were just 30 seconds to go on heading for feet wet."

Oops Landing Snapshot

Kitty Hawk (CVA-63) was beginning a normal day recovery at a time when there were three carriers in the Tonkin Gulf. An F-4

Facing Page: "Fleur Near Miss" by Thomas Dunterman. (tomdunttemannart.com)

NAME QUAN LANG A/F BDA CTY VN
COORD 185854N 1050235E BE 0617-08738
MSN VA-195 8762 DATE 22 APR 71
POS KB-18 PAN FRAME 012 SP 1
PRODUCED BY NAVY CONFIDENTIAL GP-4

Post "Protective Reaction" assessment photograph. (USN via Conrad)

briefed Quan Lang so many times, the basics were videotaped. When someone new was assigned to fly with them, he was told to watch the tape.

At last, after the airfield was complete and a pair of MiGs were parked there, *Field Goal 602* and the supporting players were actually launched.

PECM and earlier reconnaissance had reported 29 radars including 7 of the deadly fire-control Fan Songs located there. The "Dynamic Duo" had flown over the site a month before when they unintentionally photographed a SAM in their vertical camera. Fully loaded with ordnance, the A-6s, F-4s, and A-6s of Air Wing 11 were waiting off the coast as the Vigilante made a high-speed, low pass down the center of the new runway, pulled up, and came back the opposite direction.

The bait was too much to resist, and the Vietnamese gunners opened up and the SAM radars went active. The attack aircraft "reacted" and rolled in to protect the Vigilante. When they left and the smoke cleared, both MiGs and most of the SAM and AAA sites had been destroyed along with an aircraft starter unit, a fire truck, and a road grader.

Not Combat

Losing an aircraft, especially if someone is killed, is always painful. Reasons vary from pilot stupidity or lack of experience to poor leadership to plain mechanical failure.

RVAH-14 on board *John F. Kennedy* (CVA-67) lost two RA-5Cs in February and October 1969.

In June, a "well, qualified, senior, aggressive Naval Aviator," flew an acceptance check flight following delivery of the A-5 from PAR.[1] After takeoff, the emergency retraction switch had to be used to raise the gear because the gear handle did not work. A quick trip to 35,000 feet and back, in the positive control airspace without clearance, completed the first part of the flight.

The remainder of the test required slow flight at a lower gross weight, so the pilot selected afterburner and went into a series of

Blue Tree missions had shown an airfield under construction at Quan Lang on the Song Ca River less than 20 miles from Vinh. LCDR Gastrock and LT Conrad of RVAH-6 were to plan and lead a Blue Tree. The number of supporting aircraft from Air Wing 11 would have made a decent-size Alpha strike. Like so many Blue Tree missions, conditions had to be exactly right and they briefed the elaborate mission only to be canceled, rescheduled for another brief and another scrub, and another brief and cancel. They had

Within the photo: DEST MIG →, ↑ INDICATES AAA SITE

In 1965, RVAH-13 RA-5C ready for night takeoff in full afterburner. The leading-edge drops are down and flaps lowered. RVAH-13s used Asian-style tail letters. This aircraft was shot down in 1967 with the pilot, CDR C.L. Putnam, KIA, and the RAN, LTJG Frank Prendergast, making a daring escape. (NNAM)

"This flamboyant tiger will fly no more. As a professional Naval Aviator, he is one we can and will do without. The Navy can ill afford to cater to the personal whims and ego-satisfying showmanship of those few individuals whose immaturities dictate the fate of lives and millions of dollars' worth of equipment."[2]

Traditionally, the commander of a navy air wing, CAG, flew all of the aircraft assigned to his air wing; although by the Vietnam Era, CAG was allowed to fly only two types from the ship.

CDR Billings, the commander of Air Wing 14, had asked to fly a Vigilante while the ship was in port at Cubi Point for the holidays. LTJG Beaver thought another RAN an inappropriate choice and complained to his CO. He was allowed to take the flight with CAG.

What went wrong will never be known, but on New Year's Day 1970, the Vigilante (BuNo 148928) went into a steep dive with the engines at high thrust. Beaver tried frantically to talk to the pilot. When there was no response, he ejected (the RA-5C did not have a system where the RAN could eject the pilot. The pilot could eject the RAN). Unfortunately, they were going faster than Mach 1. Beaver's lower connection to his seat-pan was found unfastened; he had probably released it while trying to re-seat the communication leads. The high-speed ejection with a loose seat-pan broke Billy Beaver's neck, tore apart the parachute canopy, and he was killed. The airplane made such a deep hole that the CAG's body was not recovered.

RVAH-13 lost two a month apart in the Mediterranean aboard *Forrestal* (BuNos 149316 and 150825). There was an ejection at NAS Albany in March (BuNo 151620) and BuNo 156611 was "lost at sea" off the USS *Independence* in July.

acrobatic maneuvers to burn down. First, several wingovers were performed, then he accelerated to 0.95 Mach at 12,000 feet and pulled up, initially intending to do a barrel roll to the left. This was quickly modified to a loop, and he applied about 2½ Gs, using visual reference to the horizon and the attitude indicator.

At 90 degrees nose up, the sun partially blinded him and, as the big craft continued to 120 degrees nose up, it ran out of airspeed. The pilot attempted to pull the nose down to the horizon with back-stick pressure; however, the aircraft suddenly snapped violently to the right and entered inverted post-stall gyrations.

Various control input with stick and rudder caused the yawing oscillations to stop and violently reverse several times. The plane did roll to an upright attitude, but the uncontrolled gyrations continued from 27,000 feet down to 9,000 feet, when the pilot initiated command ejection for himself and the RAN in the back seat.

Both crewmen landed safely with minor bruises and were returned to home base by the SAR helo.

Grampaw Pettibone says: "Jumping Jupiter! If the Vigilante was expected to do acrobatics, procedures would have been published; they haven't been. Even the best of our fighters won't do a 2½ G loop at 12,000 feet. In spite of poor entry procedure and technique, and non-existent stall/spin recovery procedures, which might have prevented this accident, the primary error by this pilot was attempting the maneuvers in the first place. In combination with his other omissions/commissions, the lack of mature judgment becomes self-evident.

Reduction

There were two reasons that five, then four and, toward the end, only three RA-5Cs were assigned to a squadron. Primarily it was a lack of RA-5Cs. CRAW-1 constantly had to swap airplanes among the squadrons to balance deployment needs, maintenance, and overhaul requirements. Since the Vigilante had proven itself to be a valuable asset as the war in Southeast Asia expanded, North American built 36 new ones at its Columbus plant beginning in 1969. Even these were not enough to meet all the requirements, and every Vigilante lost from combat or otherwise, made the situation more difficult.

Also, the Vigilante was unpopular on carrier flight decks where space was at a premium. A restriction to only five of the six assigned

How It Is Done: Landing

Usually, the Vigilante flies into the break alone—fast. Occasionally, on a whim, the Vigilante and E-2 Hawkeye pilots arrange to come in together. The Vigilante on the left wing to break first. The "Hummer" nose down, turboprops screaming at redline airspeed while the Vigilante has the flaps partially down and its nose high trying to stay slow and under control while in tight formation.

Downwind, lower the flaps to a full 50 degrees, lower the gear, and have the RAN check by TV what the indicator is saying. The heavy, A-frame tailhook is lowered by a lever on the right side of the cockpit. As the flaps come down, so do the

That the only aircraft on deck are three of RVAH-6's five assigned, new, 156-series Vigilantes, indicates a CQ period before deploying on Kitty Hawk. This photo was made into a postcard. In a rare event, the five squadron aircraft had sequential BuNos from 156623 to 156627.

leading-edge slats, and the cockpit air conditioning cuts out as engine bleed air is diverted over the wing.

As the airspeed slows toward 155 knots, the angle-of-attack indexer on the glare shield lights up. Engage the auto-throttles with a switch. Check auto-throttle operation by pulling back on the stick—the throttles move forward. Push the stick and the throttles move back.

There may have been lots of fuel, out flying around, but at a max trap weight of 50,000 pounds there's only enough for four "looks at the deck." Not a time to screw up with the entire ship watching and waiting for you to trap.

Across the wake, pick up the meatball. Wings level when on the landing centerline. Start the landing scan you first learned in Pensacola—meatball, line up, angle-of-attack; meatball, line up, angle-of-attack. In the Vigilante, you fly the ball with small, tiny, tweaks of the stick to keep it dead center. Gentle touches with fingers and thumb. (An exact description borders on sexual.) The auto-throttles keep the speed correct. Their jerky movements reassuring. Nevertheless, your left hand rests on the throttles all the time . . . just in case. Lineup has to be solved early.

A turn to line up an RA5C means that the spoilers come up and their drag pulls the nose down if not anticipated. Close-in, your scan changes as angle-of-attack becomes less important, then the lineup drops out. For the last seconds, it is all "meatball, meatball, meatball." Touchdown has to be in a perfect attitude or there is the risk of a shattered nose wheel or the tailhook slamming up into the fuselage.

On a good trap at Vigilante approach speeds, you are thrown forward hard against your straps (woe to those who forget to lock their harness) and have to struggle to bring the throttles to idle, raise the flaps, press the button on the stick for nosewheel steering, switch hands to raise the tailhook, switch hands to advance the power, switch hands again to fold the wings, and taxi out of the landing area.

Facing page: LSO view: flaps down a full 50 degrees, leading edge droops down, A-frame hook down. Amber angle-of-attack indicator light steady on nose strut showing on-speed (slow was green, red was fast). In daytime, exhaust smoke showed power changes and movement of horizontal slabs changed in pitch. At night, the LSO judged attitude by the triangle of wing and approach lights. (Carlton)

Takeoff checklist from the NATOPS manual.

RA-5C pilot's cockpit. G-meter on glare shield was added well into RA-5C's service when a 4G limit was placed on the airframe.

BEFORE TAKE-OFF

RAN CHALLENGE	PILOT REPLY
1. MIC SEL	1. HOT
2. WINGS AND TAIL	2. SPREAD AND LOCKED
3. COMPASS (IFF — NORM)	3. CHECK
4. CAUTION LIGHTS	4. OFF EXCEPT ____
5. HOOK MODE SELECTOR SWITCH	5. FIELD-35° (field) NORM (ship)
6. MY HARNESS LOCKED	6. LOCKED
7. ANTI-SKID	7. ON (field) OFF (ship)
8. FLAPS/DROOPS	8. SET___/___DEGREES (30/25 degrees, field) (50/50 degrees, ship)
9. PITCH TRIM	9. CHECKED/SET (a) 6 to 8 units nose-up (field)* 12 to 14 units nose-up (ship)* (b) 3 units nose-up (field)† 8 to 11 units nose-up (ship)† (c) roll and yaw zero
10. GEAR STIFF	10. OFF (field) ON (ship)
11. PITOT ANTI-ICE	11. AS REQUIRED
12. CANOPIES	12. CLOSED, LIGHTS OUT, SEALED INFLATED
13. SEAT/CANOPY PINS	13. REMOVED
14. CHECKLIST COMPLETE	

on the carrier at one time, one of which had to be on the hangar deck, was frequently imposed.

The size of the airplane (76 feet long with a 53-foot wingspan) was much of the problem. In addition, many types of maintenance required that the internal fuel cans be removed. Because the cans were designed as part of the A-5 weapons delivery system, they were mounted on rails so they could slide out when released. (The mechanics had a "creeper" on wheels to roll back and forth while working.) Easy enough on land, but on a ship the airplane had to have its tail plus the length of the cans and space to work, over the deck.

Since most carrier-based aircraft are parked with their aft ends sticking out over the water and their main wheels at the edge of the deck, removing the cans from a Vigilante took over a large piece of flight deck real estate.

Secrets

Vigilante RAN Dennis "Lance" Lauer had been on CarQuals on the West Coast and was flying back to NAS Albany with a nugget replacement pilot (RP) when the Vigilante malfunctioned and they made an emergency stop at Holloman AFB. The next day, the "Recce RAG" (RVAH-3) sent a TA-4 for the RP—he was needed in the fleet. The instructor RAN could wait.

The day after that, the squadron TA-3 Whale brought parts and mechanics. Having noticed three very different airplanes with the same tail letters and orange bands on the tail, the air force sergeant who ran the transient line asked "Lance, just what is your outfit's mission?"

After furtive glances from side to side, and in his best James Bond voice, Lance said, "I could tell you, but then I'd have to kill you."

156 Series (RA-5D)

Because of the escalation of the war in Vietnam, 36 new Vigilantes were authorized in 1968. North American Rockwell put in the latest avionics, changed to higher thrust J79-10 jet engines, and improved the airframe by redesigning the intakes and adding a fillet to the leading edge of the wing where it joined the fuselage. The result was much better handling at approach speeds.

RAG TA-4 Skyhawk plugged in during ARF training. The Vigilante is from RVAH-6. When a tanker was available, multiple squadrons took a turn to maintain proficiency. This RA-5C is currently displayed at NAS Fallon, Nevada. (Hoskin)

The Great London–New York Air Race

In 1969, there was to be a *Daily Mail* Trans-Atlantic Air Race. The goal was to get a letter from a city post office in London to the Empire State Building's post office in the shortest time. There were a variety of classes, including commercial passenger and light airplane. A Vigilante was prepared to win the unlimited prize.

By all the designation rules, they should have been RA-5Ds. However, the politics of procurement and budget being what they were, the new batch remained RA-5Cs. Within the community, the new Vigilantes were referred to as "156 series" after their BuNos. The last of 156 Vigilantes (140 were new or rebuilt RA-5Cs) was delivered in August 1970. RVAH-1 and RVAH-6 in late 1970 were the first squadrons to take the new "156" Vigilantes to the Tonkin Gulf.

AFC (Airframe Change) 328 allowed the J79-10 to be installed in older airplanes. The modification was performed during aircraft rework after 1974 on some pre-156 RA-5Cs at the Jacksonville Overhaul Facility. RVAH-7 and RVAH-9 operated BuNos 146702, 149298, 149299, and 150831. BuNos 149276, 149287, 149301, and 151630 were also modified.[3]

Facing page: Old and new RA-5Cs in formation. Original buy in forefront (RVAH-11 AB601) and new increment, 156 series (RVAH-9 AA603), leading the flight. The leading-edge strakes on 603 are the obvious external difference. The flight must have been pre-arranged. While Vigilantes from different squadrons meeting in the air was not unusual, having a third aircraft to take photos was. Judging from the dates of the ship deployments, the picture may have been taken while both squadrons were in the Mediterranean between April and June 1973. (NNAM)

CRAW-1 CAPT G. W. Kimmons and LCDR Dave Turner went to Columbus to pick up a new Vigilante of the 156 series. The reconnaissance canoe was not installed. The J79-10 turbojets were

Intake strakes on the Vigilante displayed at the Sanford, Florida, International Airport.

CRAW-1 CAPT G. W. Kimmons and LCDR Dave Turner in a brand-new, special, RA-5C *intended for the Trans-Atlantic Race.*

"race tuned." The paint was carefully applied. North American engineers said the Mach-2 speed restriction was navy conservatism and the airplane was capable of higher speeds. On a practice run for the race at Albany, the Vigilante went to 2.5 Mach and the pilot, LCDR Robert "Beef" Renner, said he felt even faster was possible.

Dave Turner was a finalist for the racing RAN. "We planned the race to the last ounce of gas, fractions of a minute. A series of KA-3 tankers over the Atlantic was arranged. We'd carry four drop tanks, but jettison them in the Irish Sea soon after takeoff. One of our major problems was how to get into the city while wearing the full-pressure suits we had to wear because of the altitudes we were going to fly at.

"Then the navy bureaucracy put a thumbs-down on the idea. Very disappointing."[4]

Bears and SNAREs

The USS *Independence* (CVA-62) with RVAH-12 on board began a deployment by participating in NATO exercise "Royal Knight" in the Norwegian Sea above Latitude 70 North. US Phantoms landed aboard HMS *Ark Royal* and Royal Navy Phantoms aboard the *Independence*. The fighters were kept busy intercepting Soviet aircraft that came out of Murmansk and across the Barents Sea. RA-5Cs were also frequently used on such intercepts because their high-resolution

cameras brought back more usable data than the handheld cameras the F-4 RIOs fumbled with.

Infrared coverage with the AAS-21 was attempted, but flying directly overhead was too risky in the confrontational arena of flyovers and intercepts. However, by 1971 the use of airborne lasers had increased to the point where two Vigilantes of RVAH-12 (BuNos 148933 and 151727) were fitted with an articulated, infrared spectrum sensor on the top of the RA-5Cs. Known as SNARE, the highly classified equipment was in a 10-inch-tall turret that was hydraulically powered and aimed by the RAN through a viewfinder. The system had its own electronics and recorded data on 16-channel tape.

The goal of SNARE was to collect data about laser emitters and other related systems mounted on specially equipped Soviet Badger, Bear, and Bison aircraft checking out the *Independence* Battle Group. On completion of the cold-weather operations, RVAH-12 was happy to spend the remainder of its deployment in the Mediterranean. SNARE was removed as soon as the carrier headed south.

Now officially "Blue Noses" from having sailed across the Arctic Circle, flown in snowstorms and on an icy flight deck, and been in the Norwegian Sea, when a Viking figurine was found in a shop during a port visit, it was a natural as a mascot, especially since it was

While other RVAHs used a single color, RVAH-12 always had red, white, and blue markings.

Cartoon of the Viking mascot earned when RVAH-12 went north of the Arctic Circle.

Intercept of a Soviet Tu-95 Bear by RVAH-6 (author and Larry Parr) flying from Kitty Hawk in mid-Pacific Ocean, June 1975. This photo was taken by the RIO in the escorting Phantom.

holding a spear, for the *Speartips*. The RVAH-12 emblem was painted on the shield and cartoon representations appeared in squadron spaces on the ship and in newsletters. Somewhere along the line, it picked up the undignified name of "VUP" for Very Ugly Person.

Frustration Patches

During the period after the ridiculous bombing pause of 1969, known as the "Laotian Highway Patrol," most missions off the carriers in the Tonkin Gulf were close air support down south or attempts to choke the Ho Chi Minh Trail, especially at the mountain passes. (There was a sarcastic "Ski Mu Gia" patch.) For the reconnaissance squadrons there were Blue Tree missions, which actually went into North Vietnam. Blue Trees were a big deal with heavy air wing sup-

port in case a "reactive" strike became necessary and a briefing for the embarked flag staff. Then, when everyone was cocked and ready, the mission was usually scrubbed.

The patches were indicative of the attitude all the flight crews had toward the mostly meaningless missions that went on and on while the mostly meaningless peace talks in Paris went on and on. This all changed in 1972 when Operation Linebacker began.

Ad-Lib CarQual

In January 1975, John Smittle found himself again in the back cockpit of a Vigilante after 10 years, in an event that showed how close the reconnaissance community had become.[5]

RVAH-6 was scheduled to participate in a RimPac Exercise in Hawaiian waters flying from the USS *Kitty Hawk*, a West Coast carrier. However, the *Fleur* pilots were no longer carrier current and needed to be ASAP. CRAW-1 talked to AirPac, AirPac talked to AirLant, and an expedited CarQual session was arranged. *John F. Kennedy* was in the Caribbean with RVAH-1 on board. The *Smoking Tigers* hosted the RVAH-6 aircraft.

The day before heading south, one of RVAH-6's three Vigilantes went hard-down. The solution was for one of the three pilots to fly down in a back seat . . . and it certainly wasn't going to be the CO. RVAH-1 not only provided a loaner RA-5C, but a RAN as well. An offer to flip a coin for who would ride in back was rejected by the senior pilot, (senior by all of two numbers in the "Blue Book"). "'Smuts', you were a RAN once," he said, "To be fair, I'll take the back seat for the flight home."

Original patches showing the frustrations of the 1970–1971 period.

Fleur *Vigilante* at the time of the RVAH-6 Ad-Lib CarQual on JFK. BuNo 156615 had the last ever trap, a last flight to China Lake, and is now on display at the Castle Air Museum in California.

After a 2½-hour flight to *JFK*, BuNo 156638 trapped and was taxied forward of the island. It was chained down next to one of RVAH-1's Vigis that had its engines turning and preflight checks completed by that squadron's most junior pilot. Smittle climbed out of the back cockpit of the one he came in and into the still-warm front seat of the loaner Vigilante.

A RAN from RVAH-1 was standing next to 156638 and as soon as Smittle climbed down, he climbed up and strapped in. Over the intercom came "Hiya, Boom."

"Hello, Bill. You ready to go?"

"Sure am. Pre-launch check list."

Less than 10 minutes after the first trap, they were off the cat. Smittle's airplane left soon after, and there were three Vigis in the pattern. Smooth, no problems. Standard procedures. And all the pilots and RANs had all flown together before.

Jiffy Soda 196x–197x

To this day, the US Navy has been reluctant to discuss the missions around the perimeter of Cuba. Vigilante crewmembers remember flying the missions called *Jiffy Soda*, but are unsure of when they began or when the last one took place. The missions were classified and not openly talked about. The entry in the flight log book was "routine training" and there are no open records.

It was combat of a different sort. They launched from home base and were back in time for dinner with the family. From NAS Sanford and NAS Albany the Vigilante stopped in NAS Key West for fuel if needed. Once they were moved to NAS Key West, Cuba was visible soon after takeoff. The missions were short enough that an extra fueling was not required.

A *Jiffy Soda* went completely around the island of Cuba with the PECM gathering radar signatures and locations, SLR recording

Side-looking radar image of the Florida Keys.

a current image of the coastline and several miles inland while a 36-inch-focal-length camera mounted in the oblique station—or sometimes the 18-inch panoramic camera—took high-resolution photographs to correlate with the IR and SLR.

Theoretically, the RA-5C remained in international waters, but several missions were intercepted and trailed by MiGs, and lock-ups by Soviet-made fire-control radars were not uncommon.

TINS[6]: On a *Jiffy Soda* mission out of NAS Key West, a Vigi-lante pilot dropped his kneeboard with the mission code words on it so when the recall code was sent, he did not break off. Next thing he knows, there were a pair of MiG-21s with Atoll missiles on his wing. He lit the afterburners and headed for Key West. The MiG drivers (wonder if they were *Cubanos* or "advisors" from someplace else?) got caught up in the thrill of the chase and hung on until all three aircraft went booming supersonic over the city of Key West.

RVAH-5 in 1968 while attached to CVW-14 aboard the USS Constellation, 1968–1969.

RVAH-6 in 1969 in CVW- 9. A plain red stripe was added to the top of the tail. This airplane began as an A3J and was converted to an RA-5C. In 1975, it was left at Lakehurst, New Jersey, to train flight deck crews. When the aviation museum in Cape May opened, an Army Guard helicopter was airlifting it when an uncontrollable oscillation began, and BuNo 146698 was jettisoned into the Pine Barrens of New Jersey.

RVAH-9 in 1968 on Ranger with CVW-2, BuNo 147859.

The Feared Cat 4

Getting a Vigilante onto a catapult for launching was never easy (see chapter 5), but the catapult nearest the port edge of the flight deck, Number 4, was not only difficult, but scary. The geometry of the problem shows why:

- The catapult track is approximately 15 feet from the coaming on the edge of the flight deck.
- The turn radius of the main wheels of a Vigilante is 12 feet.
- Main wheels to nosewheel is 20.5 feet[7] and the pilot is 12.5 feet in front of the nose gear.

To be positioned on the cat, the nose wheel had to be run up to the edge of the deck before turning onto the cat. This meant that the pilot was 12 long feet over the side, as well as 90 feet above the sea, while looking over his shoulder at the plane director whose signals were for the direction you were going, not where you were looking. The RAN was 6 feet over the edge and in his viewfinder was a good view of white caps or, at night, a black nothingness.

- Ah, the Number 4 cat; it was all about the deck load. Many of the flight deck spotting plans kept the Vigi aft of the island, facing out toward the landing area. Depending on the launch plan, we sometimes went first to ease up spotting others and loosening the deck. So out you came, 90 degrees to the track, needing a sharp right turn and pivot onto the track. As you came across the track, you lost visual with the deck as you were now past the catwalk. The spotting director, now way past your right shoulder, was watching the nosewheel, not you. I had my RANs spin the TV camera aft so they could keep up with the nosewheel to answer my continuing question, "How much farther?"

- One evening on the *Kitty Hawk* RVAH-6 cruise; I think I was with Rob Weber. We were taxing up to Number 4, at almost 90 degrees to it. The deck was rolling a good bit and the director was working us as close to the scupper as he could. I looked out the viewfinder and all I could see was water because we were about a foot short of the scupper. The director kept signaling Weber to taxi more forward. Weber was looking at him over his right shoulder and the ship was rolling portside down a good bit and the guy wanted us to taxi more.

Director then spins you when you hit the mark for the right main mount and you give a sigh of relief. Often the ship was turning into the wind while this was going on, creating the flight deck list heading downhill. Don't go too fast or you'll hit the scupper and jump it into the catwalk—not pretty. Add a little rain and turn out the lights at night and it was a THRILL A MINUTE![8]

- I'm breaking out in a sweat just remembering it at night. The day ones were a challenge, the night ones terrible, the night ones with a wet deck that was rolling caused heart beats in your throat. I'm sure that you were extended out over the edge of the deck 12 to 13 feet before they turned you. I believe it was the final exam for the deck handlers.

Weber braked and pointed at the director and motioned for him to step farther out instead of being basically behind us. The director looked around, gave him a thumbs-up and turned us.

Afterward, we talked about it, "You want us to taxi more forward? Then you step out here with us." Hilarious . . . after the fact.[9]

- I will join others in the dislike for cat 4. I remember that the cockpit was 12 feet forward of the nose tire, and I also recall being directed to the Number 4 cat on several occasions during the darkest of nights. It took intense concentration, and trust in the director, I might add, when I was hanging many feet out over the port side as the director got the nose tire far enough out, near the scupper, until he could turn me forward and get the aircraft lined up with the cat track.

I remember several times that I got out as far as I was willing to go and shook my head, no more, and they still found a way to get me on the cat. That exercise was just about as bad as anything that the ship had to throw at you to make it interesting.[10]

To the relief of Vigilante crews, launching off Cat 4 eventually was forbidden at night in many air wings and discouraged in daylight. Like all the catapults, once lined up, it was the usual delicate touch for crossing the slippery shuttle exactly on center then stopping without cracking the hold-back.

That situation, and getting our big old Machine back aboard on those blackest of nights, are why we can certainly say we were the best of the best.[11]

Much credit goes to some talented yellow-shirts as well. Placing a Vigilante on a catapult, especially Number 4, took skill and dexterity. On most cruises, no more than two or three directors were competent enough to position an RA-5C.

Chapter 9

LINEBACKER AND BEYOND: 1972–1973

During the Vietnam War, certain locations and phrases came to mean much more than the words themselves. Yankee station, route package six, alpha strike, rolling thunder, and linebacker, which was in two phases: *Linebacker* and *Linebacker II* (the designation *Linebacker I* was only in retrospect). The political background was complex and devious with President Nixon stating, "The bastards have never been bombed like they're going to be bombed this time." The result was the fiercest fighting in the air since World War II.

US forces had been alerted to move in early April. Operation Linebacker began on 10 May 1972 with large-scale bombing operations against North Vietnam. A total of 414 sorties were flown on the first day of the operation, 294 by the navy. It was the heaviest single day of air-to-air combat during the Vietnam War, with 11 North Vietnamese MiGs shot down (and Navy Lieutenants Cunningham and Driscoll becoming the first American aces of the war in their F-4 Phantom).

Order of Battle

Three-and-a-half years of restricted bombing had given North Vietnam time to significantly improve their defenses. There were more guns, many more SAMs, more MiGs—many

View of Haiphong taken with a Vigilante's forward oblique camera. Black clouds are exploding flak. (Wattay)

of them the dangerous, supersonic MiG 21—and the gunners, operators, and pilots were trained and experienced. The stage was set for a fierce battle.

At the start of Linebacker, the *Constellation* (CVA-64), and *Kitty Hawk* (CVA-63) were recalled from port visits. The *Constellation* with RVAH-11 headed home the next month, while *Kitty Hawk* with RVAH-7 endured until November. The *Saratoga* (CVA-60) and the *America* (CVA-66) arrived after their long voyages in April and June, respectively.

Surprises for Two

After WestPac deployments, both the *Fleurs* of RVAH-6 and *Tigers* of RVAH-1 were looking forward to cruises to the Mediterranean, not being shot at, and with plenty of good liberty ports for R&R.

At a RVAH-6 all-officers meeting, when the CO was asked if the squadron was deploying to WestPac instead

Three RVAH-6 Fleur commanding officers. Left to right: CDR Bill Belay (Kitty Hawk 1970–1971 deployment), CDR Ron Ream (Forrestal 1973), CDR Jim Thompson (America 1972). All had previous combat tours flying Vigilantes. This photo was taken at the change of command ceremony when Thompson relieved Belay with Ream becoming his executive officer. (Cannelos)

Replenishment at sea (RAS) formation. A modern stores ship (AOE, seen here) can transfer food, ammunition, and fuel. During the Vietnam era, supply ships were specialized: Reefers (AF, Food), Ammunition (AE), and Oilers (AO, aircraft and ship fuel). (USN)

If the tailhook catches before the main wheels are on deck, the result is an in-flight engagement that slams the airplane down. RVAH-14 in CVW-1, landing on CVA 67. BuNo 149296 was lost at sea flying with the RAG in 1975. (THA/Swisher)

Thanh Hoa Bridge under attack. The smoke and dust show why good BDA had to wait a deadly 10 minutes. Which of many strikes this is, is unknown, but despite the impressive bomb blast, the damage was probably slight— destroying an open-span girder bridge is difficult. (Cannelos)

of the Med, CDR Jim Thompson emphatically replied "No!" while nodding his head "Yes!" The *America* left Pier 12, Naval Station Norfolk, Virginia, on 5 June amid Coast Guard craft keeping a gathering of war protestors in canoes clear of the ship.

Taking a break from preparing for a second Mediterranean deployment, the captain of the *Saratoga*, CAPT J. R. Sanderson, and his executive officer were on the sixth hole of the Mayport golf course on a Saturday when a message came from the officer-of-the-deck to call Commander Air Forces Atlantic (CNAL).

To the question, How soon could the *Saratoga* get underway for Vietnam?, Sanderson replied, "Twelve hours on one boiler, twenty-four hours on two. Half my crew is gone." He was given 72 hours.

After the emergency recall of the crew, *Saratoga* was underway in 60 hours, but with 340 sailors still not aboard. The crew was eager with transferring men volunteering to stay. CODs were arranged to shuttle passing Roosevelt Roads and got everyone back aboard.

The *Saratoga* drained the accompanying USS *Detroit* (AOE-4) of fuel off the Cape of Good Hope and maintained a 23-knot speed of advance. She held two traditional Shellback ceremonies crossing the equator but did not slow down. Sanderson had the Carrier Division (CarDiv) staff intelligence briefers on board for the transit and maintained radio silence all the way. CV-60 became the "Silent Sara."[1]

Long ship transits provide time, and a captive audience, for training lectures and briefings. (For the trip home, the motivation is gone and boredom a problem.)

Former seaman Doug Hegdahl, who had been a POW for 28 months, was on board the *America* in his capacity as an expert of Survival, Evasion, Resistance, Escape (SERE) and gave extensive briefings to the squadrons.

An example of the experience level in RVAH squadrons of the time was RVAH-6: There was combat experience in the Vigilante with pilots Jim Thompson, CO, Ron Ream, XO; RANs Emy Conrad, Colin Pemberton, Scott Follet, and other Vietnam veterans; Joe "Hoser" Satrapa, former fighter pilot and expert on air-to-air combat; Phil Pirofalo, Skyraider and Skyhawk pilot; and Fred Litvin, who had flown Photo-Crusaders. One pilot and three RANs, nuggets, were on their first trip.

Operation Linebacker had not started when on 7 May, RA-5C BuNo 151618 was shot down for the first combat loss of a Vigilante since March 1969. CDR Ron Polfer[2] and RAN LTJG Joe Kernan[3] of RVAH-7, flying from the USS *Kitty Hawk*, were taking BDA photographs of a truck park that had just been attacked near Thanh Hoa. As the aircraft was on its photo run at 4,500 feet and 600 knots, it was hit by AAA near the Dragon's Jaw[4] Bridge. The rear of the aircraft caught fire and Polfer and Kernan ejected and were captured. Both men were released from North Vietnam in March 1973.

Mines

The first action of Linebacker was six A-7 Corsairs and three A-6 Intruders dropping thirty-six 1,000-pound Mark-52 and Mark-55 naval mines into Haiphong Harbor. The mines did not activate for five days to give foreign ships in the harbor time to leave. In the next days, the harbors of Cam Pha, Hon Gay, Vinh, and Thanh Hoa, as well as the mouths of rivers, were mined. When weather and daylight permitted, Vigilantes coordinated a flyover during the drops and photographed the splashes to accurately plot mine placement.

Nuggets

Seven RVAH squadrons flew to a greater or lesser extent during the Linebacker operations. All seven had a nugget pilot. All of them were on their first deployments, which meant their first combat flights were into the high threat areas of Vietnam. As one said, "We got experienced real fast."

All did well, with some lighter moments:

- RVAH-13's LTJG Russ Campbell went to Vinh on his first combat flight. He had the volume on his ALQ warning system set so high and so many fire-control radars were active that he did not hear any radio calls while over the beach. Back on the *Enterprise*, when he learned this, he worried that he may have missed some verbal warnings. Ernie Christensen, a former Blue Angel demonstration pilot, who had been his escort in a Phantom, said, "Don't worry, kid, they couldn't have hit you; you were all over the sky."

- During his first trip near Haiphong, RVAH-6's LTJG Wes Rutledge had the escorting Phantom pilot call, "Field Goal flight, cease burner so I can keep up."

  Rutledge rapidly replied, "No-no, not now."

- Displaying a high level of panache, LTJG Jim Kiffer of RVAH-1 did a buzz job at Kep Airfield with his escorting Phantom alongside. Not recorded is the two back-seaters' reactions to the flyby. Spontaneous as it was, the North Vietnamese did not have time to react.

Buzzing Kep

"In September 1972, I [LTJG Jim Kiffer] was flying a combat mission over North Vietnam off the USS *Saratoga* (CV-60) with the RVAH-1 world-famous *Smoking Tigers*. An Alpha Strike was briefed to attack a target northeast of Hanoi in the vicinity of the Kep Airfield, which had a contingent of North Vietnamese Air Force MiG fighters. I was orbiting near the target waiting for the Alpha Strike to conclude to make a bomb damage assessment photo run with my F-4 escort, piloted by Al (Taco) Cisneros from VF-31 (who later joined the Blue Angels).[5]

"I saw Kep airfield off in the distance and decided to make an unauthorized air show to demonstrate true navy air power. We left our orbit, descended to about 50 feet, accelerated to Mach 1, and blew down the runway. The airfield was heavily defended, but we caught them by surprise. In hindsight, it was a crazy, stupid, dangerous move . . . but I was 25 years old and bulletproof! Ah, the good old days!"[6]

The daring crews on the Kep buzz job were: in the RA-5C, nugget pilot Jim Kiffer and RAN Jim Lamb (RVAH-3 instructor before joining RVAH-1). The Phantom pilot was Al Cisneros and RIO was Steve Miller of VF-31. (Digital Art by Peter Chilelli)

Checkertail returning in the evening . . . or at dawn.

Crunch

At the end of a routine flight from Cubi Point back to the *America* on a clear day with calm seas, a RVAH-6 Vigilante had the nose gear collapse. "I was in the back seat when our nose gear collapsed on landing! It felt like someone kicked a chair out from under me. Fortunately, we caught a wire and skidded to a halt in time. I opened my canopy, and instead of being several feet off the ground, the plane captain looked down at me asking if I was all right. That evening, the flight surgeon prescribed brandy for both my pilot and me."

A cartoon was soon created showing a Vigi with nose crumpled on deck, a bug-eyed RAN, and a pilot smoking a cigar saying, "Piece of cake if you're smooth."[7]

BDT and Smilin' Jack

LCDR Chuck Smith and LTJG Larry Kunz were teamed as a tactical crew in RVAH-1 aboard the USS *Saratoga*. On an earlier mission over North Vietnam, Smith looked down to his Inertial Navigation System (INS) readouts and saw the steering bar pegged to the side and distance at over 200 miles instead of the next target. "Kooner," he asked on the intercom, "where am I?"

Kunz' reply became a classic: "Well, you're 8 feet in front of me. Going faster than hell . . . and I'm working on the rest."

The tactical crew of LTJG Larry Kunz and LCDR Chuck Smith at NAS Cubi Point. Their nicknames are stenciled below the cockpits.

The sailors in the maintenance department added the nicknames they had for this colorful pilot and RAN below their normal names on the side of BuNo 156616. Smith became "Smilin' Jack," after the old comic book hero pilot, and Kunz became "BDT." He claimed it was taken from the squadron's insignia and stood for "Big Deadly Tiger" but in reality it stood for "Big Dumb Texan."

On 7 June, doing a reconnaissance run of the anchorages in the islands where foreign merchant ships moored to offload their cargo into lighters for transfer into Haiphong, they came in at 200 feet and high speed from over the Tonkin Gulf and popped up to 3,000 feet for the photo run when the ALQ gear warned of a missile launch. Evasive maneuvers left and right were to no avail and the SA-2 went into and through the fuselage. Their RA-5C was skewered by a SAM. The missile did not explode or, as Smith said, "I would not be here telling the story."

The starboard engine lost power immediately. Smith turned for deep water, and as he lit the afterburner on the other engine it also flamed out. Electrical power went and the flight controls froze. The crew ejected a half-mile southeast of the city and landed a couple of hundred yards apart in the water between the islands. Their F-4 escort (flown by a USAF exchange pilot) reported them down and the A-7E Corsair ResCAP of the VA-32 *Blue Bulls* began bombing and strafing the shore gunners.

Two SH-3 Sea King helicopters of HC-7 (callsigns *Big Mother 66* and *67*) arrived and snatched Smith from the water. The helo's mini-gun was firing inches from Smith's face as he hung in the hoist. A para-rescue swimmer leaped to assist Kunz, but jumped from too high and collapsed a lung on impact with the water. Kunz swam over and helped his "rescuer" into the sling before being hoisted aboard himself. The gunfire from both sides did not stop until the helos left the area 50 minutes after the ejections.

The day after, when Kunz learned another RAN in the squadron had turned in his wings, he was angry and said to Smith, "Hey, wasn't it you and me that got shot down?"

Linebacker II

When the North Vietnamese negotiators returned to the Paris talks, President Nixon ordered

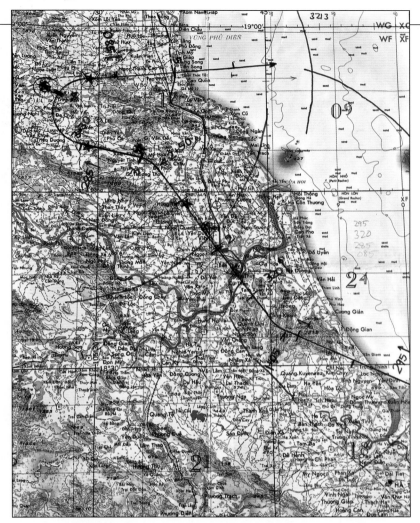

RVAH- 6's Phil Pirofalo and George Cannelos were suiting up for a hazardous daylight run in Route Pack 6 north of Haiphong near the border with China. Even at 600 knots, it meant 17 minutes over land. That mission was scrubbed before they manned up, as missions north of 20 degrees North had just been banned. A few days later, the same team was tasked to overfly seven SA-2 missile sites (each purple star on this map represents an active SA-2 missile battery), and the heavily defended city of Vinh (where course line crosses the Ca River). "There were so many missile sites, I did not bother to plot them or the antiaircraft guns." To the crew's relief, that mission was canceled by the capricious monsoon weather. (Cannelos)

With Hainan Island to the east and Hanoi, Haiphong, and Cam Pha near the Chinese border, warnings from American surveillance aircraft of approaching the buffer zone were frequent and an annoying distraction caused by the politically driven rules of engagement.

145

TGT _MOSKVA 847 LENNINGRAD_
COORD _3740N 00959E_ CTY _UR_
SENSOR _RIO_ FR_____ ALT_____
MSN NO _945_ DTG _020824Z DEC74_
BE NO_____ CLASS _FOUO_
RVAH-11 CV-60 RA-5C

Soviet helicopter carrier **Moskva** *photographed in the Mediterranean by RVAH- 11.*

Weasel SAM suppression, and electronic countermeasures support in an all-out attack on North Vietnam's air defenses. By the eleventh and final day of Linebacker II, there were few worthwhile targets left in North Vietnam.

The North Vietnamese resumed negotiations. Attacks north of the 20th parallel ceased on 30 December. The Paris Peace Accords were signed at the Majestic Hotel in Paris on 27 January 1973.

Marine Phantom Down

The weather two days before Christmas was poor, and a strike group from the *America* diverted to the south while the RVAH-6 Vigilante and its escorting Phantom of VMF-333 went north along the coastal islands on its secondary mission. Vigilante BuNo 156623, callsign *Fieldgoal 603*, was flown by the CO, CDR Jim Thompson, with his RAN, LT Emy Conrad. *Fieldgoal*'s escort was *Shamrock 210* flown by LT Col Cochran, commanding officer of VMF-333, and his RIO, Maj Karr.

a halt to attacks above the 20th parallel, again giving Hanoi and Haiphong time to rearm. Secretary of State Kissinger announced that "peace is at hand" on 26 October. The pause lasted until mid-December when the talks again broke down. The United States presented Hanoi with an ultimatum and began dropping mines in North Vietnamese ports and rivers.

The intense bombing campaign was primarily B-52s and F-111s attacking by night, with US Navy, Marine, and Air Force tactical aircraft averaging nearly 100 sorties each day. Less than a dozen were lost in the daytime during the entire campaign. The reason was obvious, the North Vietnamese defenders simply waited for nightfall and the arrival of more lucrative targets.

The losses of the big bombers had been heavy. During a 36-hour Christmas stand-down, air force planners revised their plans. When operations resumed on 26 December, 120 B-52s were supported by 113 tactical aircraft providing chaff corridors, escort fighters, Wild

VMF-333 was the first USMC fighter squadron to deploy to Vietnam on an aircraft carrier. *Triple Trey* F-4Js had bright green three-leafed shamrocks on their tails. A VMF-333 Phantom had the only Marine Corps MiG kill of the war four months previously.

Heading east at 2,900 feet and 480 knots near the island of Danh Do La, CDR Thompson saw the Phantom take a direct hit from an 85mm gun. The F-4 pitched straight down as the crew ejected. At that speed and altitude, they were in the water in seconds. Cochran and Karr were alive, although badly battered by the ejection.

The gunners on shore immediately opened up on the survivors. The Vigilante began making low passes trying to draw the gunners' attention away from the men in the water. As Conrad described it, "On some passes, I could see the face of the gunner on the quad 23mm as he was trying to track us. We were so close and moving so fast that the gun was about 45 degrees behind.

When combat gets hot, rules get lax. The crew of Fieldgoal 603, Thompson's mustache merely flamboyant, Conrad's skunk hat and full beard definitely non-regulation.

"Contact was attempted on guard channel with the downed crew. No voice was heard, but we did hear a [emergency] beeper. I kept telling them to swim south, that help was coming. The flak, large and small, was heavy. Plus I could see small arms firing all along the beach."

Hearing all the chatter on guard, an A-7 from VA-86 on the *Saratoga* arrived. Although the Corsair was rigged as a tanker and had only his cannon, the pilot made strafing runs on the beach where the small arms fire was coming from. Another A-7 with a load of Rockeye was vectored in and checked in with *Fieldgoal 603*, who was the on-scene SAR commander. As this A-7 silenced the heaviest gun with the devastating cluster bombs, the rescue helicopter *Big Mother 63* checked in. The helicopter pilot said, "I've no comms with the survivors and I'm not permitted to go in without talking to them."

CDR Thompson had barely escaped capture after his ejection in 1966 and knew how desperate Cochran and Karr would be. "You get in and pick them up right now or I'll drag my tailhook through your rotor-blades and see if you have comms when you're in the water with them."

Recruiting

A 156-series RA-5C is on display at NAS Pensacola (the historic lighthouse is in the background). A boarding stair, usually used on passenger airplanes, is pushed up to the cockpits to give people a look inside. The RAG occasionally sent a Vigilante to training bases to let student pilots and NFOs see what they might get to fly. Pensacola was where NFOs received both basic and advanced training.

The black S is for the CNO Safety Award. The panel with the switches to open and close the canopies are open, and the nose gear door has been dropped to get at the storage space inside.

There is some speculation in identifying this photograph: RVAH-3 won CNO Safety Awards in 1970 and 1971. The RAG usually did not put crew names on the fuselage unless it was for an airshow or display. LTJG Luke "Luscious" Hill was Nugget 5 and completed training in 1971 before reporting to RVAH-11. Although difficult to decipher, the other name appears to be LT Vince McManamin, who was an instructor RAN at that time. (NNAM)

RVAH-11 Vigilante, with toothy intakes, about to launch from Number 3 catapult. (NNAM)

"Luke Hill and I (Paul Habel) thought it would look neat. We hounded the CO, Murph Wright, like kids begging their parents. He finally gave in. After living with it only a few weeks, we all decided it really didn't make the Vige look like a P-40 Warhawk and changed it back." RAN Eric Briggs and pilot George Shattuck in front of RVAH-11's unique Vigilante.

The *Big Mother* SH-3 helicopter went in and picked up both survivors, although it ended up with five holes in it (one through the main rotor) from the still-active 37mm on the west peninsula. The two Marines were taken to the *America*'s sickbay and the Vigilante crew went down to see them.

As Conrad said, "It was a wild debrief as the *Trip Trey* guys were doped up and there was liberal use of medicinal brandy all around. Bad part was my wife heard most of the details within 24 hours and was extremely upset because I had been writing home telling her nothing much was happening."[8]

MiG-1, Vigi-0

On 28 December, the RVAH-13 crew of LCDR Al Agnew and LTJG Mike Haifley flew a pre-strike reconnaissance near Hanoi. The *Enterprise* was on a noon-to-midnight schedule. They had flown on the first launch of the day; this was their second mission. The escort Phantom was flown by the CO of VF-143, Gordon "Snowflake" Cornell.

As the pair accelerated away, ahead of the strike group, and went feet dry, RHAW gear was eerily silent. Following roads and a railroad to the city, the MiG calls began fast and furious, "Red, blue, bull's-eye and all quadrants!"

They made the photo run and on the way to coast-out, the escort said in a conversational tone, "*Flint Zero Three*, you better turn right."

Already keyed-up, Agnew broke into a 90 degree turn at 700 knots. There was a loud explosion and the Vigilante tumbled. "I didn't know there were that many negative G's in the whole world." Pressed against his straps and canopy, Agnew managed to reach one of the alternate ejection handles on the side of the RAPEC seat. His sense of time warped; his canopy seemed to take forever to come off. Next thing he knew, he was hanging in a parachute, surprised that its canopy was white and bright orange nylon.

The escort had seen two smoke trails from the Atoll missiles fired by a MiG-21 and watched what was left of the RA-5C crash. There was no second ejection. Mike Haifley was killed in the explosion or the crash.[9]

This was the 90th and last US aircraft shot down by a MiG during the war. BuNo 156633 was also the last of 26 RA-5C Vigilantes to be lost in Southeast Asia.

There was no wind. Peasants working in a rice paddy had to move aside to let Agnew land. He was stripped down to his "Hang Ten" T-shirt and red shorts he had gotten on Christmas a few days before. His new Seiko watch was taken. Agnew said his scariest

Standing in center are nugget Luke Hill and RVAH-11 Commanding Officer "Murph" Wright. (Shattuck)

RVAH-7 in 1972 at NAS North Island, Kitty Hawk's home port. Drop tanks were not used during Vietnam operations. (NNAM)

moment came when a Vietnamese came toward him waving a large Machete, but all he did was cut off his flight boots.

Agnew spent time in both the "Hanoi Hilton" and the POW camp called the "Zoo" where he met Jerry Coffey, the first RVAH-13 pilot to become a POW. Agnew was released on 29 March 1973. He was home before the squadron returned from deployment.[10]

Savage Sons' Mark

By 1962, the Mushmouth patch became officially unacceptable and was replaced with an Indian head and red arrow design. However, the Mushmouth lingered in the form of a Kilroy-like face peering over the tail stripe on the vertical fin of the squadron's RA-5C Vigilantes.

Facing Page Top: By 1973, RVAH squadrons were down to three aircraft. RVAH-5 borrowed a cartoon figure from the comic strip Tumble Weeds. As the CO's aircraft, 601 has "Head Savage" added to the Poohawk Chief. Left to right standing: Bob Kuntz, Don Brumbaugh, CO Joe Ausley, Bill Scott. Left to right kneeling: Doug Cook, Frank Waters, and Bob Thomas. BuNo 156632 is now on display at the Sanford Airport after a stay at NWC China Lake. (THA)

Facing Page Bottom: RVAH-7 on static display at an air show or open house. BuNo 151629 survived and is on display at the museum in Pueblo, Colorado.

What It Was Like: Air Refueling

The RA-5C carried enough fuel for most missions over Vietnam; twice as much as its usual escort, the Phantom. Also, for combat, the F-4 had Sidewinder missiles (AIM-9) on pylons below the wings, a huge fuel tank hung on the belly, and Sparrow missiles (AIM-7) partly buried in the fuselage. Although the two jets had the same engines, GE J79s, the RA5C could outrun its fighter escort because the Vigilante carried no external stores and is "clean" aerodynamically.

The refueling probe on a Vigilante is retractable to streamline the airplane for high speed. When the switch was flipped, doors popped open and an obscenely red, bent pipe with a gray tip came out of the left side of the nose. Wind across the probe and its doors made a racket.

Normal procedure was for the escort Phantom to take on fuel before going feet dry. Then, after feet wet, the Vigilante pilot gave the F-4 the flight lead as he headed for the tanker and took on fuel a second time. After the Phantom was clear, the Vigilante pilot did some practice plugs to stay proficient. A favorite stunt was after a couple of "dry" plugs, retract the probe, pull alongside the tanker to show you were clear, then light the burners and pull away in a swooping barrel roll while your escort was lazing alongside the tanker at max conserve speeds, saving every bit of fuel for the recovery.

Aerial refueling a Vigilante was difficult. The pitching moment arm was long and an up or down correction resulted in the probe twisting in an arc. Just before contact, airflow over the nose shoved the basket off to the side. The secret was to aim halfway out at the drogue's ten o'clock. Some pilots in the RA-5C selected Hydraulic Flight Isolate and moved the flap handle to 30 degrees, which put the leading-edge droops down and improved control response.

With large and stable drogue baskets, KA-3 Whales and KA-6 Intruders were favored for ARF. They also had lots of fuel to give. Bomber A-6s and the small A-4 Skyhawk became temporary tankers by hanging a self-contained D-404 buddy store on the centerline pylon, but their baskets were small and they did not have much fuel "give."

The use of A-7s made ARF awkward for Vigilantes and Crusaders, which had fuel probes on the left. Since the Corsair II had no centerline station, the right-side-probed Phantoms and other A-7s dictated that the buddy store be hung on the left. This meant the RA-5C had to fight the turbulence from the tanker's engine exhaust.

Here are a few comments from Vigilante drivers:
- On tanking from an A-7, "Needed 3/4 right lateral stick to maintain wings level. Right arm ached when complete."
- "I bent a probe on the Vigi when the A-6 tanker take-up reel [to buffer impact shock] into the pod didn't work and on contact with the basket, a huge ess-wave whipped up to the tanker and then back to me with the basket engaged. The wave yanked my probe to an unusual angle and it would not totally retract. This meant the fuel system didn't work properly and I couldn't use my bomb bay tanks. And, of course, with the basket not being able to be pushed in, I got no fuel. It was one of those days."
- "There was one cardinal rule in air-to-air refueling: The more you needed the fuel, the harder it was to plug."

RVAH-12 RA-5C approaching the basket behind a KA-6 Intruder, 1976. The emblem on the Speartip's fuselage is for the USA Bicentennial. After the KA-3 Whale was no longer available, the Intruder was favored. To see the basket at night a red light shown on the probe when it was extended. (Hoskin)

The basket of the KA-3 tanker was larger than those on other aircraft. Because of that, the A-3's stability, and the large quantity of fuel that it could transfer, it was the best carrier-based tanker. The green fuselage light identified tankers at night. Temporary tankers carrying a buddy store had green lenses on their rotating beacons. (Carlton)

The classic reconnaissance mission pair, RA-5C with F-4 Phantom from one of the two embarked fighter squadrons. (THA)

The Savage Sons, RVAH-5, deployed in Ranger (CVA-61). The mushmouth's face and fingers appear above the decorative "arrow" on the tail.

Another big change was integrated air wings on carriers now designated CV. The USS Saratoga, here in 1974, has one of the last ASW squadrons of propeller S-2 aircraft and only one RA-5C on deck. This photo was taken by a Vigilante with the squadron's third airplane buried in the hangar bay.

TINS: During a Med deployment, a group of African dignitaries were on board the carrier for a firepower demonstration. A removal of the Mushmouths was ordered and the cartoons dutifully painted over . . . on the Vigis on board. Murphy's Law was not to be denied. The RA-5C, which trapped with the VIPs watching, had come from the beach and still had the big-eyed caricature in full view.

Last Combat Mission?

CDR Dick Schaffert was the CO of Fighter Squadron 92 during that twilight period after the cease-fire. The *Constellation* was in port at Cubi Point when he was summoned to the private quarters of the Admiral's Chief of Staff.

"CAG and the Skippers of the A-6 and RA-5C [RVAH-12] squadrons were already there. There'd been a 'call' for photo reconnaissance of an area northwest of Phuc Yen, which included several crash sites of both air force and navy planes. This was reportedly in advance of possible future requests for investigation of those sites.

"The ROE [Rules of Engagement] for the mission was about as stupid as many of the other things that were imposed upon us during that crazy war! Only two aircraft would be going feet dry over North Vietnam: the Vigi photo bird and an unarmed fighter escort. The mission would be launched from Cubi Point the next day. It would be a Senior Aviators—only mission, probably with regards to its classification. Since I was the only fighter pilot in the room, I correctly guessed that'd be me and the Vigi Skipper.

"Four KA-6D tankers would be required for the mission. The Chief of Staff asked if there were any questions. I politely asked what my duties were as an 'unarmed' fighter escort. He replied, with his usual grin, 'Mark the place where the Vigi goes down if he gets hit. He'll do the same for you!'

"As I got out of the Staff car back on the ramp where my F-4s were parked, I noted that the 'spare' aircraft, which had been loaded with a Sparrow for our inspection's firing exercise, had not yet been downloaded. The Sparrow was slightly recessed into the under-belly of the Phantom, and not easy to see. I stopped by our line shack and told the Chief not to let the Ordnance crew download that missile until they heard from me.

"Allowing for a zig around the Chinese island of Hainan, it was over 1,100 miles one-way. We would take off together: the four tankers, the Vigi, and me. At a predetermined point en route, two of the tankers would top off the rest of the flight and return to Cubi. They'd refuel, and take off again so as to meet us for another refueling on the way back. The other two tankers would stay with the Vigi and me, to top us off again before we went feet dry.

"CAG cautioned that, after recovery, there was to be no recording of the flight. It would not be logged in either maintenance records or air-crew log books. It was 'never to have happened.'

"As we manned aircraft on the flight line, I somehow found something wrong with my originally assigned aircraft, and was 'forced' to take the spare. Strangely, it still had the Sparrow under its belly.

"It was a perfectly planned and executed mission. The Vigi and I went feet dry over the Hour Glass. He initially stayed high; we'd heard the Gomers painting us on their early warning radar while we were refueling over the Gulf of Tonkin. Maybe they simply couldn't believe we were doing this, because we didn't hear the Fansong radar for a SAM until we were nearing Hanoi. My RIO and I were straining our eyeballs, but we never saw a missile launch and we never heard a launch-warning warble from our electronic gear. What we did see was barrage AAA rising over the city as we passed well to the west.

"The Vigi was down on the deck, at the 'speed of heat,' and running away from my Phantom. My RIO locked him up on our radar, which greatly assisted me in keeping him in sight. The Vigi completed his photo run, turned back, and I rejoined off his wing as we raced for feet wet. The Firecan radars for the Gomer's 85mm guns were trying to lock on, as we flew down the Red River's 'Valley of Death,' but Gabriel was there with us one more time and the really bad stuff was going off behind us.

"Then we were over the Gulf, looking down at the now-deserted Yankee Station, and heading for our rendezvous with the two 'hot spin' tankers, who would escort us safely back to Cubi, and a cold San Miguel. Actually, my Ops Officer handed bottles up to our cockpits before we even unstrapped. Over and done!"[11]

Requiem

"What's it like riding in the rear cockpit of an RA-5C Vigilante with your back to two roaring J79 powerplants? What's it like after a combat hop? After the fleeting moments of blundering precision?

Cold mic.

"The cockpit becomes a quiet and serene place; not at all the open perch up front, not a magical aerodynamic window on the world, but rather an inward, introspective place. The silent dials and counters stare back as you feel the familiar aches and pulls of sitting too long under a blanket of belts and webbing. They stare and click and point, and you stare back, taking it all in.

"The Machine and you are one. Not at all a cold iron monster, not in these moments. A wave of peaceful euphoria grips you as you realize just where you've been and what you've done. Not so much why you've done it, but that you've done it against all the risks and odds and chances, and come out again clean.

"You reach inside for your Life of Georgia water bottle, pull off your mask and even lift your visor, and drink. This reflective time lasts only until landing time; then it's all business once more . . . pattern, checklists, interval, tighten your belts, place your Nav gear up front, hands on the turn and pull handles, and then . . .

. . . the trap."[12]

After Linebacker, RVAH squadrons dropped to only three aircraft assigned. The Speartips, besides consecutive BuNos, painted each nose uniquely with a pattern of red, white, and blue, using horns for their recently acquired Viking mascot. (Gehrig)

Souvenir patch that RVAH-6 had made celebrating the end of the air war. (Cannelos)

WE DIDN'T COME BACK TILL IT WAS OVER, OVER THERE --- WESTPAC 1972 - 1973

Not at all a cold iron monster.

Chapter 10

SEVEN YEARS

RVAH-5 Vigilante over NAS Key West on Boca Chica Key with stylized shore-based tail code. Gulf of Mexico at top. After storage at NWC China Lake, BuNo 156638 was moved to NAS Fallon, Nevada, and put on display.

As Vietnam flared then faded to an end and the Vigilante community adjusted to nonhazardous deployments, another move swept the squadrons south to tropical Key West. Since the navy no longer had ships, submarines, or aviation squadrons in Key West, yet another move for the Vigilante community was decreed by the new chairman of the Armed Services Committee.

Key West

Key West was a pleasant surprise, an unexpected vacation resort on a stay that lasted as long as a set of orders. The Recce Wing and RAG made the move in January 1973 with the fleet squadrons following soon after. Deployed squadrons again left from one base and came back months later to another. Some families moved six months in advance to be sure of getting base housing because places to live in the small vacation city were expensive and hard to find. RVAH-3 began a quasi-regular shuttle flight in the TA-3 on weekends.[1]

Water and beaches were close by in all directions. Many sailboat and powerboats were bought and kept in driveways or navy marinas. At the end of the day, Dads came home, shucked uniforms, and grabbed mask and fins or fishing rods, and caught dinner. For the officers and sailors returning from deployment, life as a "Conch" (a resident of the Florida Keys) could not have been more of a change from the gray steel, noise, and bustle of shipboard life. The Fort Taylor Officers Club was from a Hollywood film set.

Operationally, the base had the advantages of multiple runways and no close residents to disturb during night FCLP (the airfield is actually on Boca Chica, east of the city).

Comment from an LSO, "We used to go tarpon fishing in Key West in the salt ponds between the runways when the airplanes went in to refuel. Of course, the mosquitoes took some of the fun out of it. Since there weren't that many Vigilantes available, it took all night to get a class through a session."[2]

RVAH-14

Reconnaissance Attack Squadron 14 was the last of 10 Reconnaissance Attack Squadrons that flew the RA-5C Vigilante. Construction of the aircraft carrier USS *John F. Kennedy* (CVA-67) brought about the need for an additional carrier air wing (reconstituted CVW-1), so RVAH-14 was established at NAS Sanford, Florida, on 1 February 1968. (RVAHs would be shifted between CVWs so each big-deck carrier would have a Vigilante Squadron, unlike standard practice of keeping squadrons in the same air wing.)

Some sailors from the brand-new squadron were at a comic book convention and asked artist Roy Crane, the creator of the

RVAH-14 insignia created by Roy Crane. His imaginative portrayal gave the squadron both its callsign and nickname: Eagle Eye.

navy-oriented *Buz Sawyer* comic strip, to create a squadron emblem. The result gave them the nickname *Eagle Eyes*.[3]

The squadron spent only three short months at NAS Sanford before moving to NAS Albany, Georgia. In mid-November 1968, RVAH-14 deployed aboard *Kennedy* for the first time at sea for the ship and squadron. The shakedown was followed by a full deployment to the Mediterranean.

In September 1970, the *Eagle Eyes* were heading for the Caribbean for workups when emergency deployment orders were received due to the Lebanon Crisis.

After turnaround time in Albany, RVAH-14 began its third cruise to the Mediterranean in late 1971, again on the USS *John F. Kennedy*.

For their fourth and final deployment, the squadron switched to the USS *Independence* (CVA-62). When the Middle East flared up again, the *Independence* was part of the largest Sixth Fleet Task Force assembled since World War II.

Yom Kippur War

After the Mediterranean deployment, which included the Six Day War, Ron Pollard stayed in RVAH-5 and went to Vietnam on the *Constellation*. A tour instructing in the Recce RAG followed. The year 1973 found him involved in another Arab-Israeli war, this time as commanding Officer of RVAH-14 flying from the USS *Independence*.

"I was sent on a PECM flight covering the coast of Israel and the belligerent countries to the east. We were so intrigued with the excellent hits [on the RHAW indicators] we were getting, I stayed on track a little too long and realized I was not going to make my Charlie [landing] time. I had plenty of gas so went into max afterburner to the delight of the air controllers on the ship who computed my speed off the radar. As I approached the *Indy*, I noted the recovery was over, but the ship was still into the wind. I was cleared straight-in and I kept thinking, 'I'd better not bolter.' I didn't.

"The PECM data showed the Israeli Hawk batteries moving on the counteroffensive. That flight was the first indication that the Israeli Army had commenced their famous and successful counterattack. The attack guys didn't get to do anything, but we recce types sure stayed busy. The Yom Kippur War was followed by the OPEC oil embargo and tensions in the eastern Mediterranean stayed high."

Eject! Eject!

In May 1973, the USS *Constellation* was in the Tonkin Gulf as the war dwindled. LCDR Howard Fowler, pilot, and LTJG Art Dipadova,

Eagle Eye *RA-5C immediately after takeoff; flaps and landing gear still down and afterburners at full thrust. Tail pattern was a distinctive shade of blue not usually found on naval airplanes. BuNo 156642 was the last Vigilante built.*

RAN, of RVAH-12, ejected from BuNo 156609.

Dipadova: "Howie and I launched on a routine reconnaissance flight over the coast of South Vietnam. Although everything appeared OK to us, separation of one of the bomb bay fuel cans during the cat shot had caused a fire in the area between the engines and less than a half minute later we received the first indication that something had gone wrong: a FIRE warning light.

"Just a few seconds later the aircraft began a violent, uncontrollable roll and because of our very low altitude I decided to eject immediately. I heard the pilot's command to eject and as the aircraft rolled inverted, the sequence began. A blue-gray cloud of smoke filled the cockpit as the cartridge fired and I immediately experienced a tremendous wind blast that made my whole body shudder. The blast had ripped off my oxygen mask and turned my helmet sideways."

Frame from PLAT tape showing one fuel can from BuNo 156609 bursting into flames on the catapult track.

Fowler: "Shortly after the fire was noticed in the cockpit, we lost all control of the aircraft, causing it to roll violently and pitch downward. Art has already told you what his ride felt like. The biggest difference between his and mine is that I went out in more of an upward attitude.

"The cockpit filled with smoke from the body positioning charges, and the canopy was blown from the aircraft. With the canopy gone, all I could hear was a great blast of air (we were flying at 250 knots) as I left the airplane, and I was pressed into the seat because of the tremendous forces that were accelerating me upward.

Almost immediately, I was separated from the ejection seat and my personal [sic] chute was automatically deployed. Just as the chute blossomed, I saw the aircraft impact the water only a few feet in front of me.

"The helicopter picked us both up and we were back aboard *Connie* in only a few minutes. Considering that Art and I got out at an altitude of less than 300 feet, I feel we were both fortunate to have come out as well as we did.

"Let me just say that I wouldn't sell my interest in the North American Rocket seat for the world."[4]

Not Navy

The Vigilante was never exported. The Australian Air Force studied a version but never got further than artists' conceptual drawings. The F-111 was chosen. NAA tried to interest the US Air Force in a three-engine version (the third J79 stacked on top) as a high-altitude high-speed interceptor armed with missiles. The concept did not sell.

A pair of Marine Corps pilots were known to have flown Vigilantes while at the Patuxent River Test Center. Major Jim Read flew the A-5A and RA-5C during acceptance trials, and there is one reference to a Major Baces having "bounced off the runway" in an A3J-1.

A trio of USAF navigators had end-to-end exchange tours as RANs during the 1970s. (All were captains [O-3], but took delight in parking in "Captains Only" spaces at navy bases.) Bill Freibel had flown as bombardier-navigator in B-58 Hustler bombers and deployed in RVAH-7. Gene "Screwtop" Quist came from RF-4 Phantoms and deployed to WestPac in RVAH-6. When his tour was over he had carrier landings and a navy wife (divorced from an A-4 pilot). Quist returned to RF-4s and then flew in the exotic SR-71 Blackbird! Steve Bryan was the third, completing the RAG in 1975.

First to Go

RVAH-14, the *Eagle Eyes*, was the last RVAH squadron created (officially, navy squadrons are "established," ships are "commissioned") and the first to be disestablished in May 1974. The Mediterranean trip on the *Independence* was the last of four deployments for the squadron with the snazzy light-blue tail design.

The drawdown of the reconnaissance community had begun. Squadrons were going to sea with only four aircraft assigned. TARPS for the F-14 was under development.

For the last cruise, a stylized eagle head was added to the nose of RVAH-14's aircraft. The large flaps and steel leading-edge droops are down. Launch bridle hooked up and taut. Final checker running clear. (Johnston)

All was not serious. CDR Cliff Johns, CO of RVAH-14 waves to JFK's air boss as he mans up wearing a World War II–style helmet and goggles. His true helmet is on top of the ejection seat. (Carlton)

Cyprus Summer

In the summer of 1974, Turkey invaded Cyprus to bolster the Turkish portion of that divided island nation. War with Greece was likely. The USS *Forrestal* had had a perfect Mediterranean cruise; four months good flying punctuated by visits to the best ports in Europe.

Forrestal was in port at Naples, Italy, with other ships of its task group when orders came for an emergency sortie. The recall left hundreds of sailors and officers behind. A combat stores ship, the

Tail code AA is for CVW-17 aboard the USS Forrestal *during 1974 Mediterranean deployment. Tail antennas in a streamlined "beaver tail" above the tail cone. Seconds from launch on the Number 2 catapult. BuNo 156612 is currently displayed at NAS Key West. (Hoskin)*

USS *Concord* (AFS-12) came into Naples to carry the stranded men to their ships now patrolling off Cyprus. The passengers doubled the size of the Concord's complement—officer and enlisted. Bunks were set up in the cargo holds for the sailors while officers were squeezed into staterooms.[5]

On a night catapult shot, an engine exploded and LT Wes Rutledge and LTJG Larry Parr had to eject. Their rescue went smoothly, but BuNo 156614 was lost. Examples of the macho humor typical of carrier crews were another RAN asking, "Hey, Larr, you got my chart?" and another pilot accusing, "Wes will do anything to see tonight's movie."

NATO and United Nations commanders needed to know the extent of the Turkish buildup and Greek responses. However, normal CVW-7 flight operations were considered to be possibly provocative. Consequently, *Forrestal* did a limited launch of three aircraft, three times a day, to search the surrounding seas. First off the catapult was the E-2 Hawkeye with its immense radar and capability to search hundreds of miles of ocean. Next was an A-7 tanker (the A-6s were temporarily grounded) and then the star of the show, a Vigilante of RVAH-6.

Usually, Vigilantes could do their own searches, but there was so much shipping in that part of the Mediterranean that it was more efficient for the E-2 to vector the RA-5C from ship to ship. The

Fleur *Vigilante* about to break into the landing pattern for Forrestal. Normal flight operations in effect, the Phantoms were first in the recovery order (one is clearing the landing area, another has been turned to join the two already parked). RA-5Cs were the last jets to land. BuNo 156608 was the last *Vigilante* to fly and is now on display in Memphis. (Hoskin)

Vigilante topped off its fuel (with some difficulty from the buddy store on the A-7's left wing), dropped to 200 feet, and flew from ship to ship. Once in sight, the Vigilante adjusted its flyby heading for optimum light and camera angles. Pilots got good at reading the ship's name on the stern and jotting it on their kneeboard. Cyrillic lettering waited for photo analysis.

Between the systems on the Hawkeye and Vigilante, accurate positions, courses, and speeds were plotted for the surface contacts. Two to two-and-a-half hours later the aircraft landed. Twenty minutes after that photographs with enough detail to determine ships' names and identify cargo came out of the IOIC and into the hands of the commanders.

The rest of the air wing was permitted to fly after more than a week on this schedule, albeit in an ever-restricted amount of airspace. A month after the emergency sortie, *Forrestal* returned to Naples for a few days and then went back to Cyprus, all hopes of sunny beaches and sightseeing forgotten. After another month at sea, the crisis quieted and RVAH-6 rode across the Atlantic and flew off into NAS Key West.

Persian First

One month after CDR George Shattuck took command of RVAH-5

in the Philippines, the *Constellation* crossed the Indian Ocean and sailed into the Persian Gulf in November 1974, for one day of flight ops. The trial run was the first time an aircraft carrier had operated in that limited body of water. Shattuck flew an 18-inch PAN flight along the coast of Iran, Kargh Island, Kuwait, and returned to the ship. RVAH-5 returned to Key West on Christmas Eve day, 1974.

Saigon Evacuation

The year 1975 was grim for the United States. The dominoes had fallen. The Viet Minh were victorious in Vietnam, the Khmer Rouge had taken over Cambodia and the Pathet Lao, Laos.

The Cambodians, now styled as Kampucheans, hijacked the container ship SS *Mayaguez* and ran her ashore on a coastal island in May. The three days of rescue effort is considered the last official battle of the Vietnam War and the names of the 41 Americans killed are the last names on the Vietnam Veterans Memorial. *Coral Sea* (CV-42) was the only aircraft carrier involved, launching several airstrikes.

Frequent Wind

Saigon, soon to be renamed Ho Chi Minh City, fell in April. The only Vigilante squadron in the area was RVAH-12. The

Enterprise's deployment was extended and took CH-53 helicopters aboard for evacuation of the embassy. Reconnaissance was not required; the ship's participation included loading evacuees transferred from ships closer to shore.

Jim Pirotte was skipper of RVAH-12 on the 1974–1975 WestPac cruise. "That was the cruise that the F-14 went operational and we blew their socks off during an air show off east Africa because they had restrictions on them due to engine problems. That was a real source of pride for us!"

The *Enterprise* spent weeks cycling C-2 CODs through the deck, taking mine-sweeping gear to Haiphong. This meant no flying for the air wing and everyone was bored to death. Pirotte was in the tower one afternoon and said in that slow drawl of his, "Hopefully the North Vietnamese will launch a strike and sink us. It would be a mercy killing."

Pirate Saves 149300 a Second Time

Jim Pirotte launched from the USS *Enterprise* (CVAN-65) in the South China Sea (see chapter 6). About 6 miles from the ship, he feels and hears a horribly loud bang. Pirate quickly scans the cockpit ladder lights for fire or other warnings and rechecks his engine gauges. The fuel quantity indicators were dropping fast. Checking the rear of the Vigilante in the cockpit mirrors, he sees what appears to be a hazy contrail streaming behind. He checks with his RAN and radios other aircraft flying in the vicinity. Several aircraft come near to inspect and confirm his worst suspicion, a major fuel leak streaming from the center fuselage. There is still no fire warning, but the fuel gauges are dropping quickly.

If they were in afterburner when the leak started, the fuel would have been ignited and the airplane most likely would have exploded.

Pirate cycles through all the fuel tank selections: bomb bay cans empty, saddle tank empty, wing tank running down fast. There's not enough fuel remaining to make it to a shore base. NATOPS says, if a flame out is imminent, put the aircraft in optimum ejection configuration, relay your position and punch out. Nevertheless, he chooses to make a risky recovery back on board the *Enterprise*.

The ship controllers respond rapidly and quickly have him join on the already airborne A-6 Intruder tanker. Pirate completes the difficult low-altitude plug-in, but as fast as fuel is coming in, it is flowing out the leaks. Plugged in, the tanker leads the wounded Vigilante to a long, straight-in approach. On the ball call, the tanker detached.

RVAH-11 RA-5C on deck the USS Saratoga *in Naples, Italy. BuNo 156623 was the last fatal Vigilante crash, in February 1975.*

The crash crew and firefighting equipment are standing by. Everyone on the flight deck is watching the Vigilante with streaming, twin black smoke trails and an enormous fuel vapor cloud. There can be only one attempt. There is not enough gas for a go-around and having to tap the afterburner would be a disaster. Even a normal landing could result in a fireball on deck.

Pirate Pirotte flies an OK pass to the number-3 wire. There was no fire.[6]

Next to Go

RVAH-11's final deployment was on the *Saratoga* and began sadly. In February, after a bad landing, CDR Tom Hogan and LCDR "Tiny" Mulholland were lost at sea—the last crash and last fatalities in a Vigilante (BuNo 156623).

RVAH-11 began as a VC squadron with P2Vs and AJs. As VAH-11 they completed six full deployments with A3D Skywarriors before transitioning to the RA-5C. The checkerboard marking had been in use since AJ Savages in 1957 and were seen for the last time at the squadron's disestablishment in June 1975.

Bats

Reconnaissance Attack Squadron 13 went away in July 1976 after a uneventful trip to the Mediterranean aboard the USS *Independence* (CV-62). Formed in 1961 with A-3s at NAS Sanford, the squadron had immediately adopted the Bacardi bat as their emblem.

Double Decomm

CDR Tom Myers had the distinction of being the last commanding officer of two squadrons. "During the party after the *Hooters'* change of command, I received two messages as skipper of my first command. The first was an official directive to disestablish RVAH-9 in three months. The second message was from the enlisted party telling me they needed more beer. I'm not sure the timing of the official message could have been worse.

"So three months later, Barry Gastrock, CO of RVAH-5, and I closed our squadrons down in a joint ceremony. After almost a year on CRAW-1 Staff, I assumed command of RVAH-7."

Savage Sons

One of the oldest squadrons, RVAH-5 traced its beginning to VC-5 in 1948 when the squadron flew P2V Neptunes as bombers before becoming the first squadron to operate North American's AJ Savage.

RVAH-5 and RVAH-6 tied for the most deployments during the Vietnam conflict with five each.

RVAH-13, NAS North Island, in 1974. Bats emblem on both fuselage and tail with Oriental-style tail letters. (THA)

Dump-In Burner

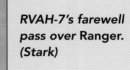

RVAH-7's farewell pass over Ranger. (Stark)

Once-in-a-lifetime shot in close formation while dumping in burner. This photo is by RAN Jim Stark with a handheld camera. A view that will never be seen again. (Stark)

RVAH-5, 1974: Poohawk Chief with Battle Efficiency "E" below canopies. While there were rumors this airplane had been on display at NAS Rota, Spain, a recent query established that it was no longer there. (THA)

During the *Savage Sons'* last deployment, *Ranger* was diverted from routine operations and deployed to the Indian Ocean for contingencies arising from the unsettled conditions in Eastern Africa. While on station, the squadron flew frequent long-range sea surveillance missions.

At the end of the ceremony, on 30 September 1977, as the rear canopy closed for the ceremonial taxi away, the RAN slid his windows closed, defiantly displaying one last Mushmouth.

Hooters

RVAH-9 began as VC-9 and flew TBM Avengers left over from World War II besides the P2V. In the AJ Savage, VC/VAH-9 conducted some of the earliest air refuelings.

RVAH-9's ninth and final deployment was on the USS *Nimitz* (CVN-68) beginning with the ship's initial training and a brief North Atlantic cruise, before going to the Mediterranean. It was only the second, and last, deployment of Vigilantes aboard the new CVN class of nuclear-powered aircraft carriers.

Back at NAS Key West, the *Hooters* in their final seven months, flew more than 500 hours, with missions including a photographic correlation mission over Panama City, Florida, for the Environmental Resources Institute, and photography of training routes in Virginia for MATWING 1 (A-6 Intruders). RVAH-9 was disestablished in a unique double ceremony with RVAH-5 on 30 September 1977.

Last Commodore

Robert V. Dean became the last commander of Recce Attack Wing One on 1 June 1978. His job was a hard one: to maintain the last squadrons at sea, plan for aircraft disposal and, most important, arrange follow-on orders for officers and sailors.

LCDR Dean completed RA-5C training with RVAH-3 in 1967 after tours as a fighter pilot and advanced jet instructor. He had combat cruises to Vietnam in the USS *Ranger* (CVA-61) and the USS *Enterprise* (CVAN-65) in RVAH-6. His third Vietnam cruise was in the USS *America* (CVA-66) as XO of RVAH-12. He fleeted up to CO of the *Speartips* for the Mediterranean cruise in the USS *Independence* (CVA-62). A tour at the Joint Reconnaissance Center of the Joint Chiefs of Staff in Washington followed before returning to Key West as Commodore.

Quo Vadis?

"Where next?" was the question asked by pilots and RANs as the community waned. In the US Navy, seniority rules. Seniors were moved around to ensure the opportunity to become commanding officers. A lucky few managed to slot directly into XO/CO billets in other types of squadrons. Several LCDRs were XOs of the last RVAH squadrons because they knew they would not be fleeting up.

Juniors had plenty of years ahead of them to establish careers in other specialties. The connection to reconnaissance was useful and some went to F-14 fighter squadrons that had TARPS pods. In between was a career limbo. Too junior to meet the criteria for command, too senior to establish themselves in another aircraft. There

were still good assignments and opportunities for promotion, but the vital step of squadron command was not there.

Over the Edge

In RVAH-1 on the *Enterprise* (CVN-65) during a 1978 deployment, RAN Jim "Beaker" Stark had a bit of excitement:

"We were halfway between San Francisco and Hawaii conducting Blue Water Ops with 12 to 14 aircraft airborne. Somehow, when we taxied out from behind the island, the Vigi's

The result of loss of nosewheel steering and brakes: tail charred by fuel from vent igniting. This aircraft was left in Cubi at the end of deployment for RVAH-7. (Stark)

Hydraulic Flight Isolation Switch was either left in the wrong position or malfunctioned, so there was no nosewheel steering or normal brakes—a very subtle abnormality as there is no indication in the cockpit.

"*Enterprise* had a perennial 1- to 2-degree port list. The turn to line up for Cat 4 brings you very close to the deck edge. The flight deck crew thought everything was normal until we went sailing past the turn point as the auxiliary brakes ran out of air pressure. I remember looking out and seeing the taxi director throw his arms up in frustration as he thought the pilot was ignoring his signals. Through the Optical View Finder I saw a rather confused green-shirt looking up at the aircraft before scrambling out of the way. Since my pilot hadn't initiated ejection and the aircraft had stopped moving, there was nothing to do but sit tight.

"I opened my canopy and was immediately showered with fog foam—my first indication that we were on fire. The fire-fighters had the tailpipe fire out in a half-minute and the main mounts were chained to the deck. Tilly [the on-deck crane] was brought over and a rope lowered down to me. I unstrapped and tied the rope around myself, jumped over the side, and was pulled up onto the flight deck. The pilot didn't want any part of the trapeze act and carefully crawled up the back of the aircraft onto the flight deck.

"The tail of the Vigilante was over the foul line and blocking the Fresnel lens. With over a dozen aircraft in the air at the end of a cycle and no bingo field, the choices were: 1. Push the RA-5C over the side 2. Re-spot the deck and launch tankers from the bow catapults, or 3. Recover using MOVLAS rigged on the starboard side. The last was

Memento

The Vigilante, which had almost gone over the side of the *Enterprise,* was left in Cubi Point as a spare airplane when RVAH-1's cruise was over. When RVAH-7 and *Ranger* (CV-61) finished the last ever deployment of the Vigilante, Buno 156627 did not go home but was left behind as a memento of US Navy presence in the Philippines.

The Vigilante was towed up the steep hill to decorate the miniature golf course. Sometime after the base was returned to the Philippines, students at a local art school were given free rein to express themselves on the Vigi canvas.

Fortunately, 156627 was moved again. This time to the Marikit-Park in the city of Olongapo and had her gray and white paint restored.

This photo of the jeepney-like result was taken by a former naval aviator who became a pilot with FedEx, which had a base at the former NAS Cubi Point. "No airplane should look like that, especially one as beautiful as the Vigilante."

Seeming to come over the wall at Marikit-Park is the repainted 156627 with the markings of Flight Service Test at NATC Patuxent River. (Philippine Info web site)

the choice, and pilots and LSOs did a superb job getting aboard in unusual circumstances. The Vigilante was hoisted back on deck and flew again in less than a month."[7]

Fleurs

RVAH-6 began with Lockheed P2V Neptunes and North American AJ Savages in 1950 as VC-6. In August 1977, RVAH-6 was on board the USS *Nimitz* (CVN-68) for that carrier's shakedown. The *Fleurs* made a 7½-month deployment with the ship to the Mediterranean, becoming only one of two Vigilante squadrons to operate on a new class CVN carrier. Disestablishment at Key West was in October 1978, it was tied with RVAH-5 for the most Vietnam deployments with five.

Smoking Tigers

Established in November 1965 as VAH-1, the *Smoking Tigers* were the first squadron to fly A3D Skywarriors. RVAH-1's final cruise was aboard the *Enterprise* to WestPac. In seven months, they had flown reconnaissance missions from the Sea of Japan to the Singapore Straits, in the Indian Ocean, and off the coast of Western Australia. Disestablishment came on 29 January 1979.

Speartips

Created as the first RVAH-only squadron (RVAH-14 followed), RVAH-12 had completed 10 full deployments (3 in combat) when in September 1978, the squadron deployed to Naval Station, Rota, Spain, in support of CVW-3 and the USS *Saratoga* (CVA-60). While deployed, the squadron maintained a detachment aboard the *Saratoga* and sent two detachments to Naval Air Facility, Sigonella, Italy, in support of special tasking requirements.

February 1979 marked the end of the last RA-5C Mediterranean deployment. Before disestablishment in July 1979, two RVAH-12 Vigilantes were flown to the Naval Weapons Center, China Lake, California. One, BuNo 156643, was flown to the Naval Air Test Center, Patuxent River, Maryland, where it was added to the Test Center Museum collection.

Dragons

RVAH-3 began as VAH-3 in Jacksonville in 1956. The RAG went before all the fleet squadrons were gone. Disestablished in August 1979, the squadron's last losses were five years before: BuNo 149296 over the sea near Key West and BuNo 151630 near Naples, Florida. All crewmembers ejected safely.

A-3, A-4, and A-5 on RVAH-3 flight line in Key West. TA-4 and RA-5 intake warning flashes have stars added to the blue section in commemoration of the USA Bicentennial in 1976. (Hoskin)

Glorious End

RVAH-7 dated back to VC-7 established in California in 1950. VAH-7 moved with its AJ Savages to Sanford where they flew Douglas A3D Skywarriors before becoming the first Vigilante squadron. Now they were the last. Only a few days after returning from the last cruise, the squadron gathered for the solemn ceremony on 22 September 1979 that disestablished the *Peacemakers*.

Their deployment on *Ranger* was a memorable finale for Vigilantes.

Deployment

Three months into the cruise, *Ranger* was on its way to a port visit in Singapore when, late at night in the crowded shipping lanes of the Singapore Straits, it collided with a tanker. The carrier limped back to Subic Bay and the shipyard filled the bow with concrete. However, because of the damage, *Ranger* could not gain enough speed to launch Vigilantes in low-wind conditions and the entire squadron was to be off-loaded to the Cubi Point Air Station.

The day before *Ranger* was to go back out to sea to continue the deployment, the RVAH-7 CO was asked if he could get the squadron off-loaded before the ship sailed. CDR Tom Myers posed the question to his senior chief petty officer who immediately turned to. What had taken three days to load aboard was on the dock, without the aircraft yet, in six hours flat with 165 happy sailors looking forward to time ashore. The aircraft flew off the ship and landed ashore the next day.

RVAH-1 had left behind an aircraft at Subic for spare parts so the three RA-5Cs assigned to RVAH-7 were usually in an up status. Over the next three months, the squadron racked up an average of more than 200 hours per month with three aircraft . . . a record.

"Being the skipper of the last squadron was a wonderful experience and I wouldn't have it any other way. Everyone who loved the Vigilante wanted to be in that last squadron and wanted to make that last cruise.

"It was a beautiful way to end the life of the fastest, most beautiful aircraft that ever graced the skies of this world. We flew anywhere we wanted, any altitude we wanted, as fast as we wanted, taking movies and pictures of each other. I had a crew where morale was so high you could walk on it."

Besides the Vigi's own cameras, VRC-50, who provided CODs for the fleet, also had a C-130 Hercules at Cubi and was happy to provide a camera platform. The result is some of the finest photographs of Vigilantes ever taken.

The *Ranger* was to stop in Japan to have its bow replaced before heading home. She stopped in Cubi Point and RVAH-7 moved back aboard. The next day, the ship sailed and the three Vigis flew out and trapped aboard. *Ranger*'s new Captain wanted to conduct flight ops while crossing the Pacific but had been ordered to load three F-4 Phantoms to transport back to the states. Added to the assigned air wing, this locked the deck. Looking to free up space, he wanted Myers

to take his three aircraft back to Subic and abandon them there. Myers argued that all had bad angle-of-attack indicators and with Monsoon weather clobbering the Philippines, he would not risk the flights. The meeting in the Captain's cabin ended. Somehow, the Vigis stayed in a down status until the flyoff.

"On the day of the flyoff, we all got airborne, joined up, and made a 'Last Pass' by the USS *Ranger* with all three aircraft dumping fuel with afterburners on, which gave us a 30-foot flame trail. It looked good.

"I tried to get everyone a 'last' something." LCDR Paul Hable [who had been in RVAH-11 during Linebacker on his first deployment] and LT Larry Parr had the last trap in BuNo 156615 and, as Habel jokes, that after one last bolter. Myself and LCDR Vince McManamin were on the last catapult shot, in BuNo 156608, for the flyoff to San Diego. There were more lasts once at home.

"We overnighted in San Diego and took off in the morning in zero-zero beach fog and flew home to Key West and arrived like a naval air squadron should, in tight formation, even if it was for the last time."

Ashore

A detachment was created in Key West[8] to retire the last three operational aircraft in the navy's inventory. CDR Myers was made OinC and made his own last flight in November. In a touch of irony, his next job, non-flying, in Washington, DC, was to manage the navy's replacement of the RA-5C, the TARPS pod on the F-14 Tomcat.

CDR Myers led a flight of two Vigis (BuNos 156615 and 156641) from Key West to a fueling stop in Texas to the disposal facility at Davis Monthan AFB, Arizona, with showy takeoffs and fast, low breaks with his wingman tucked in tight to perfect landings at all the airfields. For pilot Myers, it was his last navy flight; for RANs "Beaker" Stark and Larry Parr, these were their last flights in a Vigilante. LT Keene Little had another flight where he created a problem by overspeeding and damaging the landing gear doors of the Vigilante remaining in Key West.

Writing years later, Myers became a bit sentimental: "Under your breath, you mumble an expression of gratitude to this particular aircraft for the long, safe flight test history you have with BuNo 156615 [see "One Runway Problem" in chapter 7]. On many flight test 'firsts' that you've flown at the Naval Air Test Center, she always did what was expected, and never surprised you when you were busy with other things.

"The work of hundreds of dedicated men and women who thought of, designed, built, tested, maintained, and flew these beautiful Machines was finished. It had come full circle for us who thought of this aircraft with a respect and near-human affection."

BuNo 156615 was one of the lucky ones to avoid scrapping or being blown apart in weapons tests. She was restored and is on display at Castle Air Museum, California, in appropriate RVAH-7 squadron colors.

A selection of photographs taken by a US Navy photographer from a VRC-50 C-130 Hercules of RVAH-7 Vigilante over Subic Bay, Philippines, in October 1979. (USN)

Finality

CAPT E. O. Williams had been in the second deployable RVAH squadron, commanded RVAH-14 and the RAG, RVAH-3, and was next-to-last commander of CRAW-1. He was stationed in Memphis, Tennessee, and ready to retire, but he postponed leaving the navy until the Vigilante that was to be put on display at the air station arrived.

The last Vigilante flight on 20 November 1979 from NAS Key West to NAS Memphis did not have any of the high-speed displays that the Vigilante was famous for. The day before, all the gear doors had sustained damage and there was a hydraulic failure requiring a field arrestment (the last trap?).

When the maintenance chiefs heard that the plane might be towed across the field and cut up, they came up with a plan to pin down the gear and cap off the hydraulic lines. So the most beautiful supersonic aircraft ever to grace a carrier deck flew to Memphis no faster than 250 KIAS and had to hot refuel at Cecil Field, Florida, because of excessive fuel burn. LT Bill Westmoreland and LCDR Al Plunkett, author of the reconnaissance wing history, flew the last RA-5C BuNo 156608 to its final resting place. Only the disestablishment of the wing staff remained.

When given clearance to land, LT Westmoreland replied, "Roger, *Flare* forty, gear down and locked for final landing, the end of an era."

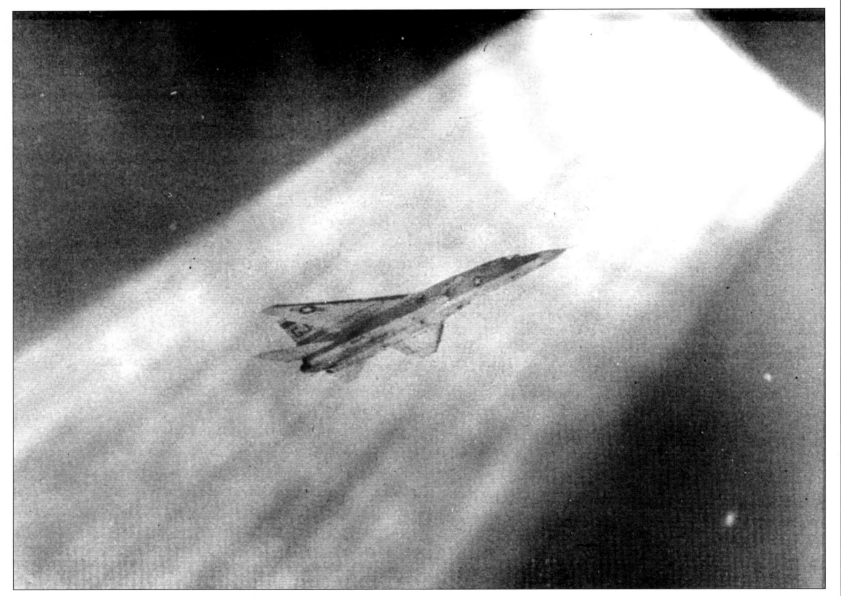

Trick of light on RAN's window gives the Vigilante an aura. (Owen)

EPILOGUE

rtists' delight! An aircraft as beautiful as the Vigilante is a natural subject for artists, both professional and amateur. From photo realism to skillful pen-and-ink drawing and even caricature, the RA-5C is captured on these pages in all forms of artistic media, style, and technique. In their own way, each illustration brings some unique aspect of the Vigi's mission to life. Complementing the illustrations in the earlier chapters, this selection is worthy of note. (All images are used with full artists' permission.)

Unbridled Elegance *by Mike Machat depicts the exact moment that a Vigilant takes flight. An actual moment in time, this aircraft from* RVAH-14 Eagle Eyes Squadron *is shown launching from the USS* John F. Kennedy *(CVA-67) during its first overseas deployment in the Mediterranean, June 1969. (Mike Machat from a painting commissioned by Brian Vaivadas)*

"VIGGIES"

© HANK CARUSO '95
#2007

The original role of the North American A-5 Vigilante was supposed to be long-range strikes at supersonic speeds, but its novel weapon tunnel delivery system didn't work as planned. Resurrected as the RA-5C with advanced camera systems, Vigis were the premier tactical recon system of the Vietnam War. The A-5 was also regularly "shot down" as a "bad guy" during mock combats at air shows. Fuel was dumped from the aircraft and torched-off by its afterburners, resulting in a spectacular trail of flame. (Aerocature and caption by Hank Caruso, aerocatures.com)

Many of their pilots had not seen the back end of the boat since receiving their wings.[1]

VFP-63 was active until disestablishment in 1982 when all the remaining RF-8G Photo-Crusaders went to Navy Reserve squadrons at Andrews AFB in Washington, DC. The last operational American Crusader was turned over to the National Air and Space Museum in 1987.[2]

Much effort went into developing a pod that could be carried on the F-14's weapons rack and remain steady enough for high-resolution photography. One of the two fighter squadrons in each air wing had TARPS with a secondary role of Reconnaissance.

Several Vigilante pilots and RANs went to the F-14 TARPS program: pilot John Carter, RANs Eddie James, and Fred Brown, as early as 1976. Pilot Jim Flaherty and RANs Randy MacDonald and Denny Lauer were together in VF-84, the first East Coast TARPS squadron.[3]

SHARP was next. Built by Raytheon, the Shared Reconnaissance Pod's initial use was on the F/A-18E/F Hornet but can be used on a wide range of aircraft mounted on a bomb rack. A SHARP pod includes a rotating midsection that allows an unobstructed, horizon-to-horizon view for dual-band electro-optic/infrared (EO/IR) sensors and subsystems capable of near real-time data link to afloat and shore-based stations.

John "Boog" Powell, the author's brother, presented this when he first learned of orders to fly Vigilantes.

Messin' with The Boss *by Dr. Carlton "Doctor Sketch" Eddy, illustrating the mismatched formation of an RA-5C and Grumman E-2 returning to the carrier as an A-6 Intruder turns final below.*

The elongated camera nose made the RF-4 the fastest of all the Phantom models. (NNAM/Gann)

RF-8G flown by reserve VFP squadron. Raised wing has photographer rating symbol and risqué set of footprints.

Fully loaded F-14 carrying Sidewinder and Sparrow missiles, fuel drop tanks, and a TARPS pod on the centerline station. (Wikipedia)

The drawdown of the Vigilante squadrons sent the US Marines to sea. The remaining Photo-Crusader assets were not sufficient to provide coverage for all the active carriers, and VMCJ squadrons were tasked to provide deployable detachments of RF-4 Photo-Phantoms.

F/A-18E during testing of a SHARP pod. (Wikipedia)

Boneyard

Tucson, Arizona's low humidity, infrequent rainfall, alkaline soil, and high altitude reduce rust and corrosion in stored airplanes. The hard Caliche soil makes it possible to move aircraft around without needing pavement. Part of the Davis-Monthan AFB, the Boneyard, officially the Military Aircraft Storage and Disposition Center (MASDC) since 1965, is an ideal storage location.[4]

Thirty-six RA-5Cs ended up at MASDC. Eight were transferred to the New Mexico Institute of Mining and Technology, which used surplus aircraft for testing of ballistics, projectiles, and aircraft metals. Five were sent to the Naval Weapons Center at China Lake, California, as targets. In 1986, the last 20 airframes were turned over to the air force, also for use as targets.

Except for the few in museums, most of which are out of doors in some not-so-friendly environments, the memory of the Vigilante will remain with the men who worked on and flew in that legendary aircraft.

In a bittersweet gesture, the officers remaining in RVAH-7 went to the scrap yard and stopped the welders for one last picture. They found a nose cone and found a way to hang it on the main bulkhead to, "At least make it look like a Vigi." Intelligence and maintenance officers are in uniform, the crews in flight suits. (Top Row, left to right): LTJG Richard Gent, LTJG Dedrich Hohorst, ENS Edwin Hamilton, CWO3 Dalbert Smiley, LTJG Quentin J. Herring, LT Larry Parr, LT Jim Stark, LT Bill Westmoreland. (Bottom row, left to right): LCDR Vince McManamin, LCDR Sam McCray, CDR Tom Myers (CO), CDR Ken Storms (XO), LT Keene Little. Which of the ten RA-5Cs scrapped at NAS Key West is unknown. (Myer)

This dramatic photo beautifully captures the graceful shape of the RA-5C. It has proven to be a very popular print over the years—one can always claim it's one of his squadron's Vigilantes!

SELECTED BIOGRAPHIES

Agnew, Al

Previously flew WV-2/EC-121 Connies and S-2 Trackers. Joined RVAH-13 during workups for WestPac. After retiring from the navy, he flew Jetstreams out of Atlanta and later a Cessna Caravan for a utility company before moving on to a Falcon 50 and Piper Cheyenne in Florence, South Carolina.

Ahern, Dave

Started in Vigilantes in January 1965, deployed in RVAH-6 on the *Constellation* then *Ranger* to WestPac. After shore duty, RVAH-1 to North Atlantic on the *America*, then RVAH-5 on *Ranger* 1976–1977. XO of RVAH-1 for its last deployment; second tour as XO for RVAH-5 until that squadron decommissioned in late 1979. After second and last Vigilnate XO tour and decommissioning, went to VAQ-33 in Norfolk as XO then CO; and moved the squadron to Key West. "You have to love it."

Bakke, Harlan "Deacon"

USNA class of 1951. First tour in patrol planes. Initial cadre when VAH-1 formed with A3D Skywarriors in 1955. Instructor in Training Command and VAH-3. Transitioned to the Vigilante in 1961 and deployed in A3J/A-5A to Mediterranean on the *Enterprise* with VAH-7. Attended RAF Staff College in England before becoming XO of RVAH-5, As CO, led the *Savage Sons'* eight-month deployment to WestPac on the *Constellation* in 1968.

Carter, John "Big Bird"

Nugget Number 3, tours in RVAH-5, RVAH-3 as instructor and LSO, and RVAH-1 before going to the F-14 TARPS program at NAS Miramar along with RANs Eddie James and Fred Brown. Made eight-month deployment to the Indian Ocean during the Iran Hostage Crisis flying F-14s in VF-143, the "World Famous Pukin' Dogs." As a civilian, two years with Doug Coleman (RVAH-5 CO) in Pensacola flying the Citation II in a contract to train new NFOs. Went to United Airlines and was Captain on Boeing B-757/767.

Cikanovich, Chris

"I was the last nugget and have a plaque to prove it." Went to RVAH-12 in its last days and wrangled orders to A-6 Intruders and was in VA-85 at Oceana with other former Vigilante crewmen: Rob "Potsie" Weber, Neil "Murry" Weisberg, and Jim "Beaker" Stark. Became qualified CVW-17 LSO and as a civilian worked in senior executive positions in Aerospace.

Coffey, Jerry

Flew RF-8 Photo-Crusaders over Cuba during the missile crisis in 1962 and instructed in the Vigilante RAG before joining RVAH-13.

After repatriation in 1973, Coffey did the illustrations for CDR Howard Rutledge's book on the POW experience, *In the Presence of Mine Enemies*. Speaker at the 2003 dedication of the RA-5C on display at the Sanford, former NAS, International Airport.

Conrad, Emerson "Emy"

Enlisted as Electronics Tech (AT) and flew as crew in WF/E-1s during Cuban Crisis. The Navy Enlisted Scientific Education Program (NESEP) at the University of Texas and a degree in Electrical Engineering. High class standing in NFO training so chose Vigilantes. Teamed with Barry Gastrock in the RAG. They had a rough start because Barry was still much single-seat from previous tour in A-4s. Emy just sat in the back until one hop where he was needed as the only way home. The pair worked together well enough to finesse orders to RVAH-6. Stayed with *Fleurs* for second combat deployment. Instructed EW and Advanced Nav in Training Command before a, "great 2½ years" as Cats & AG officer on Kennedy. Safety Center tour, but screwed over on next assignment and retired after 22 years of service.

Davis, Bob "Bull"

Earned his nickname as a bombardier-navigator in A-3 Skywarriors by hitting the bull's-eye 13 times in VAH-6. Made the transition with the squadron to the RA-5C and deployed to WestPac. Instructed in the training command and did another tour with the *Fleurs*. Earned his civil pilot's license and became an agricultural pilot in Louisiana.

deBoxtel, Lawrence "Box"

Before entering the navy, he drove racing hydroplanes and was a gymnast. First tour flying A-4 Skyhawks in VA-76 on *Intrepid*. Started Vigilantes after post-graduate school. Combat tours in RVAH-6 before becoming RAG LSO. Flew multiple airplane types in ferry squadron, VRF-32. After navy retirement, managed AgricuLTural Research Station in Virginia. Died in 2017.

Gillespie, Edward A. "Ed"

Chief test pilot at North American Aviation for many years. Flew many of the original A-5 tests as well as the last NAA-sponsored flight of a Vigilante in July 1974 (BuNo 156615). May have been the oldest continuously active test pilot. He was most proud of the fact that he landed every airplane he took off in . . . some not all in one piece, or on fire.

Gillespie first soloed in a Piper Cub in 1944. Enlisted in the Navy Aviation Midshipman Program as a 17-year-old. He completed flight training without getting a "down." After three years of flying F2H *Banshees* with VF-11 (including 80 combat missions in Korea), was offered the enticing choice of joining either the Blue Angels or attending the US Navy Test Pilot School. He graduated from Test Pilot School in February 1954.

Over the next 24 years, Gillespie performed experimental flying almost on a daily basis. He flew all series of Trojans, Buckeyes, Furies, Vigilantes, Savages, Broncos, Phantoms, Voodoos, and other lesser-known aircraft types. He stayed in the active US Naval Air Reserves for 26 years, concurrent with his civilian flying career.

After retiring from North American Rockwell in 1988, he developed and completed the flight tests on a major modification to USAF T-37 trainers. He did the test flying of a French-designed amphibian biplane and of a light jet at the Mojave test center. Died in July 2015.

Gretter, Gary "GG"

First tour he flew three types of fleet aircraft on three deployments. First was in A-4 Skyhawks to the Med in VA-172. In 1964, he deployed in A-3 Skywarriors with VAH-6. He transitioned with the squadron flew the new RA-5C Vigilante in RVAH-6 on the *Constellation*. Killed flying navy reserve F-8 Crusader in Dallas.

Johnson, Robert "Slick"

As a nugget, he was stuck in right seat of A3D for months before becoming pilot and carrier qualified. Did two cruises on 27C carriers before earning a master's degree in Aeronautical Engineering. RVAH-13 deployments on *Kitty Hawk* and the *America* flying the RA-5C. Test Pilot School at NATC Patuxent River, Maryland, and assigned to Carrier Suitability Branch testing planes on carriers. Back to Vigilantes at Albany and another deployment. Was CO of RVAH-7. Became the most junior Director, US Naval Test Pilot School in 1975. Took a job with McDonnell Aircraft in Saint Louis. Made a profession switch, got a General Contractor's license and started his own business building custom homes.

Kiffer, Jim

Nugget 4 went to RVAH-1 during Linebacker, then to RVAH-3 as an instructor and LSO. Patuxent River Test Center as LSO and pilot in carrier suitability. In RVAH-12 at the end. VX-4 doing OpsEval on F-14 TARPS. Career at Delta Airlines and took early retirement at 58.

Owen, Jim

NROTC classmate of the author. We tried to make my Fam-1 flight together when Jim was instructing after his RVAH-7 deployment, but the schedule did not work out. Did fly the next two with him. He went back to WestPac in RVAH-1 before leaving the navy and becoming an insurance adjuster.

Pirotte, James "Pirate"

The only pilot to have more than 2,000 hours in the Vigi. As he quipped when taking command of RVAH-12, "sixteen years in the community has provided the necessary volume of experience to reduce the magnitude of my mistakes. As a result, my level of incompetence has been raised beyond my fondest hope. So, after eight deployments, six in the Vigilante on six different carriers in the Med and the Western Pacific, I cannot be accused of being a rate grabber" (nautical term for one who gets promoted without being qualified). After retirement, joined other ex-Vigi drivers flying T-39 Sabreliners as civilians teaching new NFOs.

Prendergast, Frank

Awarded the Navy Cross for his escape in North Vietnam, was given his choice of duty. Completed navy flight training and did a tour of flying A-4 Skyhawks in the Med. He was never officially listed as a POW; probably because of the short duration of his stay on the beach. Left the navy. Turned down by airlines because he did not have a college degree. Became a civil servant. Died young of a massive heart attack in 1998.

Sharp, Dave

Began as a BN in A3Ds in Sanford and selected to be in the first class to train in Vigilantes in VAH-3. He was assigned to VAH-7 and sailed around the world on the *Enterprise*. CDR Ken Enney (later CO of the RAG and CRAW-1) talked junior officer Sharp into remaining in the navy, and he deployed with RVAH-7 to WestPac in 1966. Following a tour at the Naval Postgraduate School, he returned to the Vigilante community joining RVAH-12 for another cruise to WestPac aboard the USS *Kitty Hawk*. A joint tour at the Command Center in Omaha and a session at the Naval War College preceded selection for command of an RVAH squadron. He was the XO/CO for RVAH-7's penultimate cruise. After retirement, became vice-president of Flight International providing aerial services to the navy and air force from Newport News, Virginia.

Smith, John Barry

His varied career began as air crewman in P2V-5 Neptunes before earning a commission and becoming an RA-5C RAN. "I left the Navy six months later at the end of the Med cruise in Toulon, France, fooled around Europe, found myself (?), came back to the States, went to college on the GI Bill, stayed in the Navy Reserves as an AI [Air Intelligence], got my master's degree, joined the army (the navy had no military audiologists), and retired." Became a commercial civil pilot.

Williams, Edward O.

Aviation Cadet designated a Naval Aviator in October 1954. Flew the P2V-5 Neptune with Patrol Squadron 5, trained as Aircraft Maintenance Officer and instructed in Advanced Training Command at Corpus Christi, Texas. Ordered to Heavy Attack training NAS, Sanford, Florida in 1961. Flew A3D Skywarriors in VAH-11. Transitioned to the Vigilante and made a combat deployment with RVAH-l. Then back to RVAH-3 as Training and Operations Officer.

Williams went back to sea duty as XO of RVAH-14, becoming the CO in 1970 during an emergency deployment to the Mediterranean. Back in Albany, he was on CRAW-1 staff before taking over RVAH-3 until December 1972. A tour as XO of the USS *John F. Kennedy* took him briefly away from the recce community. He was the next-to-last Commodore of Reconnaissance Attack Wing ONE. His final duty was at the Training Center in Memphis, where he delayed retirement until the last Vigilante arrived.

GLOSSARY

AAA, AA, Flak, "Triple-A": interchangeable terms for guns that shoot at airplanes. AAA and AA are Antiaircraft Artillery and the shortened Antiaircraft. Triple-A is AAA pronounced and Flak from the German *FliegerAbwehrKannonen* (antiaircraft cannons).

ACLS: Automatic Carrier Landing System.

Afterburner: also AB or Burner. A way to achieve a large increase in thrust from a jet engine by injecting fuel directly into the exhaust. The J79 on A-5s and F-4s burned dirty and left a trail of black smoke. Lighting the AB got rid of the smoke.

ALQ/RHAW: used interchangeably. RHAW is the general term for Radar alerting and warning; ALQ is the particular piece of equipment. By Vietnam all aircraft carried black boxes that helped divert fire-control radars and chaff dispensers to cloud the picture. Pilot and RAN had indicators that displayed threat radars in dotted, dashed, or solid lines depending on the type, which pulsed or were steady, depending on the mode, while a variety of tones came over their helmet's earphones.

ARF: Air Refueling.

Auto Throttles: Automatic Power Compensation (APC).

Ball/Meatball: the visual landing aid on an aircraft carrier displayed two green bars of light with an amber light that moved between them. The amber light appeared round and was called the ball. The pilot tried to keep the ball between the green lights for a good approach and landing. When he first saw the ball, he made a radio call with his identification, airplane type, and fuel quantity.

Barricade: used when an airplane must be trapped. It is specially rigged and flight deck crews compete to get it up fast.

Bingo: both verb and adjective. Not the game played in churches and fire halls, but to divert to a shore base from the ship.

Beeper: an emergency locator beacon radio; automatically emitted a beeping sound on the emergency radio channel (Guard) when activated. Became more sophisticated as the Vietnam War progressed, adding a voice capability and two-channel selection. The beepers also became smaller and more reliable. Emergency radios were considered *the* most important piece of survival equipment—more important than firearms or food. The automatic activation function was later discarded because on a bad day (several aircraft downed) the beeping blocked radio communications needed for the rescue effort. The North Vietnamese also became sneaky and used captured beeper radios to lure in SAR forces.

Boat: navy pilots frequently refer to an aircraft carrier as "the boat." It is easier to say than "aircraft carrier" or even "carrier" and it teases the surface warfare officers who insist on differentiating between ships and boats.

Bolter: when an aircraft misses all the wires on a carrier deck and has to go around. A successful carrier landing is a "trap."

BuNo: Bureau Number. A number given to a Navy/Marine Corps aircraft for its lifetime. Blocks of BuNos are given to manufacturers as part of the contract to build aircraft (airplanes, helicopters, blimps, gliders, etc.).

CAG: in the old system, squadrons on a ship were part of an Air Group, hence the boss was Commander of the Air Group, CAG. With the change to air wings, he should be CAW, but that lacks *cachet*, so CAG he remains. Squadron COs are subordinate to CAG. CAG was subordinate to the ship's Captain.

CarQual: Carrier Qualify, often abbreviated CQ. A series of launches and landings at the ship with no mission except to get landings. Usually for pilots new to the airplane type or who have not seen the back end of the boat for some time.

CEP: Circular Error Probability; a measure of a weapon's or pilot's accuracy.

CO: Commanding Officer of a squadron. The second-in-command was the XO (Executive Officer). The usual progression was to be XO for a year or more then "fleet up" to be the CO.

CRAW-1: Commander of Reconnaissance Wing One. Like a CAG except the squadrons were under his command when ashore and not attached to a CVW.

Cruise: (see Deployment) to leave home port for an extended time; usually to the Mediterranean or Western Pacific (West-Pac). Sailors use the terms interchangeably. However, as one aircraft carrier commanding officer frequently reminded his crew, "We are not on a cruise! We are on deployment. The *Love Boat* goes on a cruise. Warships make deployments."

CV: C for Cruiser? V in USN designations is from the French "*voler*," meaning to fly. "Z" for lighter-than-air is based on Zeppelin and "H" is obviously for helicopter.

Deployment: (see Cruise) a planned period away from home port in the United States. For squadrons, a deployment is preceded by a turnaround cycle, which includes time at home, training, and several at-sea periods "working-up." The goal was to have replacement personnel join the squadron during the turnaround cycle.

Det: Detachment. A group taken from a larger unit for some special function. Dets formed for a limited time.

Dump: to jettison fuel. The Vigilante had a dump pipe that stuck out on the left side of the tail cone. Dumping fuel and selecting the left burner lighted the cloud of fuel so a long plume of fire followed the Vigi, a favorite maneuver at airshows.

Fam: familiarization, usually about a first flight in an airplane type.

Homeplate: also "mother." Endearing term for your carrier.

ECM: Electronic Counter Measures; an encompassing term for all electronic warfare.

JO: Junior Officer. This includes Navy ensigns and junior-grade lieutenants, LTJG, and some lieutenants, (depending on relative seniority and personal attitude). In mockery of officialdom there were organizations such as JORP (Junior Officer Retention Program) and JOPA (Junior Officer Protective Association). All navy officers had jobs in the squadron besides flying airplanes. At the bottom of the hierarchy was the SLJO (Silly Little Jobs Officer).

LDO: (see Warrant Officer) Limited Duty Officer. A specialized grade in a particular technical field. Insignia is that of a regular officer. Provides excellent technical knowledge in squadrons.

LSO: Landing Signal Officer. A pilot specially trained to assist, train, and control aircraft landing on the carrier. Called "Paddles" from the days before the visual landing system. Since the Vigilante was a challenge at the ship, LSOs competent with large, fast airplanes were a special type.

NAA number: a number assigned to aircraft produced by the North American Aviation Company. See BuNo.

Nadir: literally the lowest point. In aerial photography, nadir is the point directly below the belly of the aircraft. In the RA-5C viewfinder, nadir was indicated by a dot. When the RAN called nadir, the pilot knew they were exactly over a spot on the ground.

Nugget: a navy pilot or NFO on his first assignment after receiving his gold wings. Nugget implies a naiveté and inexperience in carrier operations. A lump of gold that needs to be beaten into shape. During Vietnam, some nuggets became "Must-pumps." While going through the RAGs, they were selected to join a squadron already deployed and received priority in training. Semi-nuggets were pilots who were "plowed back," (i.e., after receiving their wings they stayed in the Training Command as instructors).

On-the-line or on-line: military term for facing the enemy. Derived from riflemen being on the firing line. Navy carrier pilots used on-line on Yankee Station and in the Tonkin Gulf to mean pretty much the same thing—flying combat missions.

Plane-guard: helicopter that stays close to the ship during landings and takeoffs to haul aviators out of the sea. The job used to be done by escort ships (*Small Boys*).

Plug: to engage the drogue ("basket") while Air Refueling, ARF.

ORI: Operational Readiness Inspection; precursor to a deployment.

RAG: replacement training squadron. Like CAG, an obsolete term that hung on. Originally, training in a particular type of airplane was done at a Replacement Air Group. The name shifted to Replacement Air Wing, but individual squadrons were still called RAGs. The Vigilante RAG was RVAH-3 and was part of CRAW-1.

RBS: Radar Bombing System; a way to practice high-altitude bombing without dropping a bomb. RBS ranges were set up over many cities.

SAM: Surface-to-Air Missile. In Vietnam this referred to the Soviet-built SA-2 Guideline (S-75 *Dvina*) missile, which was 35 feet (10.7 meters) long and had a 130-kg (286-pound) high-explosive warhead that burst shrapnel in a fan-shaped pattern. A solid fuel booster burned for 5 seconds, dropped off, and a liquid fuel rocket fired for 22 seconds pushing the SAM to a Mach 3.5 top speed. The SA-2 was normally guided by a Fan Song fire-control radar.

SAR: Search and Rescue. Usually helicopters, but also boats, ships, and amphibious aircraft, picked up downed airmen. HC-7 kept detachments of Sikorsky SH-3s on aircraft carriers and other ships. Their callsign was *Big Mother*. Some smaller ships had Kaman HU-2s, callsign *Clementine*. Both worked close to the Vietnam coast for SAR. Their USAF counterpart was *Jolly Green*. A brave group of men.

Ship: to Naval Aviators the only ship that counts is an aircraft carrier (unless it is a smaller vessel pulling you out of the sea). They also rarely say "aircraft carrier," but simply "carrier."

Squadron: the basic unit in naval aviation. For Vigilantes a squadron was 6 aircraft (12 for the A3J), 18 officers, and more than 100 enlisted men. Squadrons were assigned to an air wing (CVW) which was assigned to a ship. Squadrons had COs.

TACAN: Tactical Aid to Navigation; a ground station that sends a signal showing bearing and distance an airplane is from it. TACAN was a backup for the RA-5C's ASB-12 navigation, which was independent of electronic signals. Navy ships had TACANs.

TINS: The abbreviation is from the question, "What is the difference between a fairy tale and a sea story?" Answer: "A fairy tale begins 'Once upon a time. . . ' A sea story begins, 'This is no s**t . . .'" TINS tales are most likely true, but unverifiable, have details wrong, and may have a bit of embellishment added.

Tonkin Gulf: a body of water bounded on the east by the Chinese island of Hainan, China, to the north, and North Vietnam to the west. The south opened into the South China Sea. The old names for Vietnam were Annam, Cochin, and Tonkin. Yankee Station was in the Tonkin Gulf northeast of the DMZ.

Torso Harness: the way aircrew fastened to the parachute and seat pan when ejection seats had the parachute as part of the seat.

Touch and Go: T&G; to land and takeoff again immediately, usually for training.

Trap: an arrested landing; ashore or afloat.

Warrant Officer: even more specialized than LDO; almost always a former enlisted man. Insignia was a bar with colored stripes across it.

WestPac: Western Pacific. WestPac includes the Pacific Ocean from the Hawaiian Islands west to the countries of Asia. The US Navy generally deployed ships to either the Mediterranean or WestPac. During the Vietnam War, going to WestPac meant time on Yankee Station in the Tonkin Gulf, on-the-line.

XO: Executive Officer, second in command of ship or squadron; casually, "Exec."

Yankee Station: a geographic point in the Tonkin Gulf used as a reference for US Navy ships, especially aircraft carriers. The equivalent southern position was called Dixie Station.

Yoke: also called a control wheel. Early aircraft had a full wheel until it was realized most of the diameter was not needed and removed until the control resembled a yoke for oxen.

END NOTES

Intro Note

1. NATOPS met with a great deal of resistance. One squadron was seen burning their manuals on the fantail of the carrier as it pulled out of port. Some humorous translations of NATOPS included "Not Applicable To Our Present Situation" and, more significantly, "Not Applicable To Older Pilots."

Chapter 1 Notes

1. The US Navy used "composite squadron" for a variety of purposes: VC squadrons flying multiple types of aircraft were used in ASW. Later, most were designated VU (Utility).
2. The Norden bombsight was developed by the US Navy with the intention of bombing ships in the wide-open areas of the ocean. Only later did the US Army Air Force adopt it for its new precision bombing policy.
3. T. Thomason, *Strike From the Sea*, Specialty Press: Forest Lake, MN, 2009.
4. The city of Sanford, Florida (the former Naval Air Station continues as an active international airport), was enthusiastic about remembering the men who spent much of their service lives there and erected a memorial to them. On a pier jutting into Lake Monroe at the end of Park Avenue is an arc of bronze plaques around a flag pole with all the Navy Enlisted Bombardier-Navigator names recorded for history.
5. John Barry Smith, per email October 2017.
6. Michael Grove and J. Miller, *Aerofax Minigraph 9*, Post-First Flight Report.

Chapter 2 Notes

1. Greg Goebel blog, airvectors.net.
2. George Klett, "The Half-life of an Aircraft," *Foundation*, Spring 2002. Klett was a captain who became an aviation engineering duty officer and instrumental in early Vigilante squadrons.
3. Ed Gillespie was the featured speaker at the first Vigilante reunion in Pensacola in 1995. I sent him my write-ups of two of the tales he told in a letter dated 5 July 1995. He returned the letter with corrections and additions.
4. Klett, *op cit.*
5. Grove and Miller, *Aerofax Minigraph 9*, Post-First Flight Report.
6. Klett, *op cit.*
7. Bob Elder, *The Hook*, Winter 1980.
8. Klett, *op cit.*
9. Cochrane later piloted herself above Mach 2 in a Canadian F-104. She had also used a Canadian Sabrejet to become the first woman to fly above Mach 1.
10. Adapted from RVAHNAVY.COM newsletter, 15 March 2008.
11. Elder, *The Hook*.
12. The nickname for the S2F was based on the sound when you pronounce the designation.
13. In the spring of 1965, the USS *Saratoga*, with RVAH-9 on board, was at the Cannes Film Festival when a Russian group came aboard and devoted their time to photographing and studying the RA-5C inlet duct system. A copy of these inlet ducts (which were very advanced for their time) appeared later on the MiG-25.
14. LT H. L. "Larry" Monroe, USN, was the BN on the altitude record Vigilante flight in December 1960. This tale is adapted from an article he wrote in *Naval Aviation News*, September 1961.

Chapter 3 Notes

1. *Naval Aviation News*, November 1960. The pilots were CDR Carl Cruse, LCDR Ed Decker, and LT Dick Wright from NATC Patuxent River.
2. George Klett, "The Half-life of an Aircraft," *Foundation*, Spring 2002.
3. Klett, *ibid.*
4. Klett, *ibid.*
5. Klett, *ibid.*
6. Greg Goebel blog, airvectors.net.
7. Norm Gandia was later Blue Angel Number-5 (1966–1967) and a test pilot for McDonnell-Douglas. Dick Truly went to the USAF test pilot school, became an astronaut on Skylab and the Shuttle, was first commander of USN Space Command, and was a NASA administrator (1989–1992).
8. Dave Sharp, per email September 2018.
9. The Naval History & Heritage Command website, history.navy.mil.

10. Harlen J. Bakke was CO of RVAH-5 from 1968 to 1969.
11. Elder, "Catwalk," *The Hook*.
12. Chief Petty Officer "Pem" Pemberton and LCDR Jim Bell, per emails February 2014.
13. Klett, *op cit.*
14. BuNos 144857, 144858, 144861 144863, 144865, and 144866.
15. Jim Owen, per emails September 2018.
16. George Cannelos, per emails September 2018.
17. Jim Owen, per email 15 October 1917.
18. Jerry Coffee flew RF-8 Crusaders over Cuba and transitioned to Vigilantes.
19. Bob Johnson, per emails September 2018 and July 2014.
20. The USAF version of the Phantom II went from F-110 to F-4 in the consolidation.

Chapter 4 Notes

1. When talking to an audience about the phrase "Alone, unarmed, and unafraid," a veteran Photo-Crusader pilot might quip, "Well, two out of three ain't bad."
2. Grove and Miller, Aerofax Minigraph 9.
3. R. Geopfarth, per correspondence November 2018.
4. Sharp, per email November 2018.
5. Geopfarth, *op cit.*
6. Printed bold face and all caps in the manual.
7. R. "Bull" Davis, per correspondence November 2018.
8. Jim Owen, per correspondence. The heavier an airplane is, the greater the force necessary to accelerate it. The Skywarrior A-3 and the RA-5C were the two heaviest aircraft to be catapulted.
9. Geopfarth, *op cit.*
10. The US Navy referred to a sailor's specialty as a "rating" and had a two- or three-letter identifier for them, followed by a number for his "Rate" (i.e., pay grade).
11. Wayne Perras, per correspondence.
12. Perras, *ibid.*
13. Gehrig, *RVAH Navy News Letter* Special edition, October 2008.
14. *CRAW-1 History,* part 4.
15. *CRAW-1 History,* part 2.
16. After a failed rescue attempt, pilot LT Klusmann was captured. After three months, he escaped to a friendly village and was returned to the United States.

Chapter 5 Notes

1. There was a VC-5 in World War II that was disestablished in 1944, so there is a break in continuity until the new VC-5 in 1948.
2. Grumman sponsored a documentary about the *Independence's* training and cruise called *Ready On Arrival.* The film is available online.
3. Cuban missions over land were called *Blue Moons*.
4. After repatriation in 1973, LCDR Jim Bell told of being tied to the sampan's mast, which struck him as ironic as the night before he had watched the 1946 movie *Two Years Before the Mast.*
5. George Cannelos, per correspondence with author.
6. James Owen, per correspondence with author.
7. J. K. Sutor ejected again in October from BuNo 149288 while the *Enterprise* was operating off California.
8. The legend is that Bacardi sent the *Bats* a case of rum for Christmas.
9. Don Brumbaugh was a freshman in college and visiting a friend who lived in the house right across the street from the crash site in DeBary, Florida. He found CDR Nolta's body in the neighbor's backyard. "When I finished the RAG, I was to be assigned to RVAH-5 when they returned from cruise in October 1971. I was looking forward to talking to Paul Stokes about the crash, but he was lost at sea when he and Everett flew into the water during night ops as they transited home from WestPac."
10. LTJG Glenn Daigle became a POW and was released in February 1973.
11. C. R. Smith later commanded the RAG, RVAH-3.
12. Richard Wells (tech rep for North American who went to sea three times with early RA-5C squadrons), per correspondence with author.

Chapter 6 Notes

1. Al Wattay, per correspondence with author.
2. Jim Owen, per email to author January 2019.
3. A result of lessons learned from the *Forrestal* fire and the *Oriskany* (CVA-34) fire nine months earlier, the navy instituted mandatory firefighting training for all hands. Full commanders found themselves battling smoke and flames alongside airmen apprentices in the scarily realistic training chambers.
4. *CRAW-1 History.*
5. He was later an admiral and commander Naval Air Forces Atlantic and died in that billet from a heart attack while jogging.
6. Terry Love, per letter in *The Hook*, Summer 2004.
7. Naval Aviation News, April 1967.
8. Naval Aviation News, October 1967.
9. Mike Haynes, per email February 2019.
10. CDR Charles James had flown AD Skyraiders during the Korean War.
11. Naval Air Rework Facility, NAS Jacksonville, Florida, was commonly called "Jax."
12. David R. Krause CDR, USN (Ret), NFO in VAH-9/RVAH-9, RVAH-3 and RVAH-1.

Chapter 7 Notes

1. Shore-based wing commanders were given the honorific "commodore" while sea-going wing commanders kept the traditional "CAG."
2. This is an unofficial number. Compiling an exact list is difficult, as it is dependent on individual memories. There were also pilots who had flown in land-based squadrons but because of their rank were thought of as nuggets.
3. Rob "Potsie" Weber Weber was a second-generation *Hooter;* his father had flown AJ Savages in VC-9 when the name was created.
4. Dick Dunleavy was one of the first NFO COs and CAGs and the first carrier captain and admiral. He eventually was a three-star admiral and, like Fallon, left his last position under controversy. However, although he was in one of the first Vigilante (A3J, VAH-7) squadrons he had had an earlier tour in A3D Skywarriors and was not a Vigilante nugget.
5. Jim Flaherty, FCLP social 2 April 2015.
6. Tom Myers, per email May 2018.
7. Gene Klein, per email March 2018.
8. Hence the advice to pilots to, "Keep the shiny side up, the dirty side down."
9. Coors was the current fad but, due to problems with refrigeration,

was unavailable east of the Mississippi.

10. Alpha was a measurement of how close the INS was to being fully aligned.

Chapter 8 Notes

1. Progressive Aircraft Repair. For Vigis it was done at NAS Jacksonville.
2. *Naval Aviation News,* May 1970. Pettibone was a curmudgeon who used to comment on accidents.
3. The unlimited category was won by an RAF Harrier "jump-jet," which had the ability to land at downtown helicopter pads.
4. The NATOPS manual shows this and turn radii to 1/100 of a foot.
5. Dan Howe, per email March 2018.
6. Dennis Lauer, per email March 2018.
7. Tom Myers, per email March 2018.
8. George Shattuck, per email April 2018.
9. Tom Myers, per email March 2018.
10. George Shattuck, per email April 2018.

Chapter 9 Notes

1. With the demise of dedicated ASW carriers, all carriers became CV or CVN.
2. Polfer had flown more than 200 missions during three tours in Southeast Asia, the first two as a Phantom pilot with VF-154 operating from the *Coral Sea* and the *Ranger.*
3. *After Kernan's return, t*he navy offered him any job he wanted, so he became the baseball coach at the Naval Academy. After retiring from the navy, Kernan became the mayor of South Bend, Indiana, and the lieutenant governor of Indiana from 2003 to 2005.
4. Thanh Hoa Bridge was given the nickname *Hàm Rông,* "Dragon's Jaw." Frustrations with destroying the bridge led US pilots to create the legend that when the bridge broke, the world would split in half.
5. Per peter-chilelli.pixels.com.
6. Jim Kiffer, per email November 2018.
7. George Cannelos, *Memoir: Part One* (unpublished). Amid all the combat action, he still noted the final moon mission in his journal: Apollo 17 was Dec. 7–19.
8. Emerson Conrad, per multiple conversations with author.
9. The MiG was downed by a F-4 from VF-142.
10. Agnew, conversation with author 2003. After his release and being cleared for duty, Agnew was asked to be on the speaking circuit. He always appeared humble, saying he had barely qualified as a POW after being held just 91 days, and quipped about being home before his squadron, "All things considered, it wasn't worth it."
11. Richard Schaffert, *Farm Boy to Fighter Pilot.* CDR Jerry Gehrig, CO RVAH-12, has combat missions in his log book well into April 1973.
12. George Cannelos, *op cit.*

Chapter 10 Notes

1. A bleed-air leak caused the crash of one TA-3. Pilot Jerry Ragen held the airplane level so all the passengers got out, but he was too low to save himself.
2. LSO Daniel Bo Howe, per e-mail 2015.
3. *Buz Sawyer* ran from 1943 to 1979. A fan commented, "The aircraft markings and numbers, and type of planes had an uncanny accuracy, plus dialog that we knew was real."
4. Elder, *The Hook,* Winter 1980.
5. This author was one of them having flown from the States to rejoin the *Fleurs.*
6. *Recce Newsletter.* Event occurred in 1974.
7. Stark, per email 2006.
8. CRAW-1 itself stayed on for administrative purposes until disestablished on 9 January 1980.

Epilogue Notes

1. During the Vietnam War, VMCJ-1 was based in Danang with a mix of airplane types. Besides RF-4s for reconnaissance, they operated EF-10 Skyknights and, later, EA-6A Intruders in the electronic warfare role.
2. The French *Aeronavale* operated F-8s until 2000.
3. RANs Jim Stark, Neal Weisberg, Ken Bixler; pilots Rob Weber and Chris Cikanovich overlapped in Intruder squadron VA-85 over a six-year period beginning in the mid-1970s. RANs Tim Baker and Jack Jones became commanding officers of VS squadrons operating S-3 Vikings.
4. The US Navy had its own facility at Litchfield Park, near Phoenix, until 1968.

INDEX

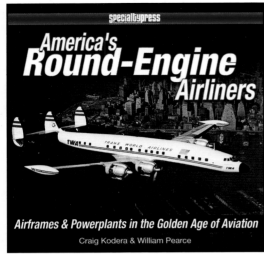

AMERICA'S ROUND-ENGINE AIRLINERS *Craig Kodera & William Pearce* The advancement and success of America's air transportation system can be linked directly to the concurrent growth of long-range, high-speed airliners and their revolutionary powerplants. This book tells the compelling story of aviation progress and development for the very first time. 10 x 10, 160 pages, 250 photos. Hardbound. *Item # SP257*

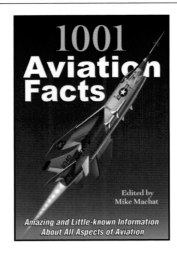

1001 AVIATION FACTS *Edited by Mike Machat* This book provides an insightful and in-depth look at aviation history by highlighting many little-known, yet very important, aviation facts. Stories are organized by category, including military, commercial, and sport aviation and features topics such as pilots, personalities, aviation movies, TV shows, and model building. Softbound, 6 x 9 inches, 384 pages, 100 photos. *Item # SP244*

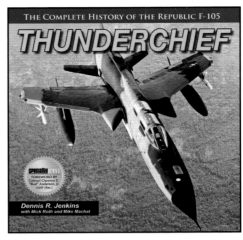

THUNDERCHIEF: The Complete History of the Republic F-105 *Dennis R. Jenkins* This book continues the story of Republic's Mach-2 F-105 Thunderchief where previous books on this aircraft left off. Author Dennis Jenkins uses rare archival air force documentation and original Republic factory material and photos never before seen by the public to tell the complete story of this legendary jet fighter-bomber. 10 x 10, 300 pages, 700 photos. Hardbound. *Item # SP259*

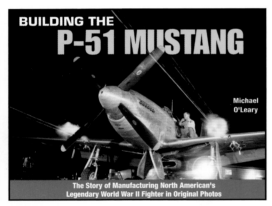

BUILDING THE P-51 MUSTANG: The Story of Manufacturing North American's Legendary World War II Fighter in Orginal Photos *Michael O'Leary* The author uses more than 300 original photos culled from his personal archive of offical North American and USAAF images, many of which have never before been seen in any publication whatsoever. This book provides a vital "missing link" in the saga of this famed World War II aircraft, and is sure to become a valued addition to libraries of P-51 modelers, historians, enthusiasts, and pilots in both the U.S. and England. 11 x 8-1/2, 240 pages, 300 b/w photos & 50 b/w illustrations. Softbound. *Item # SP190*

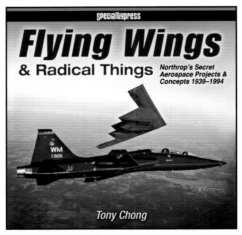

FLYING WINGS & RADICAL THINGS: Northrop's Secret Aerospace Projects & Concepts 1939–1994 *Tony Chong* This book unveils Northrop's once-secret radical designs, many for the first time, featuring stunning original factory artwork, technical drawings, and never-before-seen photographs. 10 x 10, 276 pages, 439 photos. Hardbound. *Item # SP229*

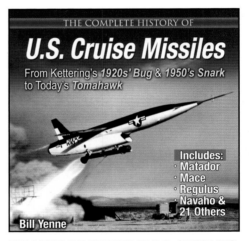

THE COMPLETE HISTORY OF U.S. CRUISE MISSILES: From Kettering's 1920s' Bug & 1950's Snark to Today's Tomahawk *Bill Yenne* Employing a considerable archive of U.S. cruise missile data and material amassed during his extensive research, author Bill Yenne has created a compelling work containing a wealth of previously unpublished photographs plus detailed technical information that is simply unavailable in any other product on the market today. 9 x 9, 204 pages, 339 photos. Softbound. *Item # SP256*

Specialty Press, 838 Lake Street South, Forest Lake, MN. Phone 800-895-4585 & 651-277-1400 Fax: 651-277-1203
www.specialtypress.com
Crécy Publishing Ltd., 1a Ringway Trading Estate, Shadowmoss Road, Manchester, M22 5LH, England. Phone: 44 161 499 0024 Fax: 44 161 499 0298
www.crecy.co.uk